The Eclipse of God

Is Religion on the Way Out?

by

Gerard M. Verschuuren

En Route Books and Media, LLC
5705 Rhodes Avenue
St. Louis, MO 63109

Cover credit: TJ Burdick

LCCN: 2018945282

Copyright © 2018 Gerard M. Verschuuren
All rights reserved.

ISBN-13: 978-0-9998814-8-4
ISBN-10: 0-9998814-8-5

TABLE OF CONTENTS

PREFACE 1
1. COSMOLOGISTS AND GOD 3
   a. How the Eclipse Sets in 3
   b. How the Sun Reclaims the Day 8
2. BIOCHEMISTS AND GOD 25
   a. How the Eclipse Sets in 25
   b. How the Sun Reclaims the Day 30
3. BIOLOGISTS AND GOD 47
   a. How the Eclipse Sets in 48
   b. How the Sun Reclaims the Day 57
4. GENETICISTS AND GOD 77
   a. How the Eclipse Sets in 78
   b. How the Sun Reclaims the Day 81
5. NEUROSCIENTISTS AND GOD 97
   a. How the Eclipse Sets in 98
   b. How the Sun Reclaims the Day 101
6. RELATIVISTS AND GOD 121
   a. How the Eclipse Sets in 122
   b. How the Sun Reclaims the Day 129
7. SECULARISTS AND GOD 155
   a. How the Eclipse Sets in 156
   b. How the Sun Reclaims the Day 160
8. ATHEISTS AND GOD 187
   a. The Eclipse Appears and Disappears 188

b. We end up with "I believe in one God." 253
9. CONCLUSION 257
10. INDEX 261
ABOUT THE AUTHOR 269

Preface

Sometimes, images help us better understand what life is all about. One of those images is the image of sun and moon. God is the Sun, and we are the Moon. They both shine light in the darkness of our world—one during the day, one during the night. But only the Sun brings us the real light. The light of the Moon is just a reflection of the Light of the Sun. In other words, the moon only provides "borrowed" light. The real light in our world is God. All the rest is just a reflection of God's light. So our prayer should be, "God, be our light. Shine in our darkness."

Another helpful image is Martin Buber's *The Eclipse of God*. God's light is always there, but sometimes, during a solar eclipse, it gets temporarily obscured by the moon, so nothing else on earth can reflect God's light. That's what we will see happening in each chapter of this book. God is the only real light, but it can get obscured by ideologies such as materialism, scientism, relativism, secularism, and atheism. And here is what it leads to: the Big Bang obscures God's creation; evolution eclipses God's Providence; genetics blocks out religion; materialism veils the spiritual world; mechanicism clouds the human mind; relativism darkens the truth; secularism overshadows morality. All of this ultimately causes an eclipse of God, but only temporarily so. God, the Light of this world, is always there, although sometimes momentarily hidden through our own doings.

Preface

This book was specifically written for all those who feel confused by ideologies that obscure God. It is hard to pinpoint one particular cause of how we feel in such God-forsaken times and places, but science is likely one of the main perpetrators, as some scientists use their scientific "authority" to churn out, with the speed of light, books that promote opinions and views that go far beyond their scientific expertise, and that robs people of any religious beliefs they might have. These prolific writers are inundating the book market, magazines, and the internet with their message that a state of conflict exists between science and religion, and that science is on the winning hand.

They loudly broadcast through the megaphones of our society their anti-religious propaganda: (1) Since there was a Big Bang, there is no creation. (2) Because there is only matter, there can be no spirit. (3) There is no purpose in life, for randomness is all there is. (4) There is no God, only a god-gene. (5) Neurons are in complete charge, so the mind is an illusion. (6) Everything is relative, for objective truth just does not exist. (7) Morality is only a matter of personal opinions and preferences. (8) All in all, God is dead, in the way Latin is dead.

All these proclamations are strongly interconnected and together make for an "export culture" that easily infiltrates foreign territory as a Trojan horse, where it then unpacks its "goodies." This leads to a destruction of what was once considered the main pillar of Western Civilization—Christianity. Media and academia seem to have joined forces to destruct this pillar. Can this avalanche be stopped? This book shows you it can. If you wonder how you and your religious faith could ever survive in such an environment, this is the right book for you.

1

Cosmologists and God

Going by best-sellers on the book market and by documentaries on TV, we might get the impression that God has been "dethroned" by new developments in cosmology. Physical cosmology is a branch of physics and astrophysics that studies the origin and evolution of the Universe. Recent advances in cosmology have transformed it from a largely speculative science into a predictive science with very close agreement between theory and observation.

This development seems to have put the science of cosmology on a collision course with the philosophy and theology of creation. Judging by the many books on this issue, belief in a Creator and his Creation seems to be at the losing end. The Universe has become "darker" than ever.

a. How the Eclipse Sets in

Astronomers have reduced our planet, so it seems, to what the late American astrophysicist Carl Sagan called "a speck of dust in the Universe." He also spoke of the Universe as "all that is, or was, or ever will be." Well, it is this speck of dust that we call home. If this planet is a speck of dust, imagine us living on it—we must be even tinier specks of dust. We are becoming tinier by the minute and end up as

Chapter 1: Cosmologists and God

plain star dust.

No wonder we seem to have been living in a God-forsaken Universe ever since. Gone is God, and gone is God's Creation. What some, or even many, physical cosmologists want to eliminate and obliterate, up to the point of a complete extermination, is something dear to most people—a belief in a Creator and his Creation. Their ultimate goal is to discard Creation by replacing it with purely "scientific" and "materialistic" concepts and explanations.

The idea behind all of this is basically very old—it is the ancient pagan philosophy of materialism (although the term itself is relatively recent). It holds that the only thing that exists is matter – that all things are composed of matter and dust, the mere result of material interactions. Its slogan is: Everything that exists is matter, and matter is all there is. It could, for instance, evolve into Lenin's dialectical materialism. Lenin's misguided ideal was that it demanded renunciation of all material rewards for the people while at the same time plunging them into gross material conditions. Lenin should have learned from this contradiction that, ultimately, human beings can only be made happy by what lifts them above the material conditions of human existence.

Matter is anything that has mass and takes up space. Although "matter" is a very old concept, in physics it has lost its prominent position because the term "mass" is well-defined, but "matter" is not. Yet, the strength of materialism is that it centers on one of the most noticeable elements in the world around us—"stuff." Studying this kind of "stuff" has been vital for our survival. It can usually be seen, touched, heard, tasted, and smelled by our five senses. We cannot disregard it; we cannot live without it. There is no denial that almost all our technological achievements are based on it. Where would we be without this "stuff"?

But materialism goes much further than that. It claims

that anything not of a material nature does not exist and is only a figment of human imagination. Materialism rejects religious faith and replaces it with its own "faith." This makes materialism a totalitarian ideology, for it allows no room for anything but itself. It asserts not only that matter is everywhere, but also that matter is all there is. Materialists dogmatically reduce or limit reality to material objects. Their creed is, "Everything that exists is material," for nothing can exist without the materials out of which it is made, so they say. In other words, matter is supposedly the only entity in this Universe; and thus physical matter has become the only fundamental reality in the minds of many. Concepts such as spirit, soul, and creation have become antiquated and outdated.

According to PBS (Public Broadcasting Service),

> It is not just biological evolution that poses challenges to traditional Christian views, scientific understanding of cosmological evolution also raises issues for people of faith. According to the Book of Genesis, God created the Universe—and all the heavenly bodies, the sun, the moon, and the stars—in six days. But according to contemporary cosmologists the Universe began with a great explosion known as the Big Bang, after which the stars and galaxies slowly formed over billions of years. Just as Darwin proposed that the evolution of life was a long, slow, and gradual process, so cosmologists now believe that our Universe evolves by long slow processes.... Ironically, the tables have now been turned with some scientists today arguing that the Big Bang demonstrates that the Universe came into being by purely natural processes needing no supernatural power.

Chapter 1: Cosmologists and God

When we summarize this long exposé in a few words, creation is considered to be on its way out, at least according to PBS. Recent developments in cosmology seem to confirm this—but the keyword is "seem." What does cosmology really tell us?

Our Universe most likely started with the Big Bang, some fourteen billion years ago. Edwin Hubble had discovered in 1929 that the distances to far away galaxies were generally proportional to their red-shifts. Red-shift is a term used to describe situations when an astronomical object is observed to being moving away from the observer, such that emission or absorption features in the object's spectrum are observed to have shifted toward longer (red) wavelengths. Hubble's observation was taken to indicate that all very distant galaxies and clusters have an apparent velocity directly away from our vantage point: the farther away, the higher their apparent velocity. This phenomenon had already been suggested in 1927 by the Belgian priest, astronomer, and physicist George Lemaître of the Catholic University of Louvain. In 1931, Lemaître went even further and suggested that the evident expansion of the Universe, if projected back in time, meant that the further in the past the smaller the Universe was, until at some finite time in the past, all the mass of the Universe was concentrated into a single point, a "primeval atom," in his own words, where and when the fabric of time and space started.

The English astronomer and mathematician Fred Hoyle is credited with coining the term Big Bang during a 1949 radio broadcast. Currently, the Big Bang theory is the prevailing cosmological model that explains the early development of the Universe. According to this theory, the Universe was once in an extremely hot and dense state which expanded rapidly. This rapid expansion caused the Universe to cool and resulted in its present continuously expanding state—not with galaxies moving through space, but rather the space between the galaxies stretching. Once it had cooled sufficiently, its energy was allowed to be converted into various subatomic particles, including protons, neutrons, and electrons. Giant clouds of these primordial elements would then coalesce through gravity to form stars and galaxies, and the heavier elements would be synthesized either within stars or during supernovae. Interestingly enough, the 92 elements we find on Planet Earth can be found all over the Universe, indicating a common origin.

There is little doubt among cosmologists that we live in the aftermath of a giant explosion that occurred around fourteen billion years ago. The first estimates of the age of the Universe based on its rate of expansion gave about a billion years, which was inconsistent with the known ages of the oldest rocks and of stars. But those first estimates turned out to be based on a mistaken calculation of the distances between galaxies. Eventually things got sorted out, and evidence for the Big Bang built up to the point where it is regarded as conclusive. Although nothing in science is final, cosmologists will tell us that the Big Bang theory is still the latest and best we have; it remains standing for now until further notice.

But there is more to it. The introduction of the Big Bang theory has not only made quite an impact on cosmology, but also on philosophy and theology. If we have to believe some of the leading physicists and astrophysicists nowadays, then the Big Bang story is the modern replacement of the "old" creation story, leaving no room for a Creator behind this Universe. There are several ways they have come up with the idea that "creation out of nothing" [*creatio ex nihilo*] is no longer a religious or philosophical concept that requires a Creator. The British cosmologist Stephen Hawking, for instance, talks about the Big Bang in terms of what he calls a

Chapter 1: Cosmologists and God

"spontaneous" creation: "Because there is a law such as gravity, the Universe can and will create itself from nothing. Spontaneous creation is the reason there is something rather than nothing." This in turn made the late astrophysicist Carl Sagan exclaim, in the preface of one of Hawking's books, that such a cosmological model has "left nothing for a creator to do." Others, such as the cosmologist Lee Smolin, also made sure there is no space left for a Creator by proclaiming that "by definition the Universe is all there is, and there can be nothing outside it." Amazing what definitions can do. They can certainly cause an eclipse of God.

Another attempt to eliminate the idea of "creation out of nothing" was made by Alexander Vilenkin. He developed an explanation of the Big Bang in terms of "quantum tunneling from nothing"—as a fluctuation of a primal vacuum. Just as sub-atomic particles appear to emerge spontaneously in vacuums in laboratories, as a result of what some have called "quantum tunneling from nothing," so the whole Universe may be the result of a similar process, he believes. Again, if true, that would be the end of any belief in a Creator. Stephen Hawking, for instance, did not get tired of declaring that science provides a "more convincing explanation" for the Universe than God. Where do these cosmologists go wrong? More than ever, we need to pray, "God, be our light. Shine in our darkness."

b. How the Sun Reclaims the Day

The outcome of what was described in the previous section is that the religious concept of creation and the religious belief in a Creator got lost in the process, thus reducing each one of us to cosmic dust. In other words, we are left alone in this Universe. The question is, of course, whether that is really a valid conclusion. In order to find out, we could get some help from philosophy and religion. We need to start with some groundwork that may seem convoluted to you at first, but it will pay off if you bear with me.

To begin with, we should explain what philosophy and theology tell us about the difference between the Creator and what the Creator created. St. Thomas Aquinas calls God a "Primary Cause," and all the causes science deals with he would refer to as "secondary causes." It is the secondary causes that we are all familiar with—"like causes having like effects." Science deals with this kind of causality. It is the causality that reigns "inside" the Universe, linking causes together in a chain of secondary causes—including the chains of causes and effects that cosmologists talk about.

How can we explain such chains of causes? Circular causation is obviously out of the question. The philosopher Michael Augros puts it simply, "You can't be your own father." You just cannot give your own existence to yourself or receive it from yourself. Infinite regression won't work either. St. Thomas uses the example of an infinite series of fathers and sons. Each son's existence is caused by his father, back in time. Theoretically, this sequence can even go back infinitely far in time. That would be an example of infinite regress. Although infinite regress is perfectly acceptable in mathematics—negative numbers go on to infinity just as positive numbers do—it is not acceptable when it comes to real beings. Real beings are not like numbers: they need causes. Just like circular causation, infinite causation going infinitely back in time does not really explain anything. Although each son's existence is caused by his father, the cause of that father must go back in time in an infinite way without ever finding a "first father" in the link of fathers— and therefore, without finding a real cause or explanation.

Besides, even if infinite causation would explain

something, it certainly does not explain everything about fathers and sons, for the question remains: what is it that enables fathers to generate sons at all. Moreover, something else would require an explanation as well: A sequence of events in time may be able to go infinitely forward through the future and back through the past, but the problem would still be that we are dealing here with time, which itself must have some other form of cause. Consequently, the explanation for all of this would not take us to another cause in this sequence of secondary causes, as Thomas calls them, but to a cause at a higher level, so to speak. That's what Thomas means by the Primary Cause. It is a Cause that exists eternally and explains the sequence of secondary causes—a Transcendent Cause, if you will, outside and above the sequence of secondary causes. Peter Kreeft compares infinite regress and infinite causation with an "endless passing of the buck. God is the one who says, 'The buck stops here.'"

And then there is the problem that any part of the chain can only do any causing unless it first exists. For something to cause itself to exist, it would have to exist before it came into existence—which is logically and philosophically impossible. Things that exist cannot explain their own existence—they are not self-explanatory nor self-sufficient. In other words, the need for causes must come to an end: There must be a cause that is not itself in need of a cause and does not come into existence—a Primary Cause or First Cause.

One could also say that the Primary Cause provides a "point of suspension" for the chain of secondary causes itself, so to speak. Augros uses the simple example of an I-beam with a hook on it from which a chain is to be hung: "If there is nothing for that whole chain to hang from, it will not hang, and nothing can be hung from it. There is nothing about those links in themselves that makes them want to hang in space.... There must also be something from which things hang and which is not itself hanging from anything." Without a Primary Cause there could not be a chain of secondary causes. It is like the framework around a spider's web; without that framework, the web could not exist. In a similar way, God is the Eternal and Infinite Cause, "in whom we live and move and have our being" (Acts 17:28).

Perhaps a word of caution first. Obviously, the "primary cause" is not understood here as the "main cause" in a series of causes. God as a Primary Cause is not a super-cause among other causes, but he is "above" and "beyond" all secondary causes, brings them into being, and lets them do their own work—acting as a secondary cause, that is. It is only thanks to the Primary Cause that creatures can become secondary causes. In other words, God is not a deity like Jupiter or Zeus—not a being stronger than other beings or superior to all other beings, not acting like all other beings. Instead, he is the very Source of all being—the Absolute Ground of all that exists. The "first" cause is not a cause before all other causes in time, but a cause before all others in causal power. It is the one and only cause of other causes that does not itself depend on any other cause. Put differently, there is no need to go back in time or in a sequence of causes to determine whether there is a First Cause.

It is classically said that the Primary Cause is un-caused—not self-caused, but the Source of all being; not a cause prior to and larger than other causes, but a Primary Cause; not a power stronger than and superior to all other powers, but an Infinite Power; not some super-being among other beings, who acts like other beings, but an Absolute Being. We are talking here about the Creator behind all that is, behind all that cannot explain itself. Without a Primary Cause, there could not be any of the secondary causes that science deals

Chapter 1: Cosmologists and God

with. Even we ourselves are contingent beings who could easily not have existed, as the reason for our existence cannot be found within ourselves—we are not self-explanatory nor self-sufficient.

Therefore, we depend for our existence on an overarching, transcending "ground," or an Absolute Ground—a "First Cause" or "Primary Cause," in terms of Thomas Aquinas. It has to be stressed again that when Aquinas describes God as the First Cause, what he meant is not merely "first" in the sense of being before the second cause in time, and not "first" in the sense of coming before the second cause in a sequence, but rather "first" in the sense of being the source of all secondary causes, having absolutely primal and underived causal power—a power from which all other causes derive their causal powers. Without a First Cause, none of the secondary causes could exist, let alone become causes themselves.

Some may wonder what then caused the First Cause, or who created the Creator. The idea behind this question is probably that "everything needs a cause," so why not the Creator? However, thinking that way would lead to an infinite regression. Instead we should rephrase the question as follows: "Everything that has come into existence needs a cause." Something that does not exist cannot bring itself into existence. But God, on the other hand, never came into existence—that is, God is the uncaused cause, the eternal cause who has always been in existence, not even self-caused. Therefore, the question "Who created God?" is illogical, just like the question "To whom is a bachelor married?" is illogical. It makes no sense to ask "What is God's cause?" because God never began to exist, and only that which begins to exist needs to have a cause.

Secondary causes, on the other hand, are contingent; that is to say, they don't have to exist, and so because they do exist, we can ask for the cause of their existence. God, in contrast, is a necessary and eternal being who did not come into existence but always has been. Since God is transcendent to the world of cause-and-effect, God is not determined by the world of causes and effects. The Primary Cause is what gives every created entity the power to be the secondary cause of something else.

Once we understand this terminology, we are probably better equipped to enter into a discussion about cosmology and creation. There seems to be a fundamental confusion in this debate concerning the idea of "creation out of nothing" [creatio ex nihilo]. Thomas Aquinas can help us disentangle some knots. He would say that when philosophers speak of creation "out of nothing," they certainly are not talking science, let alone physical cosmology. They are talking in terms of the Primary Cause, who is not a secondary cause, and thus not an object of science.

Aquinas makes an important distinction between producing [facere] and creating [creare]. Science is about "producing" something from something else—it is about secondary causes, about changes in this Universe, about changes from one thing to another thing, about "like causes having like effects." Science is about the world of secondary causes, which necessarily leaves the Primary Cause untouched. Creation, on the other hand, is about "creating" something from nothing—which is not a change at all; certainly not a change from "nothing" to "something." In other words, the Creator doesn't just take pre-existing stuff and fashion it, as does the Demiurge in Plato's Timaeus. Nor does he use some something called "nothing" and create the Universe out of that. Rather, God as Primary Cause calls the Universe into existence without using pre-existing space, matter, time, or whatever. Whereas science deals with secondary causes, creation has everything to do with the Primary Cause. This terminology may seem complex, but it will help us clear up some conceptual confusion. Here is how.

Creation is not a change, it's a cause, but of a very different, indeed unique, kind—a Primary Cause. Therefore, creating something "out of nothing" is not producing something out of nothing—which would be a conceptual mistake, for it treats nothing as a something, and it confuses "creating" with "producing." On the contrary, the Christian doctrine of creation ex nihilo claims that God creates the Universe out of nothing—which is very different from making it out of anything. Creation has everything to do with the philosophical and theological question as to why things exist at all, before they can even undergo any change. Therefore, creation—but not the Big Bang—is the reason why there is something rather than nothing (including something such as the law of gravity).

Seen in this light, Hawking's idea of a "spontaneous creation" is sheer philosophical magic, actually nonsense. Hawking was a good scientist, but that does not necessarily make him a good philosopher. For something to create itself, it would have to exist before it came into existence—which is logically and philosophically impossible. How could the Universe "create itself" from nothing—let alone cause itself? As we said before, no son can be his own father. The law of gravity cannot do the trick, for before the Universe could ever supposedly "create itself," we have to posit the existence of laws of physics—which are ultimately the set of laws which govern the existing Universe. So Hawking is actually saying that laws which have meaning only in the context of an existing Universe can generate that Universe (and themselves) before either exists—which makes again for a logical contradiction. It is like saying that you created yourself out of nothing without anything else involved.

Thomas Aquinas would join the great philosopher Aristotle in responding that whenever there is a change, there must be something that changes, for nothing comes from nothing. Plenty of nothing is still nothing—you can have "plenty" of it, but it is still nothing. All change requires an underlying material reality. So it is a mistake—a category-mistake if you will—to use arguments coming from the natural sciences to deny creation in philosophy and theology. Perhaps Albert Einstein was right after all when he said: "It has often been said, and certainly not without justification, that the man of science is a poor philosopher."

Apparently, the real nature of the concept of "creation out of nothing" has eluded many cosmologists. Hawking, as we saw, tells us that gravity would be able to "create" the Universe—spontaneously, so to speak, or automagically. And the British physical chemist Peter Atkins claims that science has a limitless power and must even be able to account for the "emergence of everything from absolutely nothing." In response to such jumbled claims, Thomas Aquinas would keep hammering on the distinction between producing and creating, or between changing and creating, or between secondary causes and Primary Cause. God, being the Primary Cause, operates in and through secondary causes, including the Big Bang. But the Big Bang does not bring anything into "being"; it works with what is already there in existence. We cannot put these two concepts on the same level, let alone in competition with each other. Creation is very different from what science is searching for. Science can only investigate what already exists, but creation is the source or cause of all that exists. Creation is about the Primary Cause, science about secondary causes.

So it needs to be stressed that creation does not mean changing a no-thing into a some-thing, or changing something into something else—like chemists change water into hydrogen and oxygen. Instead it means bringing everything into being and existence. In other words, "nothingness" is not a highly unusual kind of exotic "stuff" that is more difficult to observe or measure than other things; it is not some kind of element that has not found a position yet in the periodic system; it is in no way a material thing that can change into something else, but it is actually the absence of anything—and therefore we cannot treat no-thing as a some-thing. The theologian David Bentley Hart puts it this way: "Physical reality cannot account for its own existence for the simple reason that nature—the physical—is that which by definition already exists."

When Alexander Vilenkin tries to explain the Big Bang in terms of "quantum tunneling from nothing"—as a fluctuation of a primal vacuum—he falls into a similar trap. "Nothing" in physics is really "something," whereas in metaphysics it refers literally to no-thing. When an electron and a positron collide, they can "annihilate" and thus change into "nothing" [nihil]. What really happens is that when they annihilate, they emit a burst of energetic photons—which is certainly not "nothing" in a metaphysical sense. On the other hand, the reverse can occur too; that happens when an "empty" space is filled with an electric field, but no particles. In that situation, there is a certain probability that suddenly an electron-positron pair will pop out of "empty" space. It happens by a process called "quantum tunneling," which causes some "system" to change from one "state" (an electric field without particles) into another "state" (a changed electric field with two particles). These are different "states," but of the same "system." However, it must be realized that a pair of particles does not suddenly appear out of "nothing," but actually out of an electric field of an existing "system"— which, again, is not nothing in a metaphysical sense. Let's leave it at that.

Something similar can be said about the use of quantum tunneling at the time of the Big Bang, as if this could make a Universe suddenly pop into existing from "nothing" by a quantum fluctuation—a fluctuation of a primal vacuum. As William E. Carroll puts it succinctly, "it is still something—how else could 'it' fluctuate?" We are dealing here again with a "system" that has a set of possible "states." There is even a "no-Universe state" that precedes a "one-Universe state," so to speak. Obviously a state is a state, certainly not "nothing." It is a specific "state" of a specific, complicated quantum "system" governed by definite laws. The particle physicist Stephen Barr uses the analogy of having a bank account with no money in it: even if we have "nothing" in the bank, we still have a bank, with all that comes with it, but it happens to be in a "no-money state" for us. This kind of "nothing" is different from having no bank account at all.

Therefore, we need to recognize that the "nothing" discussed by present-day cosmologists is not absolutely nothing in the literal sense. Those who claim that a "vacuum" or "nothing" can be described mathematically with a wave function—which they consider the quantum gravity equivalent of the quantum vacuum in quantum field theory—seem to entirely miss the point that such a wave function also is something rather than nothing. Scientists sometimes use the same terms as philosophers and theologians, but they use them in a very different sense. So what scientists call a "vacuum" or "annihilation" or "nothing" is very different from the philosophical concept of "nothing" (nihil) in "creation out of nothing."

As the English physicist and Anglican priest John C. Polkinghorne puts it, "When quantum cosmologists gaily characterize their inflated vacuum fluctuation as being the scientific equivalent of *creatio ex nihilo*,... they entirely miss the point." When God created ex nihilo, he did not use some peculiar sort of stuff called nihil from which to make the Universe. Then Polkinghorne continues, "A quantum vacuum is not nihil, for it is structured by the laws of quantum mechanics and the equations of the quantum fields involved." The contention of these new theories is that the laws of physics would be sufficient to account for the origin and existence of the Universe. But that idea is based on a conceptual mix-up. A "vacuum" in physics is not "nothing," and "nothing" in philosophy is not a "vacuum"; these two terms are not the same but belong to two very different vocabularies.

Nevertheless, some scientists maintain that the origin and existence of the Universe is entirely a physical issue. If there is any metaphysical assumption lurking behind this idea, it is that the mere existence of things needs no further explanation. This view has rightly been caricaturized by the Boston College philosopher Peter Kreeft as a magical "pop theory" that has things pop into existence without any cause. A Higgs boson, for instance, cannot just pop itself into existence; it must have a cause, because it does not and cannot have the power to make itself exist, for then it would have to exist before it came into existence. This may not be a logical necessity, but it is a metaphysical necessity, for it is impossible for things to pop into being without a cause—"out of nothing," that is.

This takes us to another sort of confusion in this debate: was creation the beginning of the Universe? Let us make clear first that there is no logical contradiction in the notion of an eternal created Universe. An eternal Universe would be no less dependent upon God, the Primary Cause, than a Universe which has a beginning of time. Even if there had always been a Universe and that it never "began," even then could it only exist at any moment in time because the

Primary Cause is causing it to. It could be possible, for instance, that explosions and collapses follow each other in an endless sequence of expanding and contracting. If so, the Universe might have never had a beginning. Aristotle, for one, believed in a first cause, but not in a beginning of the Universe. But in 1215, the Fourth Lateran Council taught that the Universe was created "out of nothing at the beginning of time"—an idea which would have scandalized both ancient Greeks and nineteenth-century positivists, but which is now a commonplace of modern cosmology.

Yet, if there was a beginning—which is suggested by the Big Bang theory—we have reason to ask: was the Big Bang "preceded" by creation; was it creation that triggered the Big Bang; was creation the event that happened "before" the Big Bang took place, or could even take place? These seem to be legitimate questions, but only if we take "before" in the sense of "causally prior," not "temporarily prior." In that specific sense, creation must come "first" before any events, even a Big Bang, can follow. But creation is not an event at all. Creation concerns the origin of the Universe—its source of being—not it's beginning in time. So there is nothing before creation in time. Creation is not some distant event; instead it is the complete causing of the existence of everything that is—in the past, now, and in the future. Creation must come "first" in the order of primacy, not in the order of time. Creation itself is just not another cause in a sequence of secondary causes, but it is the cause that makes all secondary causes possible. Creation is not temporarily prior to the Big Bang, but causally prior.

It is thanks to the Big Bang Theory that we can now raise the question of the beginning of time. Obviously, the unfolding of the Universe, starting with the Big Bang, is a process that plays in time and can be studied by the physical sciences. Creation, on the other hand, cannot follow a

Chapter 1: Cosmologists and God

timeline, as time itself is a product of creation as well. Time is something that began at one point. Albert Einstein had already showed us that both time and space are part of the physical world, just as much as matter and energy. In point of fact, time can be manipulated in the laboratory. The presence of mass (and more generally energy) causes space-time to curve. And near the horizon of a black hole, where the curvature of space-time is quite finite, black holes stretch time by an infinite amount—that is, black holes cause infinite 'dilation of time.'

If time is part of the physical world, then we cannot place creation at the beginning of time, since there is no time until time has been created. Creating time "at a certain time" is just tough to do! God himself is time-less. Creation is not something that happened long ago in time, and neither is the Creator someone who did something in the distant past, as the Creator does something at all times—by keeping a contingent world in existence. Whereas the Universe may have a beginning and a timeline, creation itself does not have a beginning or a timeline; creation actually makes the beginning of the Universe and its timeline possible.

In other words, creation creates chronology, but it is not a part of chronology. If time started with the Big Bang, then it does not make sense to ask what happened "before" the Big Bang, because there was no time yet until time had been created. (It is possible, though, that something existed before the Big Bang, even though in the simplest and currently standard model of cosmology nothing did.) William E. Carroll is right when he stresses that we should never confuse temporal beginnings with metaphysical origins. Once we lose sight of this important distinction, we are in for a dangerous mix-up.

If rightly understood, creation is not a "one-time deal," but instead it copes with the question as to where this

The Eclipse of God: Is Religion on the Way Out?

Universe ultimately comes from, as to how it came into being and how it stays in existence. The answer is that it does not come from the Big Bang, but may have started with the Big Bang. Without creation, there could not be anything—no Big Bang, no gravity, no evolution, not even a timeline. Creation sets the "stage" for all of these things and keeps this world in existence. Hence, we cannot put the "seven days of creation" at the beginning of the Book of Genesis against the scenario of the Big Bang. The theologian Scott Hahn has pointed out that we might misunderstand the point of "seven days," if we do not understand that the ancient Hebrew word for seven is the same word used for "making a covenant." So, what the first chapter of the Book of Genesis is telling us is that God has created the world in a covenantal relationship with the Divine, making it a trustworthy bond that we can rely on. He faithfully keeps the world in existence.

In other words, the Book of Genesis is not a scientific theory of the world's beginning, but rather a monotheistic creed about the world's origin and foundation. The "rest of the story" would be something for science to tell—and science is definitely trying hard to do so. Take the analogy of a novel: the beginning of the novel consists of its first words or sentences; but the origin of the novel is what the author of the novel has come up with. This allows Carroll to state again, "We do not get closer to creation by getting closer to the Big Bang," because creation is not an event in the explanatory domain of cosmology—it is a metaphysical and theological concept regarding the origin of the Universe. The Big Bang did not "create" time, any more than it "created" gravity, let alone the law of gravity. Only creation ex nihilo does!

Therefore, what some cosmologists try to discard cannot be discarded by science, because creation is a philosophical and theological concept, not a scientific one. Seen in this light, there should not be any warfare between cosmology and religion. The metaphor of warfare is highly misleading; it would be more accurate to speak of an "encounter" between the two. God remains the "Maker of Heaven and Earth." God is the reason why the Universe exists and why it has laws. It is up to science to describe how those laws work.

This should be "breaking news" for all those who see a conflict between creation in religion and the Big Bang in cosmology. Some have used this make-believe conflict to claim that there has always been a conflict between science and religion. But that is a myth. Thomas Aquinas could not have said it more clearly, "The truth of our faith becomes a matter of ridicule among the infidels if any Catholic, not gifted with the necessary scientific learning, presents as dogma what scientific scrutiny shows to be false."

Yet the conflict myth remains a popular narrative. Stephen Barr testifies to this: "Ask a Catholic audience whose name they associate with the Catholic Church and science. 'Galileo!' they shout. Ask them about Lemaître, Grimaldi, Stensen, Secchi—or Piazzi—and you get blank stares. Is it any wonder the science-religion warfare myth persists?" Nevertheless, it is a make-believe conflict that wrongly assumes that science and religion are dealing with the same questions and the same concepts, so when they come up with different answers, then either science or religion must be wrong. Needless to say that religion usually is considered the loser in this conflict.

Once we understand that cosmology and creation deal with different "territories"—and therefore different concepts, different questions, and different answers—we realize that creation and cosmology are not in conflict with each other. Nowadays we often hear the question, "Are we alone in this Universe?" The answer most people expect is that there might be life somewhere else in the Universe, perhaps as much as intelligent life. That is a scientific answer. But even if this answer turns out to be true, one could still claim that we are alone in the Universe if there is no God—which makes for a religious answer. If there is a Universe without creation and without a Creator—let us assume for a moment that's possible—then we would still be alone. But most people never think of the possibility that there is also a religious sense of "being alone in the Universe," because they live in a time of God's eclipse.

Chapter 1: Cosmologists and God

2

Biochemists and God

Cosmologists are not alone in trying to obscure God. Attacks on religion have also come from scientists in the fields of chemistry and biology. Biochemistry and molecular biology are bordering fields in the life sciences. What they have in common is that they both focus on the molecular structure of chemical compounds that play a role in living systems—molecules such as DNA, proteins, hormones, neurotransmitters, and so on.

There is no doubt, scientists in these fields have tremendously enriched our lives with so many discoveries that we enormously benefit from in daily life, but they also have given us much to be suspicious of. Let's find out more.

a. How the Eclipse Sets in

The basic idea behind molecular and biochemical research is that an organism can be treated as a machine, as if it were an intricate network of "cogs and wheels," with one cause being set into motion by another cause, thus working with clockwork precision. In biochemistry, the mechanical model of cogs and wheels has been replaced by the biochemical model of enzymatic reactions—yet the outcome is the same. Through this approach, the human body has become a "machinery" of biochemical pathways. The metabolism of glucose, for instance, is a very deterministic process of breaking glucose down, step-by-step, into carbon dioxide and water, thereby releasing energy stepwise in small "packets" of ATP—and this is just one of the many intricate biochemical pathways at work in our bodies. All of life seems to be a matter of elaborate, molecular cascading pathways of cause-and-effect. In a nutshell, the secret of life can be found in its molecules.

The victory of this approach dates back to the 19th century. In the early 1800s, biologists still thought that ferments—which we now refer to as enzymes—are linked to a living cell. Destroy a cell, they said, and ferments can no longer cause fermentation after the destruction of something that they called an immaterial "life-force." Then in 1896, the German chemist Eduard Buchner mashed a group of cells with sand until they were totally destroyed. He then extracted the liquid that remained and added it to a sugar solution. He was amazed to discover that the cell-free liquid still caused fermentation, although it no longer carried the "life-force" deemed necessary to bring about fermentation. Apparently, the ferments themselves could cause fermentation, even though separate from any living organism. That discovery basically marked the end of any "life-force" idea. Biology had become a physico-chemical science.

The idea behind this "nuts-and-bolts" approach is basically old. It is called *mechanicism*—a philosophical doctrine to declare that all living beings, including human beings, are only and merely machine-like automata, which just follow all the physical laws of the Universe. They are machines that run with clockwork precision, controlled by the machinery of their bodies. Because it assumes that the only factors operating in living systems are physical factors, mechanicism is basically a form of materialism applied to living beings, but then with something like a "machine-like effect."

From then on, it was easy to conclude that if mechanicism combined with materialism can account and explain so much of the Universe, why not push it to its logical conclusion? Why not make this the complete principle of interpreting the whole of the Universe including ourselves? That is the idea probably best known from the French physician and philosopher Julien de La Mettrie who wrote a book entitled *Man a Machine* (1748). But the idea is much older. We find it already in 1637 when René Descartes argued that the world is like a machine, its pieces like clockwork mechanisms, and that the machine could be understood by taking its pieces apart, studying them, and then putting them back together to see the larger picture again. It is that nuts-and-bolts approach.

We find the same idea also in the work of one of the pioneers of biochemistry, Claude Bernard (1813-1878). As he put it, "Now, a living organism is nothing but a wonderful machine endowed with the most marvelous properties and set going by means of the most complex and delicate mechanism." The Russian physiologist Ivan Pavlov extended this approach even further into the domain of psychology: "Essentially only one thing in life interests us: our psychical constitution, the mechanism of which was and is wrapped in darkness."

Soon it became common practice to apply this technique to any kind of scientific study—not only in the physical sciences, but also in the life sciences, and even in the social sciences. This technique became so popular and so successful that more and more scientists began to believe that mechanicism is the only way of understanding their object of study. So it is probably no coincidence that many discoveries about the working of the human body were inspired by the latest technological contraptions of the time. Our understanding of many human organs came in the form of machine-like mechanisms. The camera with its lens helped us understand the working of the human eye. Bellows clarified how the lungs can do their work. Pumps revealed what the heart does for blood circulation. Computers threw some light on the working of the brain. In line with this, food is to the body what fuel does to the steam-engine. No wonder then, when things go wrong, we use technological devices to correct them: lenses, hearing aids, pace makers, and prostheses. In all these examples, the case could be made that technology was an important driving force for scientific advancement. It has been said that science has profited more from the steam engine than the steam engine from science. As a matter of fact, scientific discoveries often start with technological inventions—which is in essence some form of mechanicism.

Although most biologists nowadays won't publicly declare themselves defenders of mechanicism, they are exclusively interested in material entities and the interaction of physical and chemical factors. They may not consider a human being a real machine, but at least as some kind of mechanism. Even in healthcare, they think of a human being as a machine-like mechanism that needs to be "repaired" if it isn't working properly, so we can fix or replace parts of it as if they were parts of a machine. Thus we lose sight of the "whole" in favor of its mechanical "parts," because the "whole" is considered nothing more than the sum total of its material parts; only the parts are believed to be "real," and the rest is fiction. Thus we end up with the monopoly of molecules—or atoms, if you want to go farther "down" the ladder. Physical components have taken exclusive center stage in the mind of many biologists and biochemists.

This outcome seems to have entitled many of them to make extravagant claims about the role of molecules. Edward O. Wilson is one of them, when he exclaims, "People are DNA's way of making more DNA." James Watson said about his co-discoverer of DNA, Francis Crick, that he told "everyone within hearing distance that we had found the secret of life." From then on, life is nothing more than a string of DNA, and love is nothing but a product of molecular interactions. Francis Crick himself would add to this, "Almost all aspects of life are engineered at the molecular level, and without understanding molecules we can only have a very sketchy understanding of life itself."

To cut a long story short, it is clear that what these scientists try to discard is everything that cannot be reduced to parts, particles, molecules, quantities, and equations. Every object that exists, they say, can be taken apart, broken down into its pieces, and then be scientifically quantified, counted, and measured. Therefore, if something cannot be scientifically quantified or taken apart, it does not exist physically in time and space, and for that reason does not exist at all. Since spiritual entities in religion have never been and will never be scientifically quantified, so the reasoning goes, they are not proven to exist, and what is worse, cannot possibly exist.

In this view, we are only able to know and study material objects that can be perceived by the five senses. Because we cannot know nonmaterial things, so they say, we must conclude that such things do not exist. The material world is, in the words of Carl Sagan, "all that is, or ever was, or ever will be." What materialism and mechanism do not detect does not and cannot exist, period! It is only through science that we know things, but when it comes to everything else, we can only be dealing with fantasy or fiction. Gone are words like love, trust, faith, religion. Where do these materialists and mechanicists go wrong? We need to pray again, "God, be our light. Shine in our darkness."

b. How the Sun Reclaims the Day

The idea, or belief, that molecules are the secret of life is very widespread among scientists. The physical chemist Peter Atkins, for instance, had the arrogance to exclaim that scientists such as biochemists "are privileged ... to see further into the truth than any of their contemporaries." Somehow, it remains a timeless temptation to make extravagant claims disguised as science. However, people like Atkins fail to remember they are just specialists like any other specialists; they are specialists in doing scientific research regarding the material aspects of this world—physical, biological, or whatever—leaving everything else for other "specialists" to deal with. If they claim expertise in everything else as well, they are like plumbers trying to also fix our electricity at home—or like electricians attempting to fix our plumbing.

What gets lost in the process is that expertise in one field may not help one handle problems in another field. Scientists easily forget that they went through hyper-specialized training in a narrow field of science coupled with a lack of exposure to other disciplines and methods. So science is not what it is cracked up to be in the minds of some of its arrogant fans. Nevertheless, the tremendous power of scientific reasoning demonstrated daily in the many marvels of modern technology empowers someone like the physicist Paul Davies to think "It seems reasonable then, to have some confidence in the scientist's world-view also." It is equally reasonable, though, to question the world-view of scientists, because world-views are not scientific theories that can be tested in the lab; they are beyond scientific methodology. Besides, we might even agree with the late Nobel Laureate and biologist Konrad Lorenz that a scientist "knows more and more about less and less and finally knows everything about nothing."

Before we continue this discussion, it needs to be admitted first that mechanicism has given us a successful method of studying and analyzing nature. The *model* of a machine can be a helpful tool to better understand the working of an organism. Models simplify what is considered complex, and thus they make such complexity more accessible, controllable, and manageable. There is nothing wrong with studying an organism as a machine—the success of the machinery model proves it. But this harmless technique becomes dangerous when we claim next that an organism *is* a machine. All models are merely simplifications of reality. They are never an exact replica of what they represent; the only exact replica of an organism would be that organism itself. A road map, for instance, is a model of the countryside, but you cannot drive on a map like you drive on a road. Put differently, each model depends on "how you look at it," for all science is abstraction. Mechanicism too is a certain way of "looking" at the world in abstraction.

However, mechanicism is not just a useful method, it pretends much more in the minds of many scientists. Most "isms"—such as materialism, mechanicism, scientism, relativism, secularism, and the list goes on an on—are more than harmless techniques; they tend to turn into ideologies, doctrines, worldviews, or belief systems. They look at the world from one specific perspective, pretending this makes you see everything and all there is. But perspectives cannot be absolutized as is done with statements such as "It's all about politics." That statement may be true—at least seen from a political perspective—but it certainly does not mean that politics is all there is. Politics may be everywhere, but it is certainly not all there is. In a similar way, matter may be everywhere, but it is certainly not all there is. If matter is all there is, then one should wonder what materialism itself is. Another piece of matter?

Worldviews allow for only one way of looking at the world—one exclusive, comprehensive, universal way, so to speak. They all suffer from some form of megalomania. Worldviews are monopolistic by nature, and don't tolerate competitors. Mechanicism is one of them; it is not just a method—one out of several—but it easily becomes a dogmatic and monopolistic, authoritarian worldview that allows no room for anything but itself. However, no matter how well mechanistic models explain the workings of a human body, a human being *is* not a machine. Looking at it as if it were a machine does not make it a machine.

Mechanicism is closely linked to materialism—and that's where its shortcomings lie. Common-sense tells us there is more to life than molecules such as chemicals, genes, or hormones. As human beings, we also live by the grace of desires, plans, dreams, ideals, and loved ones, to name just a few. It is not only the genes, the hormones, and the brains that shape our behavior, but everything that we see and hear around us, plus all the dreams, hopes, ideals, plans, and expectations we foster in our minds. One could easily state, for instance, that Lavoisier destroyed water and broke it into pieces—oxygen and hydrogen. However, the designation H_2O betrays the manifold varieties of the element water. Drink H_2O, if you can. Swim in H_2O, if you want. Is water not H_2O then? Of course it is, but water is not only H_2O—it is *also* H_2O. H_2O is only one aspect of water-ness. Science is per definition partial and fragmentary.

Interestingly enough, materialism and mechanicism claim that "matter" is self-explanatory. Materialists may not explicitly express it that way, but for them matter is a "primary cause" that needs no further explanation, and is responsible not only for things coming into existence, but for their continuing in existence as well, because nothing can exist, so they say, without the materials out of which it is made. But can they really maintain this position as an alternative to God being the Primary Cause? It is very doubtful. Matter is anything that has mass and takes up space, so it is subject to motion and change. The Primary Cause, on the other hand, cannot be subject to motion and change. Michael Augros brings this argument to a close, "Matter itself is a *product*, receiving its very existence from the action of something before it." So God as the only Primary Cause, uncaused and motionless, remains standing; it is God who brings matter into existence and keeps it in existence. Matter cannot do so on its own. That's why matter cannot be a primary cause, no matter how "fundamental" it is in life.

Besides, one could argue that matter cannot possibly be self-explanatory. Explaining matter in purely material terms is no explanation at all, but more like a circular argument. Saying that things are what they are and that they work the way they work is not a very satisfying explanation. Material things cannot account for their own existence for the simple reason that matter is that which by definition already exists. Instead, this is the point where a serious question should pop up: why is there something like matter rather than nothing? Those who say that questions like these are not legitimate questions actually choose to adopt something like a "black-box theory"—no more questions asked! But that theory is hard to accept. If we say that nothing explains itself, and leave it at that, then we have come to the ir-rational conclusion that this Universe is absurd. If we follow instead a road to understanding, we restore rationality by stating that nothing explains itself, not even matter, and therefore needs

Chapter 2: Biochemists and God

an explanation "beyond" itself.

This makes one wonder why many people find the materialistic dogma so credible? The simple answer is: because the world of our sense-experience and of our imagination and memory is filled with nothing but individual objects, all of which are physical bodies, material things, or their attributes. The fact that the world we perceive through our senses and all the things we can imagine and remember are individual physical things or material embodiments gives great credibility to the materialistic thesis that the world of real existences is entirely material, and that nothing immaterial really exists. So when Francis Crick exclaimed, "without understanding molecules we can only have a very sketchy understanding of life itself," he was perhaps right, but he may not have realized you cannot turn this statement around: although understanding molecules does certainly add to our understanding of life, understanding life is nevertheless more than understanding molecules, for there is arguably more to life than molecules. In addition, there is more to human life than animal life. What goes beyond molecules, for example, are the *beliefs* human beings foster, no matter whether it is in science or in religion.

Beliefs belong to the immaterial world of thoughts, and thoughts in turn can be true or false—which sets them apart from all the material things we encounter in this world. How could mechanicism and materialism ever deal with thoughts? In a world of molecules, there is only talk of being small, heavy, strong, and what have you—but not of being true and false, or right and wrong. Suddenly, we find ourselves in a non-material world where things are not large or small, light or heavy, hard or soft—but true or false, and right or wrong instead. Thoughts have no mass, no size, no color. So materialism leaves us only one choice: there would be no world of true and false, there would be no world of non-material thoughts, and good logic would be as misleading as bad logic. Mechanicism claims that all mental states (thoughts, emotions, desires, personality traits, etc.) are really and only physical states of a machine—perhaps a complex one, but nevertheless a machine. If this were true then what we perceive as a mental state (love, hatred, envy, joy) would simply be a certain pattern of electrical activity in our brain cells. But as Stephen Barr notes, "One pattern of nerve impulses cannot be truer or less true than another pattern, any more than a toothache can be truer or less true than another toothache."

As a matter of fact, the way we know the contents of our own thoughts is not by using any of our five senses to apprehend it, or by some scientist taking a measurement, or by someone else telling us so; rather, we have direct, unimpeded access to our own thoughts. We are directly aware of what we think and know. We simply introspect, and we know. People have known the contents of their own minds from time immemorial without knowing anything about brains. So thoughts must be more than material brain waves—in the same way as love is more than a chemical reaction. The burden of proof is on whoever denies this. We will discuss this issue further in 5.b.

The problem of materialism and mechanicism is that those who reduce reality to material objects merely *assume*, in advance, that nonmaterial objects cannot exist. First they limit themselves to material things, and then they claim there are only material things. But those who deny the existence of anything immaterial do not seem to realize that they thereby also deny the existence of their very own denial, since all statements, including denials, are immaterial—they are either true or false. A world-view—for that's what it is—claiming there are only material things is as fragile as the "material" that supposedly generated this world-view. In

Chapter 2: Biochemists and God

contrast, it is rather commonsense that the world of facts, laws, and beliefs is an immaterial world—perhaps dealing with and referring to the material world, but definitely distinct from the material world. The physician Tod Worner poses a serious question: "If matter is all there is, what is the mathematical constant *pi*?" If materialism is true, then universal, immutable, and abstract concepts truly cannot exist by themselves. And yet they do.

In addition, one could adduce some simple examples that show that there must be more than matter, even in science. Fr. Joe Heschmeyer uses the example of isomers in chemistry. When two or more (different) compounds share the same molecular formula but different structural formulas, they are called isomers. For instance, there are three different compounds with the molecular formula C_3H_8O: methoxyethane, propanol, and rubbing alcohol. These are different substances, with different chemical properties. Yet these differences are not material—they're immaterial. That is, each of the three substances is made up of the same atoms, so they are materially identical. It is the arrangement of those molecules that determines whether the substance will be methoxyethane, propanol, or rubbing alcohol. The same matter, in different forms, produces different substances. Their differences are immaterial, rather than material.

Then another question arises: did mechanicism obscure God? It certainly did. If there is anything left of God, it is at best the God who sets the world's machinery in motion. This is the God of *deism* who once made the world, but as a watch-maker who makes a watch, lets it run its own course, and then abandons it to itself—the "hands-off" approach, so to speak, of an absent landlord. That is a kind of god we can easily dispense with. In contrast to deism, *theism* tells us that the Creator of this world remains very involved with this world, not only by sustaining and preserving what he has created, but also by guiding its further development. Whereas in deism we are in search of God, in theism God is also in search of us. It is obvious that mechanicism leaves no room for theism.

The question remains, of course, whether the God of theism can still be actively present in a law-abiding Universe and a world of "law and order"—other than by keeping everything in existence. To answer this question in the affirmative, a simple analogy might be helpful, imperfect as all analogies are but yet very telling. When watching a game on the golf course or on the pool table, we see balls following precisely determined courses of cause and effect; they follow physical laws and are subject to a cause-and-effect mechanism. Yet there is one element that does not seem to fit in this cascade of causes and effects—the players of the game themselves. Although we have here a cascade of physical causes and effects, there is much more going on during these games: the players have a very specific intention in mind, which eludes and transcends the laws of science. They don't go against the laws of nature, they do not change the laws of nature—yet they do go beyond those laws by using and steering them for their own purposes. People who are unable to look beyond these physical laws and causes are completely missing out on what the game is all about.

Something similar could perhaps be said about God's presence in this Universe and his Providence: God is not the god of deism but the God of theism. He is actively present in this world, not by going against the laws of nature and its secondary causes, or by supplementing or replacing them, but rather by letting them be the way they are and yet steering them in a certain direction without overstepping the autonomy of secondary causes. Is that all there is to it? Certainly not. But perhaps this analogy opens the door to

Chapter 2: Biochemists and God

better understand what God's presence is like in the world of theism. Nature is ruled by its own laws of nature, yet it is not autonomous, for it is God who upholds and directs the world by his creative, steering, and sustaining activity.

What usually comes with materialism and mechanicism is another ideology, namely the conviction that science is the only method to give us reliable knowledge about ourselves and the world around us. The connection is obvious: if there is only material stuff in the Universe, and if science deals exclusively with "matter," science must be the ideal method to study the Universe—actually the *only* method to give us reliable knowledge. This view is called *scientism*.

Let us stress first that having a conviction is not the same as having knowledge, and does not entail knowledge; conviction is feeling certain about something, whereas knowledge regards the issue itself being certain. Science on its own says nothing at all about things outside the natural world—it cannot even say that the physical world is all there is, which is what materialism postulates. When scientists declare there is nothing outside the domain of science, they are not making a statement that can be tested with scientific tools and methods. So their claim is definitely something from outside the domain of science, for one can only make a statement *about* science from *outside* science. Nevertheless, many scientists have the conviction that science provides the *only* way of finding reliable knowledge. They have a strong conviction about what counts as knowledge, and a very restrictive one at that.

To those who claim scientific superiority as their strong conviction, we should point out that science certainly is no know-all or cure-all. I know of a Jesuit biologist who used to tease his parishioners and challenge his students with a quip: "You don't need to tell me anything about life—I am a biologist." Coming from his mouth, it was a joke! But in the mouths of some scientists it is not. Students in our schools—from elementary school to college—deserve to be taught genuine science, so they and their parents should not settle for some kind of ideology. Hence, in teaching science, it should also be made clear what its limitations are—such is part of teaching genuine science as well. Teach it, but do not preach it, otherwise science becomes a semi-religion. Science becomes involved in an identity crisis, says the late physicist Fr. Stanley Jaki, "when it ignores its own method or when it lets philosophers, eager to promote their agnosticism and subjectivism, take over as the spokesmen for science."

Yet, teaching science and training future scientists usually is done with an assumption—often unspoken—that the scientific method is not only the best method there is, but also the one and only method we have to understand the world. This is what we called earlier the ideology of scientism. Supporters of scientism claim that science provides the one and only valid way of finding truth. They pretend that all our questions have a scientific answer phrased in terms of particles, quantities, and equations. They like to broadcast that there is no other point of view than the "scientific" world-view. They believe there is no corner of the Universe, no dimension of reality, no feature of human existence beyond its reach. In other words, they have a dogmatic, unshakable belief in the omni-competence of science. It is a creed that makes for a semi-religion. What is wrong with that?

A first reason for questioning the viewpoint of scientism is a very simple objection: those who defend scientism seem to be unaware of the fact that scientism itself does not follow its own rule. How could science ever prove all by itself that science is the only way of finding truth? There is no experiment that could do the trick. Science cannot pull itself

Chapter 2: Biochemists and God

up by its own bootstraps—any more than an electric generator is able to run on its own power. One cannot talk *about* science without stepping *outside* science. Well, scientism steps outside science to claim that there is nothing outside science and that there is no other point of view—which does not seem to be a very scientific move. Whatever you neglect you cannot just reject.

Consequently, the truth of the statement "no statements are true unless they can be proven scientifically" cannot itself be proven scientifically. It is not a scientific discovery but at best a philosophical or metaphysical viewpoint—and a poor one at that. It declares everything outside science as a despicable form of metaphysics, in defiance of the fact that all those who reject metaphysics are in fact committing their own version of metaphysics. Scientism rejects any religious faith and replaces it with its own "faith." This makes scientism a totalitarian ideology, for it allows no room for anything but itself.

A second reason for rejecting scientism is that a method as successful as the one that science provides does not disqualify any other methods. A blood test, for instance, is an excellent method to assess a person's health. But there are many other reliable methods, such as X-rays, MRIs, etc., depending on what we are trying to assess. But a blood test on its own cannot be used to prove that a blood test is the best and only method there is. Yet, that is somehow similar to what scientism does; it steps outside science and then claims, in an unscientific way, that science has the only legitimate method that offers us the only reliable view on the world. First scientism declares one particular method, science, as far superior and then claims that this disqualifies any other methods. It makes for megalomania: science is a know-all and cure-all.

The late University of California at Berkeley philosopher

of science Paul Feyerabend, for instance, comes to the opposite conclusion when he says that "science should be taught as one view among many and not as the one and only road to truth and reality." Even the "positivistic" philosopher Gilbert Ryle expressed a similar view: "[T]he nuclear physicist, the theologian, the historian, the lyric poet and the man in the street produce very different, yet compatible and even complementary pictures of one and the same 'world.'" Science provides only one of these views. The astonishing successes of science have not been gained by answering every kind of question, but precisely by refusing to do so.

A third argument against scientism is the following: scientific knowledge does not even qualify as a superior form of knowledge; it may be more easily testable than other kinds, but it is also very restricted and therefore requires additional forms of knowledge. Mathematical knowledge, for instance, is the most secure form of knowledge but it is basically about nothing. Other kinds of knowledge may arguably be more significant but that makes them less secure. Einstein said it right, "As far as the laws of mathematics refer to reality, they are not certain; and as far as they are certain, they do not refer to reality." So there must be many other forms of knowledge. Consider the analogy used by the philosopher Edward Feser: A metal detector is a perfect tool to locate metals, but that does not mean there is nothing more to this world than metals.

Those who protest that this analogy is no good, on the grounds that metal detectors detect only part of reality while physics detects the whole of it are simply begging the question again, for whether physics really does describe the whole of reality is precisely what is at issue. An instrument can only detect what it is designed to detect. And that is exactly where scientism goes wrong: Instead of letting reality determine which techniques are appropriate for which parts of reality, scientism lets its favorite technique dictate what is considered "real" in life—in denial of the fact that science has purchased success at the cost of limiting its ambition.

To best characterize this restricted attitude of scientism, an image used by the late psychologist Abraham Maslow might be helpful: If you only have a hammer, every problem begins to look like a nail. So instead of idolizing our "scientific hammer," we should acknowledge that not everything is a "nail." Even if we were to agree that the scientific method gives us better testable results than other sources of knowledge, this would not entitle us to claim that only the scientific method gives us genuine knowledge of reality. Admittedly, it is true that if science does not go to its limits, it is a failure, but it is equally true that, as soon as science oversteps its limits, it becomes arrogant—a know-it-all. No wonder this has led some to criticize scientism as a form of circular reasoning. The late philosopher Ralph Barton Perry expressed this as follows: "A certain type of method is accredited by its applicability to a certain type of fact; and this type of fact, in turn, is accredited by its lending itself to a certain type of method." That's how we keep circling around.

A fourth argument against scientism is that science is about material things, yet it requires immaterial things such as logic and mathematics. G. K. Chesterton liked to ask his readers, "Why should not good logic be as misleading as bad logic? They are both movements in the brain of a bewildered ape?" Logic and mathematics are not physical and therefore not testable by the natural sciences—and yet they cannot be rejected by science. In fact, science heavily relies on logic and mathematics to interpret the data that scientific observation and experimentation provide. Logic and reason are perfect examples of the kinds of immaterial phenomena that we all know exist, but naturalistic science cannot measure, analyze, or account for. Yet, these immaterial things are true and demonstrable, even though they are beyond scientific observation.

Take, for instance, the mathematical concept of "pi" (π). It is not a material object like a melon; it is certainly more than a certain pattern of neurons firing in the brain; it is not even a property of material things, for there are no pi-sided melons—perhaps close, but never exactly. Instead, it is a precise and definite concept with logical relationships to other equally precise concepts. And concepts are mental, immaterial entities. To reduce them to a "creation of neurons" obscures the fact that "neuron" itself is an abstract concept. That would make again for a vicious circle: the very idea that concepts are nothing but neurons firing is itself nothing but neurons firing. Those who claim that mental concepts are merely products of neurons should realize that talking about neurons requires the concept of *neuron* to begin with.

Ironically, scientism itself is one of those immaterial things. First, scientists decide to limit themselves to what is material and can be dissected, counted, measured, and quantified. From then on, everything that cannot be dissected, measured, counted, or quantified is off-limits for science. But then scientism kicks in and says that there is nothing else in this world than what is material and can be dissected, measured, counted, or quantified. However, this verdict itself is not material and cannot be dissected, counted, measured, or quantified. It is more like a boomerang that destroys its own claims.

A fifth reason for rejecting scientism is that no science, not even physics, is able to declare itself a superior form of knowledge. Some scientists have argued, for example, that physics always has the last word in observation, for the observers themselves are physical. But why not say then that psychology always has the last word, because these observers are interesting psychological objects as well? Neither statement makes sense; observers are neither physical nor psychological, but they can indeed be studied from a physical, biological, psychological, or even statistical viewpoint—which is an entirely different matter. Often scientism results from hyper-specialized training coupled with a lack of exposure to other disciplines and methods, in spite of the fact that the findings of science are always partial and fragmentary.

In fact, there is no science of "all there is." Someday there may be a "Grand Unified Theory" (GUT) in physics," but that is not the same as a "Grand Unified Theory of Everything." A theory of *everything* would also have to explain why some people believe that theory and some do not. Limiting oneself exclusively to a particular viewpoint such as physics is in itself at best a metaphysical decision. However, to quote Shakespeare, "There are more things in heaven and earth, Horatio, than are dreamt of in your philosophy." One cannot give science the metaphysical power it does not possess. To make science the arbiter of metaphysics is to banish not only God from the world but also, love, hate, and meaning.

A sixth argument against scientism is of a historical nature. The first legendary pioneers of science in England were very much aware of the fact that there is more to life than science. When the *Royal Society of London* was founded in 1660, its members explicitly demarcated their area of investigation and realized very clearly that they were going to leave many other domains untouched. In its charter, King Charles II assigned to the fellows of the Society the privilege of enjoying intelligence and knowledge, but with the following important stipulation: "provided in matters of things philosophical, mathematical, and mechanical." ("Philosophical" meant "scientific" back then.) That's how the domains of knowledge were separated; it was this "partition" that led to a division of labor between the sciences and other fields of human interest. By accepting this separation, science bought its own territory, but certainly at the expense of inclusiveness; the rest of the "estate" was reserved for others to manage. On the one hand, it gave to scientists all that could "methodically" be solved by dissecting, counting, and measuring. On the other hand, these scientists agreed to keep their hands off of all other domains—education, legislation, justice, ethics, philosophy, and certainly religion.

In spite of all the above objections, scientism is still very much alive, albeit mostly hidden underground. The physicist Hendrik Casimir—the Casimir effect of quantum-mechanical attraction was named after him—once said, "We have made science our God." Indeed, science has become a semi-religion of which the scientists are the priests. Science is supposed to explain *everything* but in a much better way than God once did in their opinion. It is in this frame of mind that Stephen Hawking once exclaimed, "[O]ur goal is a complete understanding of the events around us and of our own existence." Indeed, scientism likes to broadcast, "It's all about science." Well, science may be everywhere nowadays, but science is certainly not all there is.

Scientism pops up its ugly head each time we hear statements like "X is *nothing but* Y." The list is virtually endless: "Love is nothing but a chemical reaction"; "Thoughts are nothing but a series of impulses"; "Humans are nothing but glorified animals"; "You are nothing but a pack of neurons"; "You are nothing but a bundle of instincts"; "Religion is nothing but a genetic predisposition." C. S. Lewis famously dubbed this attitude "nothing-buttery." It is an ideology under the guise of science. It treats scientific models as if they are exact replicas of what they represent.

Chapter 2: Biochemists and God

Scientists who buy into this rhetoric are advised by Ard A. Louis, professor of theoretical physics at the University of Oxford, to tell the person they love that he or she has enough phosphor (P) for 2000 matches, enough iron (Fe) for one nail, enough chlorine (Cl) to disinfect a swimming pool, and enough fat to make 0.1 bars of soap. That might be the best remedy to cure them from nothing-buttery.

Besides, "nothing-buttery" is basically suicidal. If indeed we were nothing but a "pack of neurons," this very statement would not be worth more than its molecular origin, and neither would we ourselves who are making such a statement. Claims of "nothing-buttery" just defeat and destroy themselves. They cut off the very branch that the person who makes such claims is—or actually was—sitting on. This should put a science like biochemistry in its proper place: It is a great specialty, but there must be more to life than molecules. When we "physicalize" or "biologize" some particular phenomenon, we sacrifice precisely those features that give it a character distinctive from physics or biology. Nothing-buttery ultimately obscures everything outside its scope, including God. So we need to pray again, "God, be our light. Shine in our darkness."

3

Biologists and God

You don't have to believe in evolution to know that human beings are part of the animal world, seen from a biological point of view, because we share all characteristics animals have—we all breed, feed, bleed, and excrete. Even St. Thomas Aquinas knew this, more than six decades before Charles Darwin. He called human beings animals, but set them apart as rational animals [animal rationale or rationabile]. Aquinas did not need any learned biology to see the obvious truth that humans are first of all animals. The mammals among them, for instance, share more or less the same morphological structure, in spite of obvious differences in appearance. Just the fact that all of them have seven cervical vertebrae illustrates this point—no matter whether it is in the sturdy neck of a rhino or the long neck of a giraffe. So there are similarities and dissimilarities in the animal world.

As to how these similarities and differences came about, biologists may disagree. The large majority of them would find an explanation in the process of evolution. A smaller majority of them would go for a more specific biological theory of evolution—a number of interconnected theories such as Charles Darwin's theory of natural selection and

Chapter 3: Biologists and God

Gregor Mendel's theory of genetics combined. It is this latter group of biologists—sometimes identified as Neo-Darwinists—that has, in the minds of many, done away with any kind of religious ideas about the origin and diversity of life, including a Creator. So we need to find out whether this is a justified view.

Furthermore, many biologists tend to glorify the role "chance" plays in evolution—supposedly at the cost of other explanations such as design and purpose in this Universe. Chance is supposedly "blind." It changes life into a purposeless accident. "Chance is the only source of true novelty," Francis Crick once said. If that is true, we end up living in a world of "blind fate"—a world in which the light of God has been obscured. Is that really possible?

a. How the Eclipse Sets in

Most scientists support the Neo-Darwinian theory of evolution—and I admit being one of them. The defenders of this theory argue that all organisms descend from previous generations by more or less gradual modifications, mainly based on a process of mutation (creating new alleles, and even new genes) combined with natural selection (favoring certain alleles over others). This is often called "descent with modification."

This may be the right moment to make an important distinction. There is a biological theory of evolution—sometimes called "synthetic evolutionary theory"—and then there is an ideological version of this theory—often identified with "Darwinism" or "Neo-Darwinism." The latter version is usually promoted as one of those "isms" with a worldview pretention. At the very moment biologists change evolution and its evolutionary theory into an ideology, it becomes evolutionism, which is based on some kind of belief in the omni-competence of biology, stating that everything in life can be and must be explained by evolution. In a sense it is a semi-religion that has "Mother Nature"—whatever that means—assume the role of God. It is a worldview that takes the place of any religious beliefs, and does so in the name of science.

One philosopher who quickly grasped the worldview potentials of Darwin's theory was Herbert Spencer (1820-1903). Spencer applied Darwin's theory of natural selection to a wide assortment of phenomena, ranging from psychology to sociology and up to ethics—and he rephrased the theory in terms of "survival of the fittest." It became a magic wand that is supposed to explain everything in life, from thoughts to beliefs to morals. He was soon followed by Thomas Huxley. Sometimes called "Darwin's bulldog," Huxley not only defended Darwin's scientific claims but also its worldview pretentions. He dismissed religion as a source of moral authority, and believed the mental characteristics of human beings are as much a product of evolution as their physical aspects. That's when Darwinism became a secular religion with an eschatology based on evolutionary progress. That's also when evolutionism "dethroned" God and obscured his Light.

From here it is only a small step to the Spencerian idea that human society is an arena of struggle in which "supremacists" should survive, at the cost of "misfits." This idea soon became the cornerstone of eugenics—the study and practice of selective breeding applied to humans, with the aim of actively improving the human gene pool. Eugenics basically asserts that we should breed humans like we breed animals—hence we should be able to kill them like we kill animals. The "interventions" advocated and practiced by eugenicists involved a wide range of "degenerates" or "unfits"—the poor, the blind, the mentally ill, entire "racial"

Chapter 3: Biologists and God

groups such as Jews, Blacks, Roma ("Gypsies"); all of these were deemed "unfit" to live according to their despotic dogma called "survival of the fittest." And this, in turn, led to practices such as segregation, sterilization, genocide, preemptive abortions, euthanasia, designer babies, and in the more extreme case of Nazi Germany, mass extermination. G. B. Shaw once predicted that "part of eugenic politics would finally land us in an extensive use of the lethal chamber."

Currently, the latest breed of eugenicists urges parents to have the "best" children by using what they call a pre-implantation genetic diagnosis (PGD). In this procedure, a single cell is extracted from an IVF embryo and then tested to see which embryos make the genetic cut. The embryos that "fail" the test are discarded or donated to research. The ones that "pass" have a chance to be transferred into a womb. It is hard to defend this with the slogan "Man's power over Nature," for that is what C.S. Lewis once called "a power exercised by some men over other men with Nature as its instrument." Yet, this is what happens when the science of evolutionary theory becomes a pseudo-science, the ideology of evolutionism.

Unfortunately, the distinction we just made between evolutionary theory and evolutionism is not always recognized by biologists. They easily slide, often unknowingly, from the science into the ideology. Whereas evolutionary theory is only a theory or hypothesis, evolutionism is a dogmatic stand. Like all other scientific theories, evolutionary theory is open to revision. It can be wrong (only a few biologists think so), it can be incomplete (many think so), or it can be the best we have right now (I tend to think so). Let us focus on the scientific part first before we discuss some of its worldview implications.

Darwin's theory of natural selection basically attempts to

explain nature's beautiful design in terms of physical causes and laws of nature. In other words, it deals like all other sciences with secondary causes, not the Primary Cause. Charles Darwin used to say that evolution follows laws in the same way as planets and comets follow laws in physics. The fact, for instance, that the caterpillars of a white cabbage butterfly are green rather than white (which is caused by alleles of certain genes), makes these slow organisms feeding on green cabbage less conspicuous to predators and thus more successful in survival and reproduction—which ultimately increases the frequency of alleles that cause the green color in future generations. The green color of caterpillars has a selective advantage over other colors, and therefore increases its frequency through better chances of reproduction. In other words, the green color is a successful design in the world of these caterpillars. Natural selection promotes good designs over bad designs, which makes them increase their representation in future generations. In short, natural selection promotes those (secondary) causes which have successful effects.

What Darwin basically did is he replaced explanation by divine, supernatural intervention with a physical, natural explanation based on natural causes that have successful effects, since Darwin considered it to be his scientific duty as a scientist to come up with physical and natural causes and laws. He wanted to explain how adaptations originated from within the natural world. Instead of seeing purpose in nature, and thus a Creator behind the purpose, science came to see only the operation of impersonal laws. According to Darwin, there is no longer any need in biology for a cosmic designer, for it has been the laws of science that shaped and sculpted the world in which we live.

In other words, the phenomenon of design in nature—also called teleology—is not to be explained in anthropomorphic or deistic terms, but in terms of a "materialistic" process of mutation and natural selection. But soon the denial of purpose and design in nature became virtually the denial of God. Richard Dawkins, for instance, acknowledges that biology is about "things that give the appearance of having been designed for a purpose." But all it is, in his view, is merely an "appearance." It is here that evolutionary theory may easily slip into evolutionism. It tries to keep its scientific vocabulary clean—free of "purpose" terminology, that is—but then invalidly concludes that there is no design or purpose at all in evolution, and therefore no Designer.

Not surprisingly, most biologists prefer to avoid the term teleology in favor of the term teleonomy, because in their eyes the term teleology may carry some historical baggage—with connotations of intention, purpose, foresight, or even divine planning. They introduced this new term to describe the study of goal-directed features and functions which are not guided by the conscious forethought of man or any supernatural deity. Whereas artificial selection, as done in selective breeding, promotes causes with a desired effect, natural selection promotes causes with a successful effect—which should be clearly distinguished from an "intended" effect, according to these biologists. As a consequence, the "hand of the Creator" has been replaced by the "hand" of natural selection.

This calls for some unambiguous terminology in biology. Green caterpillars achieve a goal without having that goal as a "purpose in mind"; they were just born that way. Or think of hormones that reach their target cells through the blood stream. Yes, they do in fact reach their target cells, but not so because they have a purpose that makes them intentionally go there; on their way through the blood stream, they happen to encounter specific receptors on specific target cells where they bind. Hormones do not seek like humans seek in a purposeful manner. Whereas intentions and purposes may be something in the mind of a product-maker, functions are a feature of the product itself. They function as if they are steered by a purpose—"as if" is the keyword here.

How could such seemingly purposeful behavior come along without being intended? According to biologists, it is not only natural selection that weeded out the good from the bad, but there is also a great deal of "chance" involved, especially when it comes to mutations, which is the "modification" part of "descent by modification." As a matter of fact, "chance"—or the more technical term "randomness"—plays a pivotal role in the biological theory of evolution. What do terms like these stand for?

By "random" biologists mean several things. First of all, mutations are considered random in the sense of "spontaneous." We know that certain factors increase mutations, but we don't know when they happen. Second, mutations are—as far as we know—"unpredictable" as to when and where they strike. We cannot predict at what location in the DNA mutations will hit and what changes they might generate there. Third, mutations are random in the sense of "arbitrary," because mutations do not select their target but hit indiscriminately—"good and bad" spots alike, so to speak. Fourth, mutations are also random in the sense of "aimless," because they occur without any connection to immediate or future needs of the organism. There is no physical mechanism that detects which mutations would be beneficial and then causes those mutations to occur, so they lack any "fore-sight."

Apparently, randomness in biology is a very technical (and confusing) concept, mainly borrowed from statistics and probability calculus and used when events are independent of each other. Randomness has no memory and

Chapter 3: Biologists and God

no foresight. In that sense, mutations are "statistically random"—they just happen one way or the other, but there is no direct connection with other events such as past changes, environmental changes, or immediate and future needs, so the former do not affect the latter, nor the other way around. Obviously, there is no purpose or direction to randomness or chance; if you do not believe this, just test it at a slot machine. Chance is considered "blind"; it has no "favorites," no memory, and no foresight. No wonder then most biologists take something like DNA as a random product of evolution, based on random mutations.

On the other hand, no matter how prevalent "chance" and "randomness" are in biology, those who hail "chance" as an all-pervading phenomenon have to deal with the fact that our Universe seems rather "fine-tuned"—instead of accidental and random. Science has shown us that the conditions for life in the Universe can only occur when certain universal fundamental physical constants lie within a very narrow range. Therefore, if any of several fundamental constants were only slightly different, the Universe would most likely not be favorable to the establishment and development of matter, astronomical structures, elemental diversity, or life as we understand it. William Paley, as early as 1802, pointed out that if the law of gravity had not been a so-called inverse square law, then the earth and the other planets would not be able to remain in stable orbits around the sun. And there are many more cases like these. In other words, the odds against a Universe like ours appear to be enormous.

What are these fundamental physical constants? They are physical constants that are dimensionless, which means that their values cannot be calculated, but are determined only by physical measurement. This is one of the unsolved problems of physics, because their numerical values are not understood in terms of any widely accepted theory. As

The Eclipse of God: Is Religion on the Way Out?

Stephen Hawking has noted, "The laws of science, as we know them at present, contain many fundamental numbers, like the size of the electric charge of the electron and the ratio of the masses of the proton and the electron. ... The remarkable fact is that the values of these numbers seem to have been very finely adjusted to make possible the development of life."

What do we make of these physical constants? Whereas some scientists try to tell us that we were not "meant to be here," these physical constants seem to indicate that the Universe was designed with life in mind, even human life. That's why some scientists call them "anthropic coincidences," which are features that happen to be—just coincidently—exactly what is required for the emergence of life to be possible in this Universe. These specific characteristics of the laws of physics seem to coincide exactly with what is needed for the Universe to be able to produce life, including intelligent beings like ourselves. Had any of these features be different, life would not have been possible, and certainly not intelligent life.

These are the facts, but as to how we explain or interpret them is another issue. What we just discussed does not seem to look good for the all-hailed concept of chance and randomness. Not surprisingly then, some scientists have come up with a "chance" explanation for the "oddity" of the Universe we live in. One of them is the astrophysicist Stephen Hawking. He explains "fine-tuning" as randomness in disguise by postulating some "basic stuff" underlying Universe formation. His explanation is worded by Michael Augros as follows. "This fertile nothing spews out Universes quite randomly, and so the fundamental constants in them must represent nearly all possible quantitative variations. Most of them, presumably, do not allow life. But some of them inevitably will. And the fact that we happen to live in a life-friendly one is neither a matter of design nor a wild coincidence." Apparently, Hawking thought he had brought randomness back into the picture.

But no matter which explanation we favor, the ultimate outcome remains the same: a world without purpose, without design, without meaning. Many scientists like to echo this message. The chemist Peter Atkins tells us, "We are children of chaos. ... Gone is purpose; all that is left is direction. This is the bleakness we have to accept as we peer deeply and dispassionately into the heart of the Universe." Or take this one from the biologist Douglas Futuyama: "[W]e need not invoke, nor can we find any evidence for, any design, goal, or purpose anywhere in the natural world."

The biologist Richard Dawkins is happy to join this crowd: "The Universe we observe has precisely the properties we should expect if there is, at bottom, no design, no purpose, no evil and no good, nothing but blind pitiless indifference." It is also the same Dawkins who made chance and randomness into a capricious, blind agent, almost a deity, or a "blind watchmaker" at best, according to the title of one of his books. But perhaps the most arrogant claim comes from the late paleontologist George Gaylord Simpson, who ventured to proclaim from his quasi-scientific pulpit, that "man is the result of a purposeless and natural process that did not have him in mind." In all these cases, evolutionary theory has become evolutionism—pretending to be the only valid and all-inclusive explanation of life by claiming monopoly over any other explanations.

Brainwashed by these very vocal paragons of evolutionism, many people nowadays find themselves stuck in a world of chance and randomness. The whole drama of life has become a meaningless competition. If it is indeed "chance" that ultimately drives evolution, there does not seem to be any space left for some goal or direction in evolution, let alone for a Creator. In the eyes of Dawkins, evolution leaves the designer with nothing to do. The general idea is clear: There is no purpose, no design, and therefore no Designer. We seem to live in an accidental, purposeless, and meaningless Universe. This idea has certainly caused a complete eclipse of God. Where do these biologists go wrong? We need to pray again, "God, be our light. Shine in our darkness."

b.   How the Sun Reclaims the Day

Let us make clear first that "chance" and "randomness" are very technical, statistical concepts. Some suggest that we should replace the term "random" with the more technical sounding term "stochastic," because the word "random" has so many confusing overtones. Tossing a coin is a stochastic process. There is randomness involved because the outcome is independent of what the one who tosses the coin would like to happen, and it is also independent of previous and future tosses. For example, we cannot know the outcome of a dice roll before it occurs, nor can we explain how it turns out the way it does; there are too many variables and causes acting together, such as the speed at which we throw the dice, and the way the dice bounce when they first impact the table. Yet, in the aggregate, we are able to make predictions to a certain extent in terms of probabilities. But key is that randomness has no memory and no foresight.

As we saw before with regard to materialism (see 2.b), devotees of randomness follow a similar strategy: they somehow declare chance to be the ultimate primary cause of this Universe, thus making randomness a cause that needs no further explanation. However, if randomness is the basis for change in the Universe, it must be a secondary cause and cannot be itself a primary cause. Chance events occur within nature, so chance itself cannot be a primary cause. That's why it makes no sense to capitalize "Chance" and declare it a self-explanatory principle of nature—something like the blind deity of "Doom" or "Fate." Randomness plays a very legitimate role in the sciences, but it cannot play the same role outside the domain of science. Randomness is just another created entity, another secondary cause—and therefore not the ultimate explanation of everything else in this Universe.

Our first question is then whether "chance" still leaves room for "purposes." It could very well be stated that chance does not rule out purpose. It may not seem that way, though, because the natural sciences have eliminated the term "purpose" from their vocabulary. The concept of "purpose" was taken out of astronomy by Nicolas Copernicus, out of physics by Isaac Newton, and out of biology by Charles Darwin. Astronomers do not seek the purpose of comets or supernovas, nor do chemists search for the purpose of hydrogen bonds. The sun does not rise every morning because it "wants" to, but because it follows physical laws. Water does not "seek its own level" in an intentional way. Even plants do not "seek" the light, but they do respond to the light in their environment through a light-sensing hormone, called auxin, which makes plant shoots curve towards light. Eye patterns on butterfly wings have the effect of warning enemies; that is a function of eye patterns, but not a purpose of butterflies. In all such cases, "purposes" have been replaced with causal mechanisms. The concept of purpose just plays no part in scientific explanations.

But did science really eliminate purposes? Is this the end of "purposes"? Not really. When scientists removed "purposes" from scientific discourse, they removed them as secondary causes, but they left their reference to the Primary Cause untouched. So they did not make purposes disappear

The Eclipse of God: Is Religion on the Way Out?

entirely; they just moved them from inside to outside the scientific domain. The fact that "purposes" are missing on scientific maps does not mean they do not exist at all; they are not completely out of the picture, although they are out of the scientific picture. The fact, for instance, that houses are missing on highway maps, or that human beings are missing on astronomical maps, does not entitle us to deny their existence; whatever we neglect we can never just reject for that reason. Removing purposes from the territory of science may have been a very legitimate move, but this does not entitle us to remove them from our discourse completely. There are strong indications that they cannot possibly be removed that way.

We need to ask those who keep denying the existence of any purposes at all some pertinent philosophical questions. If there is no purpose in the Universe at all, how were we ever to know there is no such thing as a purpose? As C. S. Lewis put it, "[I]f there were no light in the Universe and therefore no creatures with eyes, we would never know it was dark." Besides, we should ask those who deny the existence of purposes what the purpose is of trying to prove or claim that there is no purpose in life. As a matter of fact, denying that there are purposes in life defeats its own claim. If it is your purpose to remove all purposes from life, you are also wiping out your own purpose of doing so. Ironically, those whose purpose it is to eradicate all purposes from life have lost even the very purpose of acting that way.

That is why it is most striking to see how some people still make it their main purpose in life to claim that there are no purposes in life at all. Some even make this their mission. Scientists have to face the problem that one cannot make statements like these as scientists. First they eliminate the concept of purpose from science, but then they keep using it by rejecting it. True, once "purpose" has been eliminated

Chapter 3: Biologists and God

from science, it can no longer be used, let alone be explained, by science, as it is from now on beyond science's reach. Darwinism, for instance, just does not know whether evolution has a purpose or not, for the simple reason that the word "purpose" does not exist in its scientific vocabulary. The British philosopher and former atheist Anthony Flew probably worded it well when he said, "How can a Universe of mindless matter produce beings with intrinsic ends, self-replication capabilities, and 'coded chemistry'? Here we are not dealing with biology, but an entirely different category of problem." David Bentley Hart says about purposes that to bracket them out of one's investigations "is a matter of method, but to deny their reality altogether is a matter of metaphysics."

Apparently, it is hard, if not impossible, to deny the existence of purposes entirely. In a Universe without purposes, there could not even be any man-made machines, since such machines, curiously enough, are always made for a purpose; the world of technology is per definition purpose-driven, based on purposes that designers and engineers have in mind. Therefore, we could never ban purposes from the Universe by saying the Universe is just a machine that runs with clockwork precision, as some scientists have tried. The analogy of a machine was an unfortunate choice made by these proponents of mechanicism. There are no machines without a designer or inventor. The analogy actually gives meaning to a world of design involving the great Designer—God. So using the machine metaphor to claim there is no purpose in this Universe is a bit odd, to say the least.

Yet, "chance" remains standing tall in biology. But we have to add that it needs to be put it in its proper place in order to see what its real power is. The fact that all creatures are contingent—could not have existed, that is—does not entail they are "accidental" in the sense of mere products of blind fate. Yet, some scientists keep falling for the timeless temptation to capitalize the word "chance" by changing it into the goddess of Fate or Doom or Blind Fate. Again, they slip from a theory about evolution into a dogma of evolutionism. However, science has nothing to say about chance with a capital C. Fate is far beyond its reach, for it is in essence a worldview notion, not a scientific one. Interpreting the word random as "senseless" or "meaningless" changes life into a mere play of whimsical and fortuitous events. By so doing, we turn "Chance" into a capricious, blind agent, so we end up with the deity of chaos versus the God of order.

Let's face it, chaos is what it is—chaos! It is not some enigmatic form of "pre-order," but it is precisely what it says—chaos. C. S. Lewis once remarked, "Before you switched on the light in the cellar, there was (if you want to call it so) 'pre-light'; but the English for that is 'darkness.'" Well, the same holds for "chaos": Chaos is not pre-order, but it is what it is—chaos! Chaos and chance can never create the order found in the living and nonliving world—just as blindness can never create sight. Therefore, scientists have no right as scientists to decree that we are unintended, unplanned, unguided, fortuitous creatures or mere products of a blind and purposeless fate. That is beyond their competence as scientists.

When scientists speak of randomness in science, they are talking in statistical terms, in the sense of how things in this Universe are related to each other—not how they are related to a Higher Power, God. At the very moment they take chance as a fate issue—in the sense of "being meaningless, unintended, and purposeless"—they have left the territory of science. In the words of the particle physicist Stephen Barr, "one must distinguish between words used by scientists and words used scientifically." Therefore, no matter how biologists believe evolution operates, chance with a capital C is beyond their reach and expertise; they cannot speak about it scientifically. Science may be everywhere, but science is not all there is. Scientists as scientists are not qualified to make such judgments. The question as to whether evolution has a meaning, destination, or purpose takes us into the domains of philosophy and religion. But if science cannot invoke a goddess of fate, how then should we see "chance" in relation to the God of Creation?

First of all, we should make an important distinction between randomness in science and Providence in religion. When we speak of randomness in science, according to Stephen Barr, we are talking in statistical terms, in the sense of how things in this Universe are related to each other (for example, we exist thanks to our parents). But when we speak of Providence in religion, we are talking about how things in this Universe are related to God—not to each other (we exist thanks to God). When it comes to God, randomness has lost its original meaning. St. Padre Pio was apt to say in various ways that it is God who arranges the coincidences. He once asked a man who claimed such-and-such event had happened by chance: "And who, do you suppose, arranged the chances?" Science has no answer to this question—not even the answer "nobody did." Science always creates a fragmented reality that only religion can piece together. The proposition that the physical Universe is a closed system that does not allow for Providence is not itself a law of physics, but an assumption that can be traced back to materialism. It denies ahead of time—a priori, if you will—that Providence is even possible in a closed Universe.

In contrast, anything that seems to be random from a scientific point of view may very well be included in God's eternal plan. As a matter of fact, Thomas Aquinas once said, "Whoever believes that everything is a matter of chance, does not believe that God exists." How can this be? Well, someone like Thomas Aquinas would argue that God's position with respect to time is such that, unlike us, he does not have to wait for the future to unfold in order to know its contents. God is in no way a temporal being, but rather the Creator of time, with complete and equal access to all of its contents. But if God exists entirely outside of time—in a kind of eternal present to which all that occurs in time is equally accessible—God would indeed be able to comprehend all of history, the past and the present as well as the future, just as though they were now occurring. As the Book of Proverbs (16:33) says, "The lot is cast into the lap, but its every decision is from the Lord."

For this reason, religion emphasizes Providence, but that does not mean it has to shy away from randomness. The Bible has several examples of chance being used by casting lots. The eleven apostles used chance to have God elect a new, twelfth apostle: "Then they gave lots to them, and the lot fell upon Matthias" (Acts 1:26). Temple Priests were chosen by lot: "According to the custom of the priesthood, he was chosen by lot to enter the temple of the Lord and burn incense" (Luke 1:9). The Old Testament mentions another case: "Then Saul said, 'Cast the lot between me and my son Jonathan.' And Jonathan was taken." (1 Samuel 14:42). Apparently, there is no conflict per se between chance and Providence. Casting a lot is accidental seen from our perspective but not from God's perspective

As said earlier, Creation by God accounts for the existence of things, not for changes in things (see 1.b). An evolving Universe is still a created Universe. The concept of randomness in science is about the relationship between secondary causes, but it has nothing to say about how secondary causes are related to the Primary Cause. As to how things in the Universe are related to the Maker of the

Universe is a completely different story—and not a scientific one. Confusing primary and secondary causality is actually a "category mistake." That is the reason why a molecule like DNA may appear to us as driven by chance, from a biological point of view, but seen from God's perspective, the outcome could very well be entirely specified. That's the reason why Francis Collins, former head of the Human Genome Project, calls DNA "God's language." St. John Henry Cardinal Newman wrote in an 1868 letter: "'the accidental evolution of organic beings' is ... accidental to us, not to God." As said earlier, purposes were removed from science as secondary causes, but they still exist in connection with the Primary Cause—which is called Providence.

God's creative power is exercised throughout the entire course of cosmic history, in whatever ways that history has unfolded. God creates a Universe in which things have their own causal agency, their own true self-sufficiency. As William E. Carroll observes, "No explanation of cosmological processes, nor biological change for that matter, regardless of how radically random or contingent such an explanation claims to be, challenges the metaphysical account of creation, that is, of the dependence of the existence of all things upon God as cause." God is not a rival or contender for created causes, but rather the One who makes all secondary causes be their own causes. Earlier (see 2.b) we discussed how the analogy of playing at the golf court or at the pool table may help us better understand the role of God's Providence.

This takes us back to the issue of teleology, for teleology assumes some form of design behind the Universe and in the process of evolution. Biologists seem to have an ambivalent, contentious relationship with teleology and design. On the one hand, they keep using expressions such as "in order to" or "for the sake of" or "for the purpose of"—for instance, the heart pumps "for the sake of" circulating blood—which sounds rather teleological. On the other hand, they feel they should reject such statements as unscientific. Just as physicists reject "for the sake of" statements—for instance, when the temperature rises, gases do not expand "in order to" keep the pressure constant—so should biologists too, they think. This latter stand makes them reject any notion of design in evolution, as it reminds them of William Paley's natural theology that speaks of a "Watch-Maker," a design-Designer. They consider this a form of teleology that reeks of "intentions" and "purposes," whereas it is their general conviction there is no "planning and foresight" in evolution but only chance.

Is this the end of the design concept? Not really. George Bernard Shaw once said that Charles Darwin had thrown William Paley's "watch" into the ocean. Well, what Darwin did throw away was Paley's "watchmaker," but certainly not his legendary watch; if he did throw anything away, it was Paley's design-Designer, but certainly not the design concept itself. As a matter of fact, the concept of "design" is an artifact analogy that is as basic to Darwin's evolutionary theory as it is to Paley's natural theology. Since the heart has a design like a pump, it is a successful design that works "in order to" or "for the sake of" circulating blood—and thus is a great target for natural selection. The only difference is that someone like Paley was saying why these things are the way they are, while thinking he was also describing how they had come about.

Apparently, even Darwin himself did not discard design or what comes with it, teleology. Michael Ruse, a philosopher of biology, was right when he said that after Darwin, the heart still existed "for" circulation; the cause of its existence may have been different, but its teleology was not. As strange as it may sound, Darwin put "design" and "usefulness" back into the picture, but in a veiled way. His evolutionary theory still requires some kind of design in the background. That's why life scientists can hardly resist using teleological or design-like expressions, because natural selection works on causes with a "successful" effect—"for the purpose of," so to speak. Even the term "success" does not make sense without assuming teleology.

This brings the design concept back into the discussion. We should realize, though, that there is some potential confusion lurking here, because the word "design" in English can refer simply to a pattern, or to a purpose, or to both. Richard Dawkins, for instance, maintains that Darwinian evolution is not teleological as the term "selection" in natural selection suggests. He considers natural selection to be simply a filter to which a pool of randomly generated mutations is subjected. When he says, "good genes tend to fall through the sieve into the next generation; bad genes tend to end up in bodies that die young or without reproducing," he seems to forget that the terms "good" and "bad" already are teleological terms. His filter does not just randomly filter; it filters according to design criteria, which makes the outcome "good" or "bad." That's where teleology comes in. The result may not be an "intended" effect, like in artificial selection, but it is at least more or less a "successful" effect in evolution. However, "success" is in itself a teleological concept that is connected with another teleological concept, "design."

This takes us to the heart of the matter: Why do certain biological designs "work," and why are they "successful" and "effective" in reaching their "goal"? What is it that makes them "fit" to certain degrees? Fit for what? Or put differently: what is it that carries certain designs or patterns through the process of natural selection? The answer would go along these lines. The Universe has an overall set of restraints harnessing individual designs and making them "fit" or "successful" to a certain degree. Without a metaphysical design in the "background," biological as well as technological designs could not work at all. A heart could not pump blood if it did not follow hydrodynamic laws; a bird's wing would not let the bird fly if it did not follow aerodynamic laws. It is the "rules and laws of the cosmic design" that restrict the range of possible end results and make them more or less successful. It is the cosmic design that regulates which designs, in the sense of mere patterns, are designs with a successful outcome or purpose. That is where both meanings of the term "design" come together.

It is the cosmic design that explains which biological designs are successful in reproduction and survival—as much so as the cosmic design regulates which bridges are successful technological designs, and which are failures. Given the cosmic design, some biological designs are "better" than others in having a "better outcome" than others—a better "fit," so to speak. Natural selection can only select those specific biological designs that are in accordance with the rules and laws of the cosmic design (again, designers, engineers, and architects must aim for the same thing). Leon Kass, a University of Chicago professor and physician, could not have worded it better: Organisms "are not teleological because they have survived; on the contrary, they have survived (in part) because they are teleological." To put it differently, organisms have survived because their biological design squares well with the cosmic design. They must have "something" in their biological design that carried them through the process of natural selection. This "something" is a fit with the cosmic design. Natural selection does not explain a "fit" but uses a "fit" in order to select.

If this is right, then the filter of evolution is not natural selection the way Dawkins thinks it is. Instead, the cosmic design is the real filter. The cosmic design does not filter just randomly; it filters according to design criteria. The result may not be an "intended" effect, like in artificial selection, but is at least a more or less "successful" effect in evolution. It is the cosmic design that regulates which biological designs "work," and thus are fit and successful. That's the ultimate filter of evolution. Apparently, there is no way to avoid teleology.

Even Darwin himself always felt uneasy about his term "natural selection," because it leads almost automatically to the obvious question "Selection by whom or by what?" Indeed, the implication of a "selecting agent" is looming large. Darwin certainly tried to avoid this implication by saying he had as much right to use metaphorical language as physicists do. In his own words, "who objects to an author speaking of the attraction of gravity as ruling the movements of the planets? Everyone knows what is meant and is implied by such metaphorical expressions." Yet, in many passages, he refers to "nature," some kind of feminine deity, as the agent of selection. Eventually, his colleague Alfred Wallace convinced Darwin to replace the term "natural selection" with Spencer's notion of "survival of the fittest" in the 5th edition of his book. Nevertheless, the question of "Selection by whom or by what," remains legitimate. Although Darwin wanted to avoid this question, there is an answer for it: selection is done by the cosmic design.

Each time biologists are speaking of being "fit" or "successful," they are actually talking teleology—or teleonomy, if you will. Certain biological features of organisms are "successful" and "effective" in reaching their "goal" because they have a design that enables such a goal. If they were not design-like, they simply would not work. Natural selection does not create the fit—it can only select what fits. A good fit comes from somewhere else—the cosmic design. The fittest are not defined by their survival—that would create a tautology—but by their design. Consequently, biological fitness is not an outcome of natural selection but a condition for natural selection. Natural selection does not create teleology, but its working is based on teleology. To put this in a catchphrase: the cosmic design is indeed a teleological concept, but not in the sense of a goal the Universe is directed to in the future, but as a framework the Universe started with from the very beginning—which in turn explains how new designs will work out in the future. Without a cosmic design in Creation, there could be no such thing as natural selection.

The following analogy may explain the importance of the "cosmic design" concept for evolution a bit further. A river follows a "path of least resistance" according to the "topographic design" of the landscape. In a similar way, the "stream" of evolution follows a path somehow regulated by the cosmic design of our Universe. The "cosmic design" concept explains how there can be so much potentiality in this Universe. The Belgian biochemist, cell-biologist, and Nobel Laureate Christian de Duve describes the origin of life as follows: "the pathway followed by the biogenic process up to the ancestral cell was almost entirely preordained by the intrinsic properties of the materials involved." We could rephrase this as follows: those intrinsic properties are part of the cosmic design. Interestingly, the German evolutionary biologist Andreas Wagner has found that adaptations are not just driven by chance, but by a set of laws that allow nature to discover new molecules and mechanisms in a fraction of the time that random variation would take. Obviously, those laws must also be part of the cosmic design.

In other words, evolution follows the "path of least resistance" in the "landscape" of the cosmic design. It does not just flow in a random manner. Somehow the cosmic design creates the "bed" in which the stream of evolution meanders. The success of any biological design can only be explained against a background of cosmic design. Richard Dawkins tried to ridicule this idea with the image of "a puddle of water, fitting itself snugly into a depression in the ground, the depression uncannily being exactly the same shape as the puddle." But this still poses the question where the shape of "the depression in the ground" comes from.

So the next question would be: where does this cosmic design come from? It is hard to deny that it finds its origin in Creation. We talked earlier in this chapter about cosmological fine-tuning (CFT), about the fact that our Universe is "fine-tuned" for life. Now we can add that this fine-tuning does not need any special interventions by God during the evolution of the cosmos, for the laws of nature and the physical constants at issue are preordained, built into the very fabric of reality. They are part of the cosmic design. In this design, everything appears to be a matter of cause-and-effect, with like causes having like effects. Our Universe is a law-abiding Universe—a Universe of law-and-order, certainly not chaos. There is no need for periodic divine interventions. Besides, mutations and natural selection are part of Creation, but God is not; God is not a secondary cause in his own Creation.

Even Isaac Newton did fall for this timeless temptation of having God keep a "divine foot" in the door, when he called upon God's active intervention to periodically reform the solar system from increasing irregularities, and to prevent the stars from falling in on each other. When Newton called on such special interventions by the Creator in the working of the Universe, the philosopher Gottfried Leibniz quipped, "God Almighty wants to wind up his watch from time to time: otherwise it would cease to move. He had not, it seems, sufficient foresight to make it a perpetual motion." Today, we know God does not have to make these interventions in Newton's Universe, because science can now explain them with the proper laws (which are God's laws anyway). Newton wrongfully made the Primary Cause periodically act like a secondary cause. In contrast, we should claim that God did not outfit the Universe with a defective, incomplete design. God's cosmic design is complete; it lets all secondary causes follow their own causality.

This latter conviction goes ultimately back to one of our fundamental religious beliefs that there is a trustworthy Creator God who created a "reliable" Universe—not a haunted house or a bizarre fairy tale. We can orient ourselves in it, feel secure in it, and make plans for its and our future. This fact made even the astronomer Fred Hoyle, once an outspoken atheist, exclaim, "A common sense interpretation of the facts suggests that a superintellect has monkeyed with physics, as well as with chemistry and biology." This seems to indicate that the Universe, far from being overwhelmingly hostile to us, as Steven Weinberg thought, is actually amazingly and gratuitously hospitable.

Michael Augros makes a strong case for a designed Universe. His reasoning is, "If the first cause is intelligent, then all things are the products of its intelligence, and living things are just what they always appeared to be—designed." He also explains why there can be cases of "bad design." In his own words, "If secondary causes, unlike the Primary Cause, are not infallible, if they are defectible, then we might well blame them, rather than the first cause, for any flaws we find (or think we find)."

Does evolution really operate within the context of a preexisting background of cosmic design? Many scientists won't answer this question in the affirmative; they see evolution rather as the gradual development of biological order out of physical chaos. Daniel Bennett, for instance, thinks that religion has it wrong—"upside down" in his own words—by claiming that science places order at the end of an evolutionary process, whereas God's creation is supposed to start with order from the very beginning. Is this really true?

It is true that evolution seems to have a time arrow moving from "what is less complex" to "what is more complex," but the simple is in no way less orderly than the complex; something as simple as a snowflake actually shows a very intricate order. In other words, there is no reason to think that the process of building more order begins with and is being steered by "disorder" or "chaos." Although science tries to explain that order comes from below, religion keeps maintaining that order comes from Above, from its very beginning. The order we see in nature does not and cannot come from chaos, but must come from a more fundamental, preexisting order at a deeper level—which is the cosmic order of Creation governing everything that happens in the Universe, including the process of evolution. G. K. Chesterton once "seriously joked" about a conspiracy of order in our world of regularity: "One elephant having a trunk was odd, but all elephants having trunks looked like a plot."

To explain the underlying order of our Universe, Stephen Barr uses the following example. Shaking jars of variously shaped candies won't create much more order, but shaking a jar with round candies would, as round candies have an underlying order—that is, at a "deeper" level"—which allows for a "hexagonal closest packing" structure. It is the cosmic design that is at the basis of this kind of order. Barr describes this principle as follows: "Order has to be built in for order to come out." Such an approach might help us understand that evolution has an underlying order of biological designs and genetic constraints—making the stream of evolution run in the bed of a cosmic design. Like water, natural selection follows the path of "least resistance." Does this mean there is an end-goal in evolution? In a way it does not—like water is not intentionally seeking its own level. In another way, it certainly does—similar to the way water ends up at its lowest level.

There "must" be some form of preexisting order, as no order could ever come forth from a purely chaotic Universe. In a world of chaos and pure randomness, there wouldn't even be room for science, because science is a very orderly enterprise that studies order by definition (even statistics is a very orderly enterprise). In contrast, those who believe order emerges from chaos should realize that chaos is what it is—chaos! When a die constantly throws a one, we would say it must be loaded. Well, our world seems to be "loaded" too—loaded with cosmic design. Even the very laws of nature and its physical constants are part of this "pre-loaded" cosmic design. That's why Charles Darwin had to admit in a letter to Asa Gray: "I am inclined to look at everything as resulting from designed laws" (italics added).

Chaos and chance can never create the order found in the living and nonliving world—as little as blindness can create sight. As the old saying goes, "what chance creates, chance destroys," because there is no purpose or direction to chance in itself; as we discussed earlier, chance has no memory and no foresight. It is the other way around: chance is only intelligible in terms of the order which it lacks; a previous order must exist before any chance event can even occur. If there were no order, there could be no chance, because chance needs the order of preexisting causes coming together to produce unexpected results. Blaise Pascal once remarked, "If the nose of Cleopatra had been shorter, the whole face of the earth would have been changed."

Chapter 3: Biologists and God

The Catechism of the Catholic Church (CCC) puts all of this together as follows: The world "is not the product of any necessity whatever, nor of blind fate or chance" (CCC 295). In his first homily as pontiff, in 2005, Pope Benedict XVI insisted: "We are not some casual and meaningless product of evolution. Each of us is the result of a thought of God. Each of us is willed, each of us is loved, each of us is necessary." This is and remains true, even in a world seemingly stripped off by science. That's why we can believe in science as well as religion. Scientists tend to lose sight of the larger picture when they focus on the details. That's what Alexander Pope noticed about the atheists of his day in the mid-eighteenth century: "See Nature in some partial narrow shape, And let the Author of the Whole escape...."

Yet, some think that people who believe in science as well as religion are "schizophrenic," by celebrating religion on Sundays and science on weekdays When they are occupied with science, they are critical, look for proofs, and believe something only if it has been proven. Then in their leisure time, especially on Sundays, they turn a switch while in church. They set their understanding to zero and their gaze on infinity. They swallow everything without any proof. Isn't that what they do?

Of course not. We all live in the very same world—no matter whether we look at it from a religious or a scientific viewpoint. Seeing the world from both the perspective of science and the perspective of religion is something the English theoretical physicist and Anglican priest John Polkinghorne describes as seeing the world with "two eyes instead of one." He explains: "Seeing the world with two eyes—having binocular vision—enables me to understand more than I could with either eye on its own." Besides, the person of faith and the person of science are ultimately one and the same person. Together, science and religion make us whole and wholesome, whereas in isolation, they are incomplete and under-performing—with each one being only one side of the coin. Therefore, science should be protected from religion as much as religion should be protected from science. Never render to science what is God's. So honor the fences. Yet, no matter on which side of the fence you happen to be, don't forget that you do have a neighbor, as we will show in the rest of this book. Thanks to God, there is still light in a world that science seems to have darkened according to some.

4
Geneticists and God

Genetics has come a long way since the Augustinian monk Gregor Mendel began working with garden peas. He used seven different pairs of contrasting traits—such as seed shape (round vs. wrinkled) and stem length (short vs. tall). When plants with round peas were crossed with plants with wrinkled peas, all the offspring produced round seeds. Because one trait seemed to "dominate" over the other trait, Mendel called such traits dominant. When he let these new plants pollinate themselves, he found that 75% produced round seeds, but 25% wrinkled seeds again—which is a ratio of 3:1. In other words, the characteristic of wrinkled seeds had receded only temporarily, so he called that trait recessive. That was the first milestone in the soon rapidly unfolding history of genetics.

Much has happened since those modest beginnings. Nowadays we know that it is through DNA that such traits are passed on to the new generation. Thanks to the Human Genome Project, geneticists have been able to map all the genes on the 23 pairs of human chromosomes and to sequence the 3.2 billion DNA base pairs that make up the human genome. Now we know we share over 98% of our DNA with chimpanzees. This shows just how small differences in DNA can make a huge difference in the way life takes shape. This doesn't mean, of course, we are 98% chimp. We share also 50% of our genetic makeup with a banana—which does not make us 50% banana. But we do share some basic, common mechanisms.

a. How the Eclipse Sets in

Not surprisingly, the Human Genome Project has caused quite a stir. It made many people believe that DNA holds the complete script for a person's entire life, which made them want to know their "personal genomics." The science journal Nature listed "Personal Genomics Goes Mainstream" as a top news story of 2008. The new genomics has now become our latest crystal ball. No wonder the expectations are high. Sidney Brenner, one of the DNA pioneers, said not too long ago he could compute an entire organism, humans included, if he were given its DNA sequence and a large enough computer. With a like mind, the American molecular biologist Walter Gilbert had the audacity to claim that "when we have the complete sequence of the human genome we will know what it is to be human." That certainly sounds like another instance of "nothing-buttery" (see 2.b): We are nothing but a series of DNA strings.

Most geneticists will admit, when forced to do so, that the development of a human being is not only a matter of nature—shorthand for genes and DNA—but also of nurture— the impact of the environment, including upbringing. Yet, they tend to exclusively focus on what can be studied in the lab: DNA. As a consequence, we have been bombarded and will be more bombarded with a series of new genes: a gene for alcohol addiction, a gene for homosexuality, a gene for homophobia, a gene for depression, a gene for kleptomania, a gene for stuttering, a gene for skepticism, a gene for altruism, and the list could go on and on. All these assumed genes have been tried but they were never able to receive sufficient evidence.

Because genes determine everything in human life, so the mantra goes, they must also determine whether we are religious or not, and what it is that we believe in our religion. So it should not come as a surprise that one of the latest new genes that has entered the field is a gene for religion. The discussion about a gene for religion has become very animated due to a 2005 book of the human geneticist Dean Hamer that he gave the provocative title *The God Gene: How Faith Is Hardwired into Our Genes*. The god-gene hypothesis was basically invented by Hamer, who now claims he has in fact discovered a gene that he decided to call the "god gene." To be more precise, he is talking about a gene for spirituality, which he deceptively dubbed as a "god gene."

Hamer theorized that if our sense of spirituality has a genetic basis, then those who rank higher in spirituality should share some genetic link that those who ranked lower do not. What did he mean by "spirituality"? He measured it by using a "self-transcendence" scale developed by the psychologist Robert Cloninger, so he could quantify how "spiritual" someone is, assuming that spirituality can be quantified by psychometric measurements. What impressed Hamer is that the self-transcendence measure had been shown to be heritable by classical twin studies. So Hamer felt he was on his way to a huge discovery.

What about the term "self-transcendence"? It is a word used by psychologists to describe spiritual feelings that are independent of what they call "traditional religion." Hence it is not based on belief in God, frequency of prayer, or any other conventional religious practice. Self-transcendent people tend to see everything, including themselves, as part of one great totality. They have a strong sense of "oneness" with people, places, and things. Self-transcendent individuals are also considered "mystical." They are fascinated with things that cannot be explained by science. They are creative but may also be prone to psychosis. In short, they are "spiritual," if you redefine this in a certain way.

In order to identify some of the specific genes possibly involved in self-transcendence, Hamer analyzed DNA and personality score data from over thousand individuals. He asked them to fill out a detailed questionnaire—a standard test called a "Temperament and Character Inventory"—including a section that asked them to rate their feelings of "absentmindedness, connectedness with nature, belief in extrasensory perception, and other traits." He assumed that the answers would provide a measure of the subjects' affinity for what he called spirituality.

Then he went poking around in their genes to see if he could find the DNA responsible for their differences. With over 21,000 genes and 3.2 billion chemical bases in the human genome, he limited his search for the "spiritual gene" to nine genes known to produce monoamines (brain chemicals that regulate mood and motor control) and then identified one particular gene, VMAT2, as showing a significant correlation with affinity for spirituality. VMAT2 is a gene that codes for a vesicular monoamine transporter that plays a key role in regulating the levels of the brain chemicals serotonin, dopamine, and norepinephrine. These monoamine transmitters are in turn postulated to play an important role in regulating the brain activities associated with mystic and spiritual experiences (see 5.b).

When he analyzed this gene further, he discovered that those with the nucleic acid cytosine in one particular spot on the gene ranked high in spirituality, whereas those with the nucleic acid adenine in the same spot ranked lower. So he concluded that a single change in a single base in the middle of the "god gene"—at position 33050 of the human genome map, to be precise—seemed directly related to the ability to experience self-transcendence. He even gave an explanation as to why the "spiritual" allele for this gene would give its carrier a selective advantage: Spiritual individuals are believed to be favored by natural selection because they are provided with an innate sense of optimism, which produces positive effects at either a physical or psychological level.

In general, the goal of studies like these is to reduce religion to spirituality and then tie spirituality to a gene or a set of genes. It is in line with what the biologist Richard Dawkins says, "There was something built into the human brain by natural selection which was once useful, and which now manifests itself as religion." What these scientists try to achieve is explaining the evolutionary roots of religion, but what they end up doing is discarding the very essence of religion. They may think they put God in a new light, but in fact they obscured God.

What are we to make of all of this? Let me mention first that Hamer rushed into print with his book without any peer review and without publishing his results in a credible and reputable scientific journal—plus, which is even more serious, his findings have not been replicated. All of this probably gives us ample reason to not take his work too seriously on face value—or to put it nicely, it definitely deserves further scrutiny. Yet, the discussion keeps going on. Who could ever believe that God could be obscured by genes! Where do these geneticists go wrong? We should pray, "God, be our light. Shine in our darkness."

b. How the Sun Reclaims the Day

It has become more or less epidemic to replace the term religion with spirituality—the New Age version of religion, of the "god within." People who no longer claim they are "religious" still tend to call themselves "spiritual." It is often a nature-based spirituality that allows them to find something of the divine in forests, lakes, and mountains, where their "spiritual needs" are being met. They find God in nature, not in the pews. That explains why spirituality seems to be on the rise, whereas religion is experiencing a decline. As G. K. Chesterton put it, "Of all horrible religions the most horrible is the worship of the god within ... That Jones shall worship the god within turns out ultimately to mean that Jones shall worship Jones." Nonetheless, let us assume for a moment that spirituality does have something to do with religion. What happens when geneticists reduce religion to a set of genes tied to spirituality? There are several serious objections against this kind of approach, especially Hamer's approach. Let's analyze them step by step.

First of all, a more general remark. Hamer has proved himself to be an expert in inventing genes—once it was a "gay gene" (in 1994), now a "god gene" (in 2005). Unfortunately for him, the field of behavioral genetics is littered with failed links between particular genes and behavioral traits. Many of these were inventions that have never made it to becoming discoveries. In science, discoveries always start as inventions—usually called hypotheses. However, not all inventions lead to discoveries. To use an analogy, the person who invented "Atlantis" did not discover Atlantis; it remains a legendary island until further notice. The same in science: Most inventions do not lead to discoveries. Yet some scientists think they have made a discovery when all they have in mind is an invention, a conjecture, a hypothesis. As a consequence, we have been flooded with all kinds of new genes. However, a hypothesis is only an invention in the mind until it has been proven to be a discovery in reality. As someone said, given the damaging fate of Hamer's so-called "gay gene," it is strange to see him so impatient to trumpet the discovery of his "god gene."

Reason #2. The assumed link between gene VMAT2 and religious experiences is rather weak. First of all, why did Hamer limit his search to nine genes known to produce monoamines? If a certain allele were indeed the cause of being spiritual, we should expect that the number of people possessing this spiritual allele should at least be proportionate to those who consider themselves spiritual. In addition, all those possessing the "right" allele should have spiritual experiences; otherwise the presence of cytosine cannot be the cause of spirituality. Hamer failed to test for any of these ramifications. If our belief in the divine is due to our genetic wiring, how can one not believe in God when the wires are connected? There is arguably more to being "hard-wired" for religion.

Reason #3. The results of twin studies only speak of some 40% to 50% heritability of spirituality and/or religion, which raises the question of what to make of the residual percentages. Twin studies remain very controversial, even when done with identical twins who were separated by adoption. First of all, similarities between identical twins are not only the result of their identical alleles but also of nearly identical surroundings. Their strong resemblances make it even more likely that others will treat them the same way in life. Moreover, they themselves often strongly desire to become and be more like each other. So, we would easily over-estimate the impact of genes. Second, even if twins become separated at an early age, we need to take into account that these similarities get reinforced the longer it takes before they get separated. Let's not forget that, for nine months, they shared their mother's womb, including her voice, her hormones, her food, and her emotions. Besides, adoption usually takes place in an environment that is very similar to the original one, often just around the block or with relatives or friends. So, we tend to easily over-estimate the impact of genes again. All of this makes research on identical twins, even when adopted, rather limited.

Reason #4. Even if it were true that we are genetically hard-wired for religion, what could this possibly mean? Clearly, we are not hard-wired for a particular religion; there are more than 7,000 identified varieties. "Born a Catholic" does not mean always a Catholic. Plenty are the cases of people who, in the course of their lives, decided to become atheists or chose the opposite by leaving atheism behind (see 8.a). But in any of these cases, these changes were almost certainly not caused by genetic changes. Even if some part of spirituality is wired in the brain, the particular forms and practices of religion are still cultural and can be passed from one person to another by learning or imitation, and can be changed by further experiences in life. In a sense, Voltaire was right when he said, "All men are born with a nose and ten fingers, but no one was born with a knowledge of God." In that respect, religion is similar to science. No one is genetically determined to join a religious or scientific community (although some might be better genetically equipped or inclined to do so). Members of both communities are in search of the truth, but in order to do so, both require schooling in the form of training and study.

Nevertheless, it is often argued by geneticists that the presence of religion in all cultures of all ages indicates that the idea of God must be preloaded in the genome. However, that comes close to a circular argument: The cultural universality of religion suggests a genetic basis; since there is a genetic basis, religion is a universal phenomenon in human cultures. Serious questions remain: If man did invent God for social reasons, how would those beliefs get into one's genes? While it is possible for one's genes to change behavior, there is no clear evidence to suggest that one's behavior can change genes. When dentists pull wisdom teeth, they are not pulling genes, so people from the next generation will struggle again with their wisdom teeth. These "external" changes did not make it into the genes.

Reason #5. We are dealing here with genes that are allegedly connected with behavioral traits. Such hypothetical genes are supposed to control traits with very complicated and variable patterns of behavior. They make for very complicated similarities that come in many varieties. Most of them were once claimed, and then had to be retracted. So if we cannot even link individual genes to personalities, how can we possibly link them to religion? There are too many intervening steps involved—such as other genes, environmental effects on gene expression, cultural factors, upbringing, and personal experiences—to make such a simplistic link.

Even if we admit that genes do have an effect on how religious you are, upbringing still might have a big impact on the "brand" of religion you take on—not to mention experiences such as illnesses or the loss of dear ones. Just as genes don't tell you how to vote, neither do genes tell you what to believe. Curiously enough, Hamer's "god gene" accounted for only 1% of the variance in the test scores of his subjects, prompting Francis Collins, former head of the Human Genome Project, to characterize Hamer's thesis as "wildly overstated." Do we really believe we can compute a person's religion, if we were given the entire DNA sequence and a large enough computer?

Reason #6. It is very doubtful if all this genetic talk has actually anything to do with religion taken as a belief in a Transcendent Being, God. Perhaps genetics can tell us something about mystical experiences, but the idea that people believe in God because of mystical experiences is silly.

Chapter 4: Geneticists and God

One need not feel anything, let alone have a mystical experience, to believe in the existence of God. Arguably, most individuals who believe in God have never experienced God in a mystical way. Quite a few believe in God, or reject God, for purely intellectual reasons. Others simply have an intuitive awareness of God's existence. So the label "god gene" is very deceiving, to say the least—which Hamer did acknowledge himself, though. He admitted, "My findings are agnostic on the existence of God. If there's a God, there's a God. Just knowing what brain chemicals are involved in acknowledging that is not going to change the fact." Kudos to Hamer for this confession.

Reason #7. A "feeling of transcendence" is not necessarily a religious experience, and if Hamer is right, it is in fact merely a biological one. The monoamines involved in the feeling of self-transcendence are the same monoamines that are jumbled by ecstasy, LSD, and other mind-altering drugs. The theologian Jason Dulle comes to the right conclusion: "If the feeling of transcendence is a biological experience rather than a religious experience, then studies performed on that experience only tell us about biology, not religion. The question of God's existence remains a philosophical question, not a biological question." The core issue is whether religion comes from "above," or from "below" during the process of evolution.

While biology can tell us a lot about human beings, it does not tell us anything about God. Besides, spirituality may actually have little to do with God. It could very well be an emotional feeling, whereas religion is not just a feeling but rather a conviction about facts and truths as stated in a Creed, for instance ("I believe in..."). To put it more directly, God's existence is not dependent on our experience of him. The existence of God is a factual issue of yes or no. God either exists or he doesn't—that's not a matter of opinion or feeling. You can have your own opinions and feelings, but you can't have your own facts.

Reason #8. Religious belief is not merely a belief that is credible, believable, or acceptable to a certain degree, but it is the very basis on which our rationality and morality, all our thinking and doing, are based (see 5.b and 6.b). Without this religious belief, rationality and morality would be baseless; we need some beliefs so that we may understand. Albert Einstein was right when he said that science without religion is lame (but he also rightly added that religion without science is blind). It is faith in a Creator that makes us understand ourselves and makes us comprehend the Universe—thus turning science into a faith-based enterprise, based on a belief in a Creator God who has given this world its order and its laws, so we can explore, understand, explain, and predict, because God created a "trustworthy" Universe. Therefore, denying that there is a Creator is actually an acid eating away not only the foundation of science, but of all rationality and all morality.

Our Universe must somehow possess an "inner logic" accessible to human reasoning—an intrinsic "rationality" that governs everything science is trying to decipher. Albert Einstein expressed very emphatically his "confidence in the rational nature of reality and in its being accessible, to some degree, to human reason. When this feeling is missing, science degenerates into mindless empiricism." At the very moment we claim that this belief is merely a product of genes, we have undermined all our own activities, scientific and otherwise. If this is true, then genetics as a science cannot explain religion or any religious beliefs, for it must assume certain religious beliefs before it can even start its explanatory job. It is thanks to God that scientists have reason to trust their own scientific reasoning.

Reason #9. All of this prompts the question as to why

Chapter 4: Geneticists and God

Hamer wants to reduce religion and faith in God to something else, to something like spiritual experiences, and ultimately to genetic instructions. The answer can perhaps be found in some underlying philosophical assumption he entertains—the assumption that biology can fully explain everything in life, including religious faith, beliefs, and experiences. It is a deep-seated dream of certain scientists. The sociobiologists E. O. Wilson once triumphantly exclaimed, "[W]e have come to the crucial stage in the history of biology when religion itself is subject to the explanations of the natural sciences."

This presupposition is based on the view that all reality can be reduced to a scientific explanation—a view we discussed earlier as scientism (see 2.b). However, if there is only material stuff, then there is not even the possibility of spirituality. Then there is no longer room for spiritual reality—perhaps for emotions and sensations that we consider spiritual, but not for a reality behind and beyond those experiences. Hence, the "spiritual allele" of the "god gene" cannot be spiritual at all and can certainly not cause a religious experience. It may cause a natural sensation of self-transcendence that some have unwittingly interpreted as an encounter with the Divine. Before Hamer can reduce spirituality to biology, he must demonstrate that man is only flesh, rather than flesh and spirit. Alas for him, science does not have that capacity. It may study man as if man is merely flesh, but it cannot transform man into mere flesh.

Reason #10. Last but not least, we need to touch on a more general issue regarding any kind of research in genetics. Typically, geneticists assume that genes and their DNA determine many features and characteristics of an individual. That is surely a valid assumption, but it may easily become a dogma or creed: "It's all in the genes, and only in the genes!" James Watson, the co-discoverer of DNA, trumpeted this dogma to everyone: "We used to think that our fate was in our stars. Now we know, in large part, that our fate is in our genes." What this geneticist says is no longer genetics.

According to this ideology, even those kinds of behavior that we think are our own choosing—lifestyle choices, moral decisions, religious beliefs, and the like—would require us to postulate a gene for what we decide, believe, or choose. This is the doctrine of genetic determinism. Because it is rather rampant in genetics, new hypothetical genes just keep coming and going. We could even invent a gene that makes one believe in the all-powerfulness of genetics. That is where science borders science fiction, or actually turns into it. People who believe in strict genetic determinism—and a number of geneticists do, albeit a minority probably—are of the opinion that what some call their "free will" must, like anything else, be determined by genes and DNA as well. Why should we bother to say anything at all, if all is determined?

There are some real flaws in the doctrine of strict genetic determinism. One of its problems is that it leads us into logical trouble. Determinism is a doctrine that wants us to believe that everything is predetermined. But how could it make us believe so, for wouldn't our beliefs be as predestined as anything else in life? Why debate free will at all if people are already determined to either believe in it or not? If genes really determine everything in our lives, then they would also determine our choice to believe or not to believe that genes determine everything. In other words, people who defend complete determinism—let us call them determinists—want us to choose their conviction that human beings cannot choose. So instead one could as well decide not to choose their conviction—which leaves our capacity of "free will" intact. Put briefly, not everything in life can be a matter of genes. We can either do certain things or not do them; do them this way or that way. It makes no sense to praise or blame someone for his deeds if what he did had to happen anyway.

Therefore, we can still maintain that we are not at the mercy of our genes, and that our genes are not our destiny; they are like a hand of cards we are dealt, but we can play them differently. Human behavior is arguably more often than not a matter of lifestyle choices rather than the outcome of a set of genetic instructions. Humans are in control of those choices. Human beings are free to choose whether to act or not to act—and in choosing, their choices cause them to act as much so as genes can cause us to act. People who do not care about what is true or false and about what is right or wrong have chosen not to care; they have decided not to become a "good cause." However, having a free will is essential for us to be masters of our actions, instead of victims—by allowing us to make our own choices and decisions in life, especially so when it comes to religion. To put it in more sneering terms, people who do not believe this must have a gene that makes them think that way.

So, what is our final verdict on what Hamer was trying to do with his "god-gene"? He had to assume ahead of time that religion has biological roots, which is why he was searching for a spiritual gene in the first place. But he went farther than searching: He strongly believes biology can (fully) explain religious faith and experience, because we are only flesh, not spirit.

The key issue is that we are dealing here with beliefs, and beliefs are not material entities like genes—for unlike genes, they can be true or false. If I believe that genes determine everything, I have no reason to suppose my belief is true, and hence I have no reason for supposing that genes determine everything, including my religion. The assumption that genes determine everything is a "boomerang theory" in optima forma—it defeats itself, for once we consider it to be true, it becomes false. Since molecules can make no claim to truth, any more than they can err, we seem compelled to acknowledge the existence of cognitive events in addition to molecular events in order for us to make claims of a cognitive nature. One cannot have it both ways. If materialism is true, there is no space for religion—but neither for the science of genetics. If materialism is false, then there is still room left for science, but then also for religion.

Ironically, for some enigmatic reason, materialism has quite a spiritual appeal to it. It is definitely a philosophical position—certainly not a conclusion of the empirical sciences. The theory that all knowledge is limited to what can be empirically known is itself incapable of being known or demonstrated on empirical grounds. Scientists actually acknowledge the existence of immaterial things when they come up with explanations based on scientific laws. In so doing, they explain material things and events by using non-material laws of nature. This makes one wonder what immaterial laws are doing in a world of material entities. That is actually rather odd, for laws are unlike anything else in this material world. Right in the middle of our comfortable, spacious, temporal, transient, and piecemeal world of causes and effects, something pops up that we call "laws of nature"—physical and biological laws, mathematical laws, and even moral laws.

Unlike all material things surrounding us, laws of nature do not have any of the features that apply to the material world. A law such as the law of gravity is not located somewhere in space, not even in our minds, for that is just a mental "picture" of the law. In a physical sense, laws are nowhere, and yet they are everywhere and apply to the entire Universe; they are universal. Laws are also beyond time—

timeless entities that cannot emerge nor perish in the history of the Universe; we may discover them at a certain time, but they were already there before we discovered them. Neither are laws subject to change, for they will always remain true, even before we came to know them. And here is the most important difference: Not only are laws universal, as we find the same law applied all over the Universe, over and over again, but they also are necessary, which means that things in this Universe cannot be different from what is expressed in those laws of nature (of course, God could have created them differently). That makes them absolute: They are without exceptions.

In addition to laws of nature, there are many more immaterial things that eludes us—things such as thoughts, values, beliefs, emotions, hopes, dreams, and ideals. There is no way materialism can deal with them—other than denying them, but then is must also deny itself. This gives us ample reason to claim there is still space left for religion in the "material" world studied by science and genetics—but, of course, only on condition that we allow for a world-view that goes beyond materialism. Limiting oneself exclusively to one particular viewpoint is in itself at best a philosophical decision, but certainly not a scientific one.

Seen within a more comprehensive framework, reality is like a jewel with many facets that can be looked at from various angles, from different viewpoints. Reality cannot be looked at from "nowhere"; we necessarily look at the world from a specific perspective, and then may change perspective at any time. Just like the "physical eye" sees colors in nature, so the "artistic eye" sees beauty in nature, the "rational eye" sees truths and untruths, the "moral eye" sees rights and wrongs, and the "religious eye" sees everything in relationship to its Creator. All these "eyes" claim to be in search of reality, but each one "sees" a different aspect of it—

and therefore sees different "facts."

Let us look at a more specific example. The "biological eye" sees every beginning of new life as a fertilization process—a product of procreation. The "religious eye," on the other hand, sees it as a gift from Above—a product of creation. These two perspectives may be different, but certainly not contradictory, as both of them are valid and show us different "facts." A fertilized egg cell is the beginning of a human life, but it is not its origin. For the religious believer, the origin of every human life is God, for it is in God that we live, move, and have our being. To put it differently: At the beginning of one's life is a fertilized egg cell, but in the beginning of one's life is God. Although we have come here through our parents, we may as well claim that all of us have come to this world from God. Either perspective is valid and cannot claim exclusiveness.

This may not be all there is to religion, but it is at least an important part of religion. Hamer and his like-minded colleagues wish to deny this and reduce religion to a series of self-transcending feelings and mystical experiences, thus missing the core of what they are trying to study and explain. To say that some gene creates "religious or spiritual experiences" entirely misses the point as to what religion is all about. Religion is not about those experiences per se, but about what they reveal to us about the "other side," about what is "above" us and transcends us. Religion is not about hallucinations, delusions, and illusions, but about a real, yet unseen, heavenly world—about something or someone beyond and behind this world. It is not merely about feelings and experiences but also about certain beliefs as to what is true or false and what is right or wrong in this Universe. In short, it is a belief in facts. It sees God's presence and work in this world. So it is based on empirical evidence, not to be confused with the experimental evidence most natural

Chapter 4: Geneticists and God

sciences use in addition. In religion we reason from the "seen" to the "unseen," from visible data to invisible facts.

Here is one more example to end with. Religion is one way of coping with our knowledge that death is inevitable. Religion diminishes the hurt of death's certainty and permanence and the pain of losing a loved one with the prospect of reuniting in another life—not as a form of wishful thinking but as a pillar of religious faith, not as a product of genes but as a given revealed to and embraced by the human mind. Humanity has always known this—intuitively if you will—from its very beginning. In early primeval history, we find already evidence of elaborate burials; such burials with grave goods indicate a belief in an after-life, for the goods are there because they are considered useful to the deceased in their future lives.

How different this is in the animal world. Take, for instance, the observation of female apes that continue carrying their dead newborns around for quite a while, without having any idea of what is happening until at last they give up and drop the dead remains of their newborn. In Guinea, West Africa, chimpanzee mothers were seen in nature carrying and grooming their offspring's lifeless bodies for up to sixty-eight days. By the time the corpses were finally abandoned, the bodies had mummified and developed an intense smell of decay. Ironically, evolutionists gave this observation a peculiar twist: These, they say, must be sixty-eight days of actually mourning the dead! Only human beings could come up with such an explanation. Arguably, this sixty-eight-day period is not a time of "mourning," but rather a time of "ignoring." Besides, we should ask such evolutionists where the burial and the grave are once this period of "mourning" was over.

Apparently, only the "finite" human mind is able to catch a glimpse of the Infinite. This capacity of the human mind is rightly called self-transcendence—referring to the transcendence of something or someone more than our own selves, and certainly not in the sense Hamer uses that term. We can even say about ourselves "I am only human"—thus comparing ourselves, not with something "below" us (such as a cat, a dog, or an ape), but with something, or rather Someone, "above" us and transcending us. I cannot transcend myself on my own, of course, but because I myself was made in the image of God, I perceive more than myself whenever I perceive myself completely.

Man's drive for self-transcendence seems to be so universal that it can be found even in the earliest archaeological data, such as art and burial rituals—which made some biologists claim it "must" therefore be encoded in our genome. Blaise Pascal—the mathematician, physicist, and philosopher—had a better explanation. He used to speak of a hole in each one of us, an "infinite abyss that can be filled only with an infinite and immutable object; in other words by God himself." It is very unlikely that this hole is programmed in our genes—and neither is religion. Isn't it amazing how science can enlighten and blind us at the same time by uncovering the material world while, at the same time, obscuring the immaterial world that lies behind its undertakings. Where does our intractable tendency of self-transcendence come from? Christians would say: because we were made in the image and likeness of God.

Chapter 4: Geneticists and God

5
Neuroscientists and God

Neuroscience has experienced quite a boom lately. Neuroscientists have discovered that specific regions in the brain are associated with particular cognitive and other mental functions. These discoveries provide compelling evidence for the idea that the human mind has something to do with activities of the human brain. This is a relatively recent discovery, since never before the mind had been associated with the brain. People have known the contents of their own minds from time immemorial without knowing anything about brains.

But times have changed. Scanning techniques such as an electroencephalogram (EEG) or functional magnetic resonance imaging (fMRI measures brain activity by detecting associated changes in blood flow) have opened up the brain for us as the center of various mental activities of the mind. Many neuroscientists think that through their discoveries in the human brain they have unraveled the mystery of the human mind. The part of the body that we "think" with traces us back to the animal world, so in their view that's where brain and mind must have found their origin. This has darkened not only the mind, but also the Maker of the mind.

Chapter 5: Neuroscientists and God

a. How the Eclipse Sets in

It should not come as a surprise that impressive discoveries in the field of neuroscience have set the stage for extravagant claims. In the words of the DNA co-discoverer Francis Crick, "The astonishing hypothesis is that 'you,' your joys and your sorrows, your memories and your ambitions, your sense of personal identity and free will are, in fact, no more than the behavior of a vast assembly of nerve cells and their associated molecules." Then he adds, "As Lewis Carroll's Alice might have phrased it: 'You're nothing but a pack of neurons.'" Apparently, Crick had made Alice's phrase his own—we are nothing but a pack of neurons. Marvin Minsky, a pioneer in the field of artificial intelligence would add to this that human beings are mere meat-machines—just machines, albeit made of meat. And the biologist Richard Dawkins likes to declare that mind is only a feature of matter that emerges when matter is organized in certain complex ways.

It is a tempting step from seeing some correlation between mind actions and brain activities to claiming that the mind is nothing more than a series of brain processes—another case of "nothing-buttery" (see 2.b). In the view of many neuroscientists, the brain has effectively replaced what some call mind, spirit, or even soul. The general conviction behind such claims is that mental phenomena are identical to neural phenomena, that the mental is "nothing but" the neural, that the mind is "nothing more" than the brain, that the mental is just an "illusion"—in short, that thoughts are merely "brain waves." This made George Bernard Shaw exclaim triumphantly, "We know now that the soul is the body, and the body the soul."

According to many neuroscientists, anyone invoking the mind as a control source of the brain would bring in an unnecessary, elusive entity that does not really exist. The British philosopher Gilbert Ryle sarcastically calls this the "ghost in the machine" theory. This idea is connected with the so-called "homunculus fallacy," according to which consciousness is the work of the mind—the inner entity that thinks and sees and feels and which is "the real me inside." When Descartes compares the mind with a pilot in his ship, he seems to suggest that our minds are the pilots behind our eyes and behind everything our body does.

Most neuroscientists reject this idea because it casts no light on the consciousness of a human being by simply re-describing it as the consciousness of some inner little being [homunculus]—and that's why they consider it a fallacy. So they eliminated this mysterious being and decided on the autonomy and monopoly of the brain. The mind could not possibly be "inside" the brain or the body, they said, because minds themselves are not spatial. The brain is all there is to it, so there is no longer any "room" left for the mind, let alone the soul.

Someone who phrased these developments in more philosophical terms is Gilbert Ryle himself. He considers mind-talk an example of a "category mistake," an illusion produced by the misuse of ordinary language. It is like the person who asks at the end of a tour through all the facilities and laboratories of Oxford University, "Now, where is the university?" That person is under the misapprehension that the university is something over and above all that he had been shown on the tour. But there clearly is no additional building for him to see.

Ryle also uses the analogy of a foreigner being shown a cricket match. After being pointed out batsmen, bowlers, and fielders, the foreigner asks: "Who is left to contribute the famous element of team-spirit?" That foreigner is making the same category-mistake. In a similar way, the word "mind" is

Chapter 5: Neuroscientists and God

not something extra beyond or behind a complex of brain activities and bodily actions. Our "beliefs," for instance, are not mental entities, but merely the propensities or tendencies to act and speak in a particular way through the brain. Mental activities are merely bodily dispositions in this view.

Neuro-scientists love to speak in terms of a neuronal network—a fancy set of cogwheels. They even compare this network with what is going on in a computer. These days, the computer has replaced the clock and watch as the latest contraption that makes us tick. So the computer has become the favorite imagery of the human brain. The reasoning goes as follows. Neurons either do or do not fire an electric impulse—in the same way as transistors either do or do not conduct an electric current. So it looks as if the brain "thinks" like a computer "thinks." Of course, they stress, it is not literally a matter of thinking but rather of processing. Thus, all our thinking can be explained in computer terminology. Whatever is going on in the brain—say, some particular thought—has a material substrate that works like a binary code, but it would not really matter whether this material substrate works with impulses, as in the brain, or with currents as in a computer. So it must be this very stream of binary code in a neuronal network that makes us tick. The outcome is that the brain is merely a computer, and the body is merely a machine. The end result is that the brain has become a mind-less brain—which is mechanicism in full glory!

Therefore, neuroscience is more often than not understood as a mind-science that has turned out to be a pure brain-science. Neuroscientists have taught us more and more about this ingenious and intricate brain instrument that makes us number one in the animal world as far as intelligence is concerned. What these neuroscientists try to discard is the mind and soul "behind" the brain. Mind-talk should be replaced with brain-talk, is their motto. All there is, in their view, are brainwaves. Presumably, what the brain carries are impulses, but no longer thoughts, plans, hopes, and dreams—just a pattern of neurons firing. Stephen Barr makes a good comparison: Just as astrologers believe that their lives are controlled by the orbits of the planets, these scientists believe that their own actions and thoughts are controlled by the orbits of the electrons in their brains. In this view, God is not only "out of sight" but also "out of mind," for there is no longer a mind. Can these claims withstand further scrutiny, or are we missing out on something essential? Where do these neuroscientists go wrong? We need to pray again, "God, be our light. Shine in our darkness."

b. How the Sun Reclaims the Day

It is hard to claim that the mind is identical to the brain. If they are considered identical, all the properties and qualities on one side of the equation should be identical to all the properties on the other side of the equation. However, if there are differences in the qualities and nature of the items on opposite sides of the equation, then we must be dealing with two realities. Well, there are several reasons why mental phenomena cannot be equated to neural phenomena. Some of these reasons are scientific, some empirical, some epistemological, and some just common sense. Let us study them in more detail.

Reason #1. One of the pioneers in neurosurgery, Wilder Penfield, made a compelling case about the difference between mental events and neural events, when he asked one of his patients during open-brain surgery to try and resist the movement of the patient's left arm that he was about to make move by stimulating the motor cortex in the right hemisphere of the brain. Then the patient grabbed his left arm with his right hand, attempting to restrict the movement that was to be induced by a surgical stimulation of the right brain. As Penfield described this, "Behind the brain action of one hemisphere was the patient's mind. Behind the action of the other hemisphere was the electrode." In other words, one action had a physical cause, whereas the other action had a mental cause. Therefore, he concluded the physical cause and the mental cause had a different origin.

From this follows, as the neurologist Viktor Frankl put it, that while the brain does condition the mind, it does not give rise to it. The neurophysiologist Sir John Eccles concluded from experiments like Penfield's "that voluntary movements can be freely initiated independently of any determining influences within the neuronal machinery of the brain itself." This observation seems to call for a mind in addition to the brain. The cognitive scientist Jerry Fodor put it most vividly and dramatically: "If it isn't literally true that my wanting is causally responsible for my reaching, and my itching is causally responsible for my scratching, and my believing is causally responsible for my saying... if none of that is literally true, then practically everything I believe about anything is false and it's the end of the world."

Reason #2. When neuroscientists claim that certain mental phenomena are associated with certain neural phenomena, they cannot conclude that these mental phenomena were caused by neural phenomena. The reason is that correlation doesn't automatically equal causation. We all know that the rooster's crow does not cause the sun to rise. The fact that regions light up on an fMRI does not explain whether this lit-up state indicates they are causing a certain mental state, or just reflecting it. Therefore, we need to find out whether certain mental phenomena always correlate with certain neural phenomena; and furthermore, whether they are proportional to the intensity of the mental phenomena. If such is not the case—and mounting evidence indicates it is not—then the assertion that the mental can be reduced or equated to the neural has actually been falsified. Brain activity may be a necessary condition for mental activity, but it does not seem to be a sufficient condition.

In fact, there are situations where the most intense subjective experiences correlate with a dampening—or even cessation—of brain activity. What comes to mind are cases of Near-Death Experiences (NDEs) or Out-of-Body Experiences (OBEs) induced by G-LOC (or G-force in aerospace physiology, a loss of consciousness occurring from excessive and sustained g-forces draining blood away from the brain causing cerebral hypoxia), cortical deactivation through the use of high-power magnetic fields, mystical experiences induced through hyper-ventilation, and brain damage caused by surgery or strokes. If this is true, then neural activity not only fails to be a sufficient condition for mental activity, but it may not even be a necessary condition.

Reason #3. Another peculiarity in this discussion is that something like pain, for instance, can be induced in a physical way, but there is no evidence that experimental stimulation of specific neuronal areas is able to produce a specific mental state, let alone a specific thought. Even if every mental event is a brain event, not every brain event is a mental event. The jump from matter to "thinking matter" appears to be enormous. The neural system is a necessary, but arguably not a sufficient explanation of thinking. As the late philosopher Mortimer J. Adler emphasized, there is a clear difference between perceptual and conceptual thought. Thinking in concepts requires universality, whereas sensorial information is only about particulars. The fact that the brain is only a necessary, but not a sufficient, condition of conceptual thought, indicates that an immaterial intellect is required besides in order to provide an adequate explanation of conceptual thinking. We can even conceptualize what we cannot visualize—something like a circle with four dimensions, for instance. That calls for something mental, not neural. Very often we do not see what receptor cells and neuron cells tell us to see, but rather what we wish to see, which is then also not a neural but a mental issue.

Nowadays, there is also growing evidence that the neuro-circuitry of the brain is not as static and unchangeable as long thought—which is called brain plasticity. This gave Dr. Norman Doidge the idea that the brain can change itself. But that would be sheer magic. Aquinas would say that whenever something undergoes change, something must be causing that change; nothing can be the cause of its own change; therefore, whenever something changes, this change must have been brought about by something other than itself. As nothing can cause itself to exist, so nothing can cause itself to change. The brain could be changed by the mind, but not by itself, for every change requires a cause. However, that would only be possible if the mind is not identical to the brain. The brain cannot rewire itself; it needs something else, the mind, causing it to rewire.

Reason #4. Identity is not just a matter of correlation. A certain mental state may be associated with a certain neural state, but that does not entail identity of the two. The mere fact that two entities are correlated means that they must be distinct entities. True, my mind can be fully occupied with a specific problem, but it is either false or makes no sense to say that my brain is then fully occupied with that problem. If this statement is true, then my mind and my brain cannot be identical. The most we could say is that a certain part of the brain is thinking about a certain problem under consideration. If there are mental states that are not brain states, then there must be some properties that distinguish brain states that are mental states from the brain states that are not mental states. These properties will have to be specifically mental, as no physical property could do the trick. Just as the brain cannot distinguish between legal and illegal narcotics, so the brain cannot tell false thoughts apart from true beliefs.

So as to evaluate the outcome of neural states as true or false, we need something that is not neural. Denying this reduces the working of the mind to the materialism of the brain. However, thoughts and concepts are mental, immaterial entities. To reduce them to a "creation of neurons in the brain" obscures the fact that "neuron" itself is an abstract concept. That would make for a vicious circle: the very idea that concepts are nothing but neurons firing is itself nothing but neurons firing. And the same holds for thoughts. To think differently is like saying that Shakespeare's thoughts are nothing but ink marks on paper.

Reason #5. The German philosopher Gottfried Leibniz once suggested to picture the brain so much enlarged that one could walk in it as if in a mill. Inside, we would only observe movements of various parts, but never anything like a thought. For this reason, he concluded thoughts must be different from physical and material movements and parts. Nowadays, the mechanical model of cogs and wheels that Leibniz used has been replaced by the chemical model of neural and biochemical pathways, but the outcome is still the same. Whereas the brain as a material entity has characteristics such as length, width, height, and weight, the mind does not have any of those; thoughts are true or false, right or wrong, but never tall or short, heavy or light—they have no mass, no size, no color. If the mental were the same as the neural, then thoughts could never be right or wrong and true or false. As John C. Polkinghorne puts it, "neural

Chapter 5: Neuroscientists and God

events simply happen, and that is that." We can think about sizes and colors of things, but the thoughts themselves do not have sizes and colors.

How can an assemblage of neurons—a group of material objects firing away—have any content? Alvin Plantinga describes the problem acutely, "A single neuron (or quark, electron, atom or whatever) presumably isn't a belief and doesn't have content; but how can belief, content, arise from physical interaction among such material entities as neurons?" Then he says, "Propositions are also mysterious and have wonderful properties: they manage to be about things; they are true or false; they can be believed; they stand in logical relations to each other. How do they manage to do those things? Well, certainly not by way of interaction among material parts." In other words, if we accept materialism, we must give up content, belief, and truth. Is that worth the price?

Reason #6. It is hard to equate the working of the mind to the working of a machine such as a computer. Computers require a human maker and would still need a human subject to give their informational output some meaning or sense. Without human subjects, computers just cannot "think." So computers cannot explain the human mind, but they must presume its existence. Computers do not create thoughts, but they may carry thoughts that were created by the mind of a human subject—for example when using a word-processing program. Consider a voice recognition system; it doesn't really understand what it is programmed to "recognize." Computers only do what we, human beings with a mind, make them do, for we have proven to be champion machine builders. So the popular slogan "Man versus Machine" is actually very deceiving; it should be "Man versus Man"—Man versus the Man who designed the machine.

The Eclipse of God: Is Religion on the Way Out?

Besides, a computer may play chess better than Kasparov or any other champion, but it plays the game for the same "reason" a calculator adds or a pump pumps—the reason being that it is a machine designed for that purpose—and not because it "wants" to or is "happy" to do so. Computers, and similar devices, do not have meaning or sense in themselves until a human subject uses them as carriers of information that receives sense and meaning from a human subject. This makes it hard to use the computer analogy to understand the human mind, for without the human mind there would be no computers. For those who like to use computer metaphors, we might suggest the following: the mind uses the brain like a programmer uses a computer. The same computer can actually run various programs—and so can the brain.

Reason #7. Denial of the human mind is self-destructive. If the mind were just the brain, its thoughts would be as fragile as the molecules they are supposedly based on. It would be sitting on a "swamp of molecules," unable to pull itself up by its bootstraps. Sociobiologists, for instance, claim we believe what we believe because what we call "truth" emerges from brains shaped by natural selection. But claims like these work like a boomerang—if they are true, they become false. The snake of this claim is eating its own tail, or rather its own head.

There is no way we can deny the mental, because denying the existence of mental activities is in itself a mental activity, and thus would lead to contradiction. Ironically, one cannot deny the mental without somewhat affirming it. Some people such as the nearly legendary biologist J. B. S. Haldane and the famous philosopher C. S. Lewis have worded this paradox along the following lines: if I believe that my beliefs are the mere product of neurons, then I have no reason to believe my belief is true—therefore, I have no reason to believe that my beliefs are the mere product of neurons. So if we are looking for a key to understanding ourselves it will not be in matter, but in mind. The brain is governed by laws of physics, chemistry, and biology, but thoughts are not. It should not surprise us then that people have known the contents of their own minds from time immemorial without knowing anything about brains. As Stephen Barr pithily puts it, "The brain does not infer the existence of the mind, the mind infers the existence of the brain."

Reason #8. In order to make any mental claims, especially so in science, such claims need to be validated as being true, otherwise they are worth nothing. If Watson and Crick, or Planck and Einstein, or Darwin and Dawkins, or any other scientists, were nothing but their neurons, then their scientific theories must be as fragile as their neurons. That would be detrimental to their claims and to their status as experts in their respective fields. If our mental activities are only the by-product of neural events, then they could be nothing more than illusions, or mere sensations at best. If we were nothing but a "pack of neurons," this very statement would not be worth more than its molecular origin, and neither would we ourselves who are making such a statement.

It requires a mind to come up with generalizations and abstractions such as the law of gravity. Newton's mind, for instance, was able to see beyond the sensorial impression of a falling apple. It has also been argued that the infinite universal meaning of an abstract concept cannot be inscribed in the finite material system of the brain. Hence, the physical world can never be studied by something purely physical, any more than neurons could ever discover neurons. The knowing subject must be more than the known object, for it requires a mind to understand the brain, and it requires a subject to study any object. To explain the mind in terms of physics obscures the fact that one would still need to have a mind first before one could even have physics. While idealists such as George Berkeley reduce reality to "mind" and deny the existence of "matter," materialists reduce reality to "matter" and deny the existence of "mind." But on what grounds do they assume reality must be of only one kind of being? Why cannot reality be of both matter and mind, both the mental and the neural? G.K. Chesterton was right, "The modern materialists are not permitted to doubt; they are forbidden to believe."

Reason #9 can be found in information theory and information technology. Crucial in information theory is the separation of content from the vehicle that transports it. No possible knowledge of the computer's materials can yield any information whatsoever about the actual content of its computations. The brain is supposed to work in the same way as a computer operates, since both use a binary code based on "ones" (1) and "zeros" (0); neurons either do (1) or do not (0) fire an electric impulse—in the same way as transistors either do (1) or do not (0) conduct an electric current. But that is where the comparison ends. Whatever is going on in the brain—say, some particular thought—may have a material substrate that works like a binary code, but it would not really matter whether this material substrate works with impulses, as in the brain, or with currents, as in a computer, or with letters, as in a book, for the simple reason that this material substrate only acts as a physical "carrier" for something immaterial—thoughts.

As said earlier, thoughts are about something mental, about something beyond themselves. To use an analogy, anything that shows up on a computer monitor remains just an "empty" collection of "ones and zeros" that do not point beyond themselves until some kind of human interpretation gives sense and meaning to the code and interprets it as being about something else. Think of what we call a picture:

a picture may carry information, but the picture itself is just a piece of paper that makes "sense" only when human beings interpret the picture as being about something. The same with books: they provide lots of information for "book worms," but to real worms they only have paper to offer. This calls for a distinction between the neural carrier of information and the mental information it carries.

Reason #10 could be found in the two components Thomas Aquinas distinguishes in the human mind—reason and intellect. While reasoning allows us to move from one thing we know to another, the intellect can create concepts through the power of abstraction. The brain can handle signals and images, but it seems that only the human mind can deal with symbols and concepts. Images can have some degree of generality—we can visualize a circle without imagining any specific size—whereas concepts have a universality that images can never have—the concept circle applies to every circle without exception. Because images are inherently ambiguous, open to various interpretations, we need concepts to give them some specific interpretation. Mental concepts transform "things" of the world into "objects" of knowledge, thus enabling humans to see with their "mental eyes" what no physical eyes could ever see before. Although animals may be able to recognize a circle when presented with a circular object, their seeming act of abstraction is closely tied to a perceptual act. Only human beings can think about circularity in general, apart from any perceived object.

Besides, the senses do not know themselves nor their own workings, but the intellect is able to know itself and its workings. Aquinas makes the following observation: sight neither sees itself nor sees that it sees. The power of self-reflection or self-consciousness—knowing that one knows something—belongs to the intellect alone. It is very hard, arguably impossible, to describe the intellect in purely material terms. So it is very questionable whether our understanding of the world is done by the brain. Michael Augros uses the following analogy: you cannot count what you are seeing without using your eyes, but that does not mean your eyes are doing the counting. Similarly, it is clear that we cannot understand anything without using our brains, but it does not follow that our brains are doing the understanding. There is always something "more" than the brain as studied by neuroscientists for them to be able to observe, investigate, and understand the brain. Our knowledge of the brain requires someone—a mind with an intellect—to know the brain. A known object always requires a knowing subject.

Reason #11. It does not seem very likely that thoughts can be induced in a physical way. We are not talking here about something like emotions or feelings (even animals have those), because those are physical and biological phenomena that can be physically induced by stimulation of certain brain areas. Neither are we referring here to memories stored in the brain—including memories of thoughts once produced by the mind—because memories can be physically stored, similar to the way thoughts can be "stored" on paper.

Thoughts, on the other hand, cannot be produced in a physical manner, neither by chemicals nor by electrodes. If we could change beliefs with chemicals, presidential candidates would be wise to use that method in their campaigns. If the thought of "two to the power of two" would physically produce the thought of "four," we could have skipped much work in school. Mathematics, for instance, is not something hard-wired in the brain. Unlike brain processes, which are subject to physical causation, thoughts are subject to mental causation based on reason and intellect, on laws of logic and mathematics.

Chapter 5: Neuroscientists and God

In addition, one could argue that the brain is as much responsible for thinking as the hand is for grasping or the leg for walking. Many of the discussions about the brain's causality of thought seem to involve the idea that if one makes the brain responsible for thought, then it would somehow become the principle agent of thought. But this is as dubious as thinking that if one makes the hand responsible for grasping, that somehow it is the principle agent of grasping, as opposed to a mere tool used by a human being. What if it were the mind that uses the brain as its organ? This might suggest that the conscious self is an autonomous agent working through a material brain. The mind needs the brain to function properly, but the brain also needs the mind to function fully. In other words, the neural system may be a necessary, but arguably not a sufficient explanation of thinking.

Reason #12 is based on an observation made by the philosopher Ludwig Wittgenstein. Picture yourself watching through a mirror how a scientist is studying your opened skull for "brain waves." Wittgenstein once noted correctly that the scientist is observing just one thing, outer brain activities, whereas the "brain-owner" is actually observing two things—the outer brain activities via the mirror as well as the inner thought processes that no one else has access to. In order to make the connection between "inner" mental states and "outer" neural states, scientists would depend on information that only the "brain-owner" can provide. The world of the mind is only accessible to the "brain-owner." This is even so in court, in spite of lie detector tests; very often the only ones to know whether they did commit the crime or not are the ones being prosecuted. What lie detector tests may detect are not thoughts, but at best physiological and emotional responses to those thoughts.

Apparently, there is no such thing as mind-reading

through brain scans or other techniques. Contemporary neuroimaging techniques make it possible only to observe directly the effects of neurological activity such as changes in intracranial blood flow. One cannot "see" cognitive activity itself, but only the effects of cognitive activity. Consequently, neuroscientists just cannot "read" a person's mind. If they want to associate certain brain activities with certain mental activities, they need to ask that person what he or she was thinking. Hence, material explanations cannot possibly lead to a full understanding of non-material phenomena. No mental event is physical, and no physical event is mental. Some speak therefore of a "third-person ontology" versus a "first-person ontology."

In this latter terminology, neural phenomena have a "third-person ontology," whereas mental phenomena have a "first-person ontology," being essentially subjective or "private," directly accessible only to the subject undergoing such mental experiences. No matter how we look at it, there seems to exist in this Universe a dualism of properties—neural versus mental, objective versus subjective. The mind has distinct features—such as intimacy, privacy, first-person perspective, and unity of conscious experience—that cannot be found in the brain and its overt, public, third-person perspective. It is the "I of the beholder" who allows the human mind to study the human brain.

Let us come to a conclusion. If one of the previous twelve arguments convinces you completely, that is enough. If they convince you only partially, perhaps all of them together provide enough compelling reason for you to reject the idea that the mental is identical to the neural, that the mind is identical to the brain, or that the soul is identical to the body. Amazingly, many neuroscientists seem to have never heard these ancient and modern arguments against their strongly held convictions. Or, having heard them, they have either

Chapter 5: Neuroscientists and God

forgotten them or willfully discarded them. The truth is that mental events seem to transcend neural events to the same degree by which life transcends chemistry and physics. We cannot just discard the mind and the soul the way the psychologist Steven Pinker thinks he can when he says, "The supposedly immaterial soul, we now know, can be bisected with a knife, altered by chemicals, started or stopped by electricity." So now the next question is what the status is of the mental, the mind, and the soul.

Those who argue that thoughts do not come from the brain but from the mind may go against mainstream thinking, but there are some very sophisticated scientific and philosophical thinkers—such as the Nobel laureate and neurobiologist Sir John Eccles, the philosopher of science and religion Richard Swinburne, and the philosopher of science Sir Karl Popper—who are mind-body dualists, taking the reality of the mental most seriously. Whether we have to go that far is another issue. Thomas Aquinas, for instance, would not agree with either monism or dualism. He would place the issue of body and mind in the wider context of the relationship between body and soul—with the mind being the intellectual part of the soul.

In Aquinas' view, body and soul are not two individual substances, like in Cartesian dualism; rather they are a unity whose nature is comprised of both material substance and immaterial form, so the body becomes what it is due to the soul (and its mind). The soul is not taken by him to be "made up" out of anything—it is not a kind of "stuff," it is not even made out of "spiritual matter" (whatever that would be). The fact that we distinguish body and soul does not entail that we can separate them, any more than the idea of a three-dimensional space means that we can separate those three dimensions. They make for a tight unity. The physicist James

'J.C.' Sanders puts it well: "Take away the soul but leave the body, and the body is a corpse; take away the body and leave the soul, and we have what we call a ghost." It is the form that makes a being a human being. Therefore, the neural is not the same as the mental because the neural is matter and the mental is form.

As a consequence, a human person is a unity of body and soul, matter and form. Biology tends to isolate the body from the person, but the body is always a person's body. And the same should be said about the soul—it is always a person's soul. Ultimately, we cannot separate the body from a person nor can we treat the soul as separate from a person. Yet, Descartes' view has permeated our culture by driving a wedge between body and soul. We tend to separate them and set them in an antagonistic relationship to each other—a master/slave relationship, so to speak.

Because of this Cartesian view, the body is often seen as a prison for the soul from which the soul wants to escape. Tendencies to disconnect them lead to dangerous consequences—such as the separation between sex and love, or between procreation and marriage. Some people, for instance, decide to undergo sex-change surgery because they have the feeling that their soul is "trapped" in the body of the opposite sex. Cases like these set the soul in a Cartesian opposition to the body; only the soul and mind are considered the "real me," manipulating the body as a slave under full control of the soul. What gets lost in this approach is that body and soul are a unity, with the soul expressing itself through the body, and the mind through the brain.

At first sight, the soul may seem an elusive idea, but actually it is a very intuitive concept. It is the soul that makes us what and who we are. Our identities do not change when we gain or lose a few particles from the collection of particles that make up our bodies. John Polkinghorne is right, "The

Chapter 5: Neuroscientists and God

atoms in each of us are being continually changed by eating and drinking, wear and tear. They cannot be the source of our experience of a continuing self." Although my body changes constantly, I myself do not—that is, my identity remains the same. In a sense, the body is something we have, but it is more accurate to say that the body is something we are. A human being is therefore an incarnated soul as well as an animated body.

The fact that an intoxicated brain cannot think well does not necessarily mean that the thinking comes from the brain. As said earlier, you cannot count what you are seeing without using your eyes, but that does not mean your eyes are doing the counting. Similarly, we cannot think without using our brains, but that does not mean our brains do the thinking. It may very well be that it is the mind that does the thinking, but does so through the "material" of the brain. Obviously, they are closely united. An intoxicated body affects the mind, and a confused mind affects the body. Stress affects the brain, and headaches affect the mind. People with an optimistic outlook on life tend to be healthier and live longer than those who have negative thoughts. Examples like these show that the unity between body and soul, or between brain and mind, is so tight that we can even speak of psycho-somatic disorders that affect this two-some together. Brain scans may not reveal the actual content of someone's thoughts, but they do tell us something about what is going on in someone's mind—in the same way as body-language can reveal something about what is going on in that person's mind.

No matter what neuroscientists tell us, from now on we should sharpen our terminology: neuro-scientists are not mind-readers, neuro-surgeons are not mind-surgeons, and neuro-science is not mind-science. Simply put, thoughts are more than brain waves—in the same way as love is more than a chemical reaction. Medical professionals can read and interpret an electroencephalogram (EEG) or a magnetic resonance image (MRI), but looking at these does not show them the mind and its thoughts—perhaps memory "traces" of thoughts, but not the thoughts themselves. Neuroscientists just cannot "read" your mind. If they want to associate certain brain activities with certain mental activities, they need to ask you what you were thinking. When Marvin Minsky called human beings mere meat-machines or machines made of meat, he had just "forgotten" that machines require a human maker and would still need a human subject to give their informational output some meaning or sense. Someday, science may understand the human brain, but it will never fully understand the human mind, for science itself depends on the working of the human mind. There is no neuro-science without the human mind. If anyone thinks that the mystery of the mind has been solved by science, it might be worth pondering the opposite—that the secret of science is to be found in the mystery of the mind.

Some may object: Doesn't this take us back to the homunculus fallacy of a "ghost in a machine"? Would the brain in its own merit not be a much safer strategy than invoking the mind as well? Not necessarily so. As Max Bennett and Peter Hacker have argued, the homunculus fallacy only keeps coming back in another form when we try to eliminate mind and soul. Now the homunculus is no longer a soul, but a brain that is supposed to "process information," to "map the world," to "construct a picture" of reality, and so on. Oddly enough, this brings the homunculus back in a hidden way, for all the expressions used here can only be understood because they describe conscious processes with which we are already familiar. To describe the resulting form of "brain-science" as an explanation of

Chapter 5: Neuroscientists and God

consciousness is very problematic, as it merely reads back into the explanation the feature that needs to be explained. It creates the unjustified impression that consciousness is a feature of the brain, and not of the person—a person being a unity of body and soul, mind and brain.

The question "what am I" may have many clear, material, and even scientific answers—ideal food for neuroscientists. But the question "who am I" is not so easy to answer. It is clearly not, in Gilbert Ryle's words, the kind of question a person asks "from a desire to know his own surname, age, sex, nationality.... He feels that there is something else in the background for which his 'I' stands ... something very important and quite unique, unique in the sense that neither it, nor anything like it, belongs to anyone else." That's basically as far as Ryle wants to go, but the question "who am I?" cannot be answered by looking at one's own body. Even if that were possible, we would still not be aware of our own identity—our "self." Thomas Aquinas summarized this well: sight neither sees itself nor sees that it sees. Perception goes in the direction from object to brain, but awareness goes in the opposite direction—from brain, or rather mind, to object. The latter relation is non-physical, yet very real.

Something similar might be said about Ryle's attempt to dissolve the mind-body problem. Ryle may think there is no university over and beyond the buildings of Oxford University. However, if there were no university in Oxford, those buildings would not be connected the way they are, or might not even exist. Of course, the university is not another building; that would indeed be a "category mistake." Yet, there is something very real about the university itself that unites all the buildings we can see and visit. And the same could be said about the mind and soul. If we try to get rid of them, we lose something that "unites" what is going on in the body, including its neuronal network. What we "see" can be best explained by what we do not "see," but is still there.

When we ask the question about our own existence—"why am I here?"—no scientific answer could possibly do the job. From the fact that two specific parents had a child, it does not logically follow that this child is or became "me." We may very well need the soul, but even more so God, to explain why each one of us exists, and what it is for us to be who we are. We cannot put our finger on what this "I" or "me" stands for. It is like my shadow—always a pace ahead of me, leaving open what the next step will be. The shadow of oneself evades capture, and yet is never very far ahead.

So we are still entitled to say that soul and mind are not identical to body and brain. The mind is the intellectual part of the soul, and together they make our bodies human. We should affirm now, contrary to what George Bernard Shaw said, that the soul is not the body, and that the body is not the soul. Because we have a mind, and because the mind is a reflection of God's mind, we can be rational and moral beings who can tell true from false as well as right from wrong (whether we always do so is another question). Since we have a mind, in addition to the body, we can make rational judgments (see 6.b.) as well as moral judgments (see 7.b). In short, we are not just machines made of meat. There must be much more to that "machine." There is no way neuroscientists can obscure this reality, and thus the reality of God.

Chapter 5: Neuroscientists and God

6

Relativists and God

Relativists claim there is no absolute truth, because they always think about truth as something relative to some particular frame of reference, such as a particular language or culture or religion. Whatever is true for me may be false for you; whatever is right for me may be wrong for someone else. All there is are our opinions about what is true or false, and about what is right or wrong.

So what, then, is wrong with opinions? Having an opinion is like saying "I know it, but of course, I just might be mistaken," without realizing that admitting you might be wrong is admitting that you do not really know at all. If you really know something, you can no longer be wrong anymore. But in a world of mere opinions, you don't really know anything. That's the difference between truths and opinions. If the world is round, then someone's opinion won't make it flat. Relativism leaves us in a cognitive desert. It creates moving targets and tells us to follow anything that moves.

Thank God, relativists only express, willingly or unwillingly, what their opinion is; they cannot coherently claim that relativism is true, for in the world of relativism there is no such thing as absolute truth. Whether their opinion is true or false is not a legitimate question in a world of relativists, at least not according to their own verdict. Despite its inconsistency, relativism has been on the rise as a

Chapter 6: Relativists and God

truthful opinion about the absence of truth. The philosopher Alan Bloom once wrote that there is this new mindset that says, "[E]very student, or nearly every student, will believe, or think he believes, that truth is relative."

a. How the Eclipse Sets in

Relativism is certainly not a recent invention. Herodotus said in his book The Histories, "Everyone without exception believes his own native customs, and the religion he was brought up in, to be the best." Then there is Protagoras who is known for the expression "Man is the measure of all things"—which must necessarily include the truths a person may claim. Pontius Pilate would follow soon with his legendary question, "What is truth?" Although the idea of relativism may have a long history, it was never really popular or widespread, but nowadays it is receiving more and more traction. It is promoted, for instance, by the late philosopher Richard M. Rorty: "Truth is what your contemporaries let you get away with." In other words, relativism promotes a sort of democratic ideal in matters of knowledge. But this democratic ideal easily turns autocratic. Benito Mussolini, of all people, once said, "From the fact that all ideologies are of equal value, that all ideologies are mere fictions, the modern relativist infers that everybody has the right to create for himself his own ideology, and to attempt to enforce it with all the energy of which he is capable." Ideologists wish to transform society and culture in such a way that their own worldview prevails.

Relativism is on the rise, in spite of the fact that science is currently one of the (perhaps last?) strongholds where truth is still respected in our culture. Why does science still hold on to its truth claims against claims of relativism? Well, if truth were at the mercy of some individuals, science would have to abandon all its universal claims. In fact, it is reality that sometimes forces scientists to revise their theories in order to come closer to the truth. They constantly need to adjust the "speculations" in their minds to the "data" of reality. The much heralded idea of falsification says that a theory is in trouble when its predictions turn out to be false—that is, not-true. This raises the age-old philosophical question: What does it mean to be true or not-true?

This reflects basically the famous question Pontius Pilate once posed: What is truth? The matter of truth is at the core of this discussion. Long ago, Aristotle famously worded the issue as follows: "To say of what is that it is or of what is not that it is not, is true." This dictum has been the starting point for all philosophical discussions about truth. It talks about something that is said or stated, on the one hand, and something that is or is not, on the other hand. So this raises the question what the relationship is between what is said or stated, usually called a statement, and what is or is not, commonly referred to as a fact in reality So the question is: what is this relationship like?

Aristotle was of the opinion that the two have a relationship of correspondence—sometimes called the correspondence theory. St. Thomas, walking in Aristotle's footsteps, speaks more specifically of a correspondence between reality and intellect [adequatio intellectus et rei]. The correspondence theory may sound trivial, but basically it only asserts that there must be a correspondence between the way reality is and what we say about reality. However, the term "correspondence" is still ambiguous. It can be taken in the sense of "corresponding to" the facts, meaning that a statement is linked to a fact, like a ledger entry corresponds to a sale. Or it can be taken in the sense of "corresponding with" the facts, meaning that a statement conforms or squares with a fact, just like a key corresponds with a key

Chapter 6: Relativists and God

hole. The latter interpretation is harder to defend than the former, for the intellect always processes sense-data in order for perception to become cognition, but let's leave it at that. More recently, at least two rival theories were developed as alternatives to the correspondence theory: the consensus theory and the pragmatist theory. What do they claim differently?

The pragmatist theory considers statements true, not so because they correspond to what is going on in reality, but because most of us accept them as true since they have been so successful. A common reason for accepting them as true is that they "work" in a satisfactory manner, which is more specifically the standpoint of pragmatism. However, the problem with this view of equating "true" with "successful" is that true explanations may indeed be useful and successful, but successful explanations are not necessarily true. The geocentrism of Ptolemy was as successful in its predictions as the heliocentrism of Copernicus at the time, but Ptolemy had it wrong, in spite of the fact that with the help of his system, ships had been able to navigate the seas for centuries, and astronomers had been able to predict eclipses. In other words, Ptolemy's geocentrism was successful and useful but not true. However, the most important point against pragmatism is that even success depends ultimately on truth in terms of correspondence, since success implies that a prediction "comes true" and corresponds to what is actually the case in reality—for instance, a predicted eclipse. So that takes us back to the correspondence theory.

The other theory, the coherence theory, declares a statement true when it is part of a coherent axiomatic system. However, this would entail that a statement being true in one system may be untrue in another system. Consequently, this kind of truth is self-made, depending on the chosen axioms—which is like saying, what is "true" in chess is not "true" in checkers. This idea comes close to relativism. However, such a definition may be helpful in mathematics and logic, but it is useless in empirical sciences. Einstein said it right, "As far as the laws of mathematics refer to reality, they are not certain; and as far as they are certain, they do not refer to reality." When we add 1 to 1 in math, the result is 2; but when we add 1 drop of water to another drop of water, the result is not 2 drops but 1 drop. Also, whether we choose either a Euclidean or a Riemannian geometry is completely up to us, but when it comes to cosmology, we need the kind of geometry that has the best correspondence between our theories and the facts. The problem is that the choice between coherent systems cannot be made on the basis of coherence but must be made on the basis of correspondence again. Maurice Merleau-Ponty said it right, "the real is coherent and probable because it is real, and not real because it is coherent." So we are back again to Aristotle and Aquinas!

Notwithstanding the shortcomings of both the coherence theory and the pragmatist theory, relativism basically rejects the correspondence theory, and therefore denies that the human mind and human reasoning have the capacity to arrive at truth. How could this happen? How did we ever come to this tragic nadir of mistrust—a complete mistrust in our capacity to capture reality? At least two factors propelled the rise of relativism in matters of truth: skepticism in philosophy and evolutionary theory in biology. Let's start with philosophy.

Skepticism in philosophy has a long history of detrimental developments, running from René Descartes (1596-1650), to John Locke (1632-1704), to David Hume (1711-1776), and to Immanuel Kant (1724-1804). It more or less started with Descartes' split between res extensa and res cogitans, with the former stripping the world of sensible qualities and the latter creating the impression that all such qualities—and the nature that underlies them, which would soon be labeled by Kant as "das Ding an sich"—are projected into the Universe by the observer. This has led to what Alfred North Whitehead rejected as "the bifurcation of nature," which splits reality into an "external" world, consisting of things that can be described in mathematical terms, and an "internal" world of the thinker or observer. Due to philosophers like these, many of us have ended up as Kantians, not knowing things in themselves, indeed not knowing that there are things at all. How are we supposed to know what this "external" world, which no human eye can ever behold, looks like, and whether it does in fact exist? So we are no longer in touch with the world around us.

Probably the main troublemaker in this process was the philosopher David Hume. He became best known for questioning the notion of causality. In order to do so, he uses the example of a billiard ball moving in a straight line toward another. There are several possibilities: the first ball stops and the second ball moves, the first ball bounces back with the second ball remaining at rest, or the first ball jumps over the second, and so on. There is no reason to conclude any of these possibilities over the others. Only through previous observation can it be predicted what will actually happen with the balls. All we observe is that the motion of the first ball is followed by the motion of the second ball—but the act of causation we cannot observe. Nor does the mind perceive the workings of cause and effect—otherwise we could determine what effects would follow from causes without ever having to rely on observation. Furthermore, we do not actually experience the necessary connection itself—we only infer it from the constant conjunction that we observe between two events. That's Hume's account in a nutshell.

No wonder Hume used this particular example because at

the time the billiard-ball model had become standard in explaining the nature of the Universe. In addition, the billiard-ball model stood for a kind of causal action that was thought to be evident, because the mechanism of this kind of action was supposedly clear and all-pervading. It was an example of "impulse," that is of one body causing changes in another body by means of contact—by pushing it or striking it. "Impulse," John Locke once wrote, is "the only way which we can conceive Bodies operate in." What Hume did, in contrast, is that he argued that this "mechanism" was really a kind of illusion produced by habit or custom. All such cases are supposedly nothing but constant conjunctions, and our perceptions of them never give us insight into the modus operandi of the connection. Causal connections, in his view, turned out to be mere "metaphysical" inventions, based on an illusion. What we thought was truth turns out to be untruth.

Since the supposed influence of a cause upon its effect was not directly evident to sense observation, Hume concluded that the connection between cause and effect was not an aspect of the real world, but only a habit of our thinking as we become accustomed to see one thing constantly conjoined to another. Causality was thus reduced to correlation at best—not a property of things but of thoughts. It was no longer an ontological reality in the world outside ourselves, but an epistemological property of the way we think about the world. We simply imagine causality. In his own words, "From causes which appear similar we expect similar effects."

This stand made Hume one of the first skeptic philosophers to question the very idea of causality—actually of objective truth in general. Hume was right, we do not see causation in the same way in which we see colors and shapes and motion. But that does not mean we don't experience causation at all. To reduce causation to a habitual connection in the mind does not do justice to our actual experience. When I hear the cock crow before dawn every morning, it never occurs to me that the cock's crowing is causing the sun to rise. Apparently, we do not equate causation with correlation. That's why we always question correlations as to whether they are based on causal relations or mere coincidences. Once we follow Hume and give up this distinction, we get into serious trouble.

The end result of this episode in philosophy is that many modern philosophers think of the human mind as something that imposes meaning on the world. There is no meaning in the world, no order, no causality, no rationality. All of this is imposed by our minds. Even truth itself is imposed by our minds; we create truth like artists create art. Consequently, there is no touchstone outside of us to corroborate our truth claims in the way the correspondence theory suggests. Relativism looms largely, bathing in skepticism.

The second factor in propelling relativism is of more recent origin—it is the evolutionary theory of biology. We can be rather brief on this one. It considers human knowledge and rationality to be merely the product of evolution after having gone through a process of natural selection. It was natural selection that shaped our knowledge about the world, so the claim goes. It promoted successful knowledge, but not necessarily truthful knowledge. Natural selection explains how our thoughts came to correspond in some way with facts in reality, for "not thinking straight" would be a disadvantage in the struggle for survival. However, if knowledge cannot be assessed as truthful but only as successful, then relativism is the only option left. Relativism ties in well with the new ideas we discussed in the previous chapters. Because the human mind is presumably nothing more than a series of brain processes in a neuronal network—a random product of evolution, they say—we have no way of knowing what we really know. There is no way anymore to distinguish fact from fiction, realities from illusions, opinions from truths, and beliefs from make-beliefs. It's all based on a certain pattern of neurons firing, tested in the furnace of natural selection.

So we end up with mere illusions: social illusions, political illusions, moral illusions, religious illusions—or more in general, cognitive illusions. As Professor David Carlin puts it, "If there is no objective truth, we are free to believe whatever we like, including utter nonsense. And if there is no objective truth, those who have power in society are free to impose, either by persuasion or force or fraud, their beliefs and values on everybody else."

It is obvious that these developments in philosophy and biology must have also obscured God. If we don't have access to "das Ding an sich," and if our knowledge is a mere product of natural selection, then we certainly don't have access to God, for God is even more unknown and unknowable than we world around us. The chasm between God and the human mind is infinitely wider than the rift between the world and the human mind.

The conclusion relativists draw from this is: just take "truth" for what it is worth—which may not be much. Some have truth actually replaced with "political correctness." In short, relativists proclaim there is no authority but themselves. The most relativists can still accept is freedom of speech, so anyone can say whatever they want, true or not. Where do these relativists go wrong? We need to pray again, "God, be our light. Shine in our darkness."

b. How the Sun Reclaims the Day

The previous section questioned our capability of

Chapter 6: Relativists and God

capturing reality and discovering truth. It painted a disconnect between what we perceive and the way the world around us really is. The end result is a destructive form of relativism and skepticism. Skeptics like Hume find a flaw in every truth we claim, including the truth of causality—they are "masters of suspicion."

Skepticism makes for a very restrained view on the world—actually so restrained that absolute skeptics cannot even know whether they have a mind to doubt with. Concerning the question whether we can prove that our knowledge of reality is real, G. K. Chesterton saw clearly that "a man must either answer that question in the affirmative, or else never answer any question, never ask any question, never even exist intellectually, to answer or to ask." And then he adds, "Most fundamental sceptics appear to survive, because they are not consistently skeptical and not at all fundamental. They will first deny everything and then admit something, if for the sake of argument or often rather of attack without argument." Why would anyone want to argue anyway, if truth does not matter?

So this poses the question: how can we claim truth back? In other words, what is wrong with the arguments of skeptical philosophers and evolutionary biologists. Let's start with the claims of biologists.

Many evolutionary biologists think that we believe what we believe because what we think is "truth" emerges from brains shaped by natural selection. At least they tacitly, or perhaps unknowingly, admit that natural selection itself is capable of capturing reality because it operates depending on the way the world "is"—which is the truth of correspondence with reality. But that's where capturing reality ends for them. As we said earlier, evolutionary biologists argue that "not thinking straight" would be a disadvantage in the struggle for survival. That argument sounds certainly attractive but is not really adequate, for several reasons.

First of all, reducing truth to a product of survival is very questionable. Natural selection cannot operate on truth claims that are not directly related to survival. Not all truths and truth claims have survival value. Many of the things we try to rationally understand are basically useless to survival, whereas illusions sometimes prove pretty useful. Truth for truth's sake is anything but survival minded. There are so many cognitive truths that have nothing to do with fitness, survival, or success. Truth trumps success. We are able to do many, many things in reasoning that have nothing to do with survival in the wild. As a matter of fact, the human intellect gives us the power to "understand" a wide variety of things that go far beyond mere survival. Knowing that the earth is round doesn't help us in the struggle for survival.

Second, success in survival does not equate to truth: True explanations may indeed be successful and useful, but successful or useful explanations are not necessarily true. Ptolemy's geocentrism, for instance, was successful and useful in navigation, but not true. So natural selection cannot be the arbiter of what is true or false. What is tested by natural selection could perhaps be the effectiveness of knowledge, but not necessarily its truthfulness. As Alvin Plantinga puts it, "Natural selection is interested, not in truth, but in appropriate behavior." That makes quite a difference. If Ptolemy's geocentrism and Copernicus's heliocentrism had to go through the filter of natural selection, either one would pass the test, but only rationality can help us decide which one is true.

Third, natural selection cannot explain that we know certain thoughts as "necessarily" true, such as 2x2=4. This kind of certainty is beyond the trial and error strategy of natural selection. Natural selection cannot possibly produce the certainty that the number 11 is a prime number. So the

Chapter 6: Relativists and God

question is how natural selection could produce the knowledge of such truths—for example, the knowledge that the laws of logic and mathematics are without any exceptions. Do those who believe that the number 11 is a prime number really have a better chance of surviving than those who do not believe this? That's hard to believe. How could natural selection ever produce in us the knowledge that the laws of logic are universally valid and allow no exceptions? That's not a matter of trial and error in the "battle for survival."

Fourth, when biologists claim that our beliefs are mere artifacts, such a claim would act like a boomerang that destroys its own truth claims. They undermine their own truth claims by cutting off the very branch that the biologists who make such claims are—or actually were—sitting on. Claiming that knowledge is only a product of natural selection makes this very claim also a product of natural selection, so it can no longer be claiming truth. If the theory of natural selection is a product of the human mind—according to a hypothesis generated by Charles Darwin's mind—and at the same time, if the human mind is supposed to be the product of natural selection, then we end up in a self-destructive vicious circle. How could we ever trust the outcome of natural selection when it comes to matters of truth? Put differently, if Darwin's thoughts were the mere product of natural selection, so would be his science, and as a consequence, none of his thoughts—or ours, for that matter—could then be trusted. That would be the end of the theory of natural selection itself.

Fifth, weighing evidence and coming to a conclusion are mental activities that cannot possibly be determined by genes; if they were, their outcome would be inevitable and predetermined. The history of science, for one thing, has repeatedly falsified this claim. It is hard to see how Newton's discovery of gravity, Mendel's discovery of genes, and Darwin's discovery of natural selection could have been catapulted by their genes. "Eureka's" don't come from genes. Their "sudden" discovery was not the result of a mutation in genes. Nor did the genes change of those who accepted these discoveries as true—they just deemed them to be true, on rational grounds, without any genetic change or interference from their genes.

So we must come to the conclusion that all attempts of evolutionary biologists to reduce the human mind to a product of genes and natural selection are doomed to fail. What remains standing is that the human mind does have direct access to reality and to the world of truths and untruths. As to how this is possible, we will see later.

Let's move from the claims of evolutionary biologists to the claims of skeptic philosophers. Where do they go wrong? In spite of contrary claims made by Hume, most people believe that we do have knowledge of an external world beyond our mental habits. When we see the sun rise every morning, we know, for instance, that there is not a different sun rising every morning. To reduce causation to a habitual connection in the mind, as Hume claims, does not do justice to our actual experience. When we hear the cock crow before dawn every morning, it never occurs to us that the cock's crowing is causing the sun to rise. Apparently, we do not equate causation with correlation. That's why we always question correlations as to whether they are based on causal relations. Once we follow Hume and give up this distinction, we run into serious trouble. Here is why.

The problem with Hume's analysis is that he came to his view because he took causality and causation as a relationship of events, assuming that "all events seem entirely loose and separate" and that "we can never observe any tie between them." As a consequence, causal connections

Chapter 6: Relativists and God

in themselves became ultimately subjective phenomena in Hume's view. What makes him think that causation is a link between "events" instead of "acting things"?

How different is Hume's view of causality compared to, for instance, Thomas Aquinas' view. Aquinas considers cause and effect to be rooted in the identity of acting things, not events. What a thing is, says Aquinas, will determine what it does. An acorn can become an oak tree, and not a butterfly, because that is its nature. The actions an entity can take are determined by what that entity is. On this latter view, when one billiard ball strikes another, it sends it rolling because of the nature of the balls and their surroundings—and not just antecedent events. The philosopher James Hill explains what this entails: When we know that billiard balls are solid and when we see one ball moving towards another, then certain effects are quite impossible. The moving ball cannot, for example, just pass through the second ball and come out the other side continuing at the same speed; nor can the first ball stop at exactly the same place as the second ball; nor can one of the balls suddenly vanish, and so on and so forth. The qualities of the balls determine the kind of effect that the impulse of the first ball will have on the second.

Aquinas' analysis seems much better than Hume's. We intuitively know there is a way things are, independent of how they may be apprehended. When we see something caused by a mirage, we know it is a mirage. Or when a stick in water, for instance, invariably appears bent, we know it is straight. Or take a statue that looks so different from different angles, yet we know it is the same statue—a phenomenon called "constancy." Although the images keep changing on the retina, we perceive constancy. To think that our apprehensions fully determine the way things are would undermine science. Albert Einstein knew very well how vital this view is for science: "The belief in an external world independent of the perceiving subject is the basis of all natural science." On the other hand, if we accept Hume's skeptic conclusions as true, the very foundation of all the sciences begins to crumble. Skepticism is a dead end.

Hence it should not surprise us that Hume's view is certainly not embraced by giant physicists such as Max Planck and Albert Einstein, who both believed that physical laws describe a reality independent of ourselves, and that the theories of science not only show how nature behaves, but why it behaves exactly as it does and not otherwise. Most scientists would in fact agree with them—although not always openly and happily. Besides, Hume's analysis would erase the important scientific distinction between causality and correlation; they would both be reduced to a series of mere subjective associations. In contrast, scientists always want to make sure that causality is not just a matter of correlation; there certainly is, for instance, a correlation between wind velocity and windmill activity, but it is only the wind that causes windmill activity, not the other way around—because of the way things are.

Although we know the world through sensations or sense impressions, they are just the media that give us access to the way things are. The Scottish philosopher John Haldane put it well when he said "One only knows about cats and dogs through sensations, but they are not themselves sensations, any more than the players in a televised football game are color patterns on a flat screen." Knowledge does rest on sensation, but that doesn't mean it is confined to it. It is "reality" that forces us sometimes to revise our thoughts. Were we to follow Hume's philosophy, however, we would end up with what the late physicist and historian of science Stanley Jaki calls "bricks without mortar." Jaki says about Hume's sensations, "the bricks he used for construction were sensory impressions. Merely stacking bricks together never produces an edifice, let alone an edifice that is supposed to be the reasoned edifice of knowledge." In science, proofs of something being true come from conformity with reality, not from systems of ideas. Who would ever want to drive across a bridge designed by an engineer whose calculations are merely based on good habits, or whose knowledge is only a product of natural selection?

In general, it could be said that evolutionary biologists and skeptic philosophers have disconnected us from reality. They tell us we have no longer direct access to the world around us. What we know about reality can no longer be assessed in terms of truth and untruth, but only as the outcome of natural selection and the result of simple habits of associating events. But after what we have seen so far, we have reason now to question these claims. Is it really true that there is no meaning in the world, no order, no causality, no rationality, and that all of this is merely imposed by our minds, shaped by natural selection? Do meaning, order, causality, and rationality only exist in our minds? Or are they also "out there"?

What is at stake here is the reliability of the human mind and the reliability of human rationality. Not only do evolutionary biologists and skeptic philosophers undermine our capacity to know the truth, their claims also eat away the foundation of human rationality. Rationality is our capacity and faculty to make rational judgements and decisions. In fact, it is rationality that gives us access to the world of truths and untruths—a world beyond our control. Rationality is our capacity for abstract thinking and having reasons for our thoughts, thus giving us access to the "unseen" world of thoughts, laws, and truths. Rationality allows us to gain knowledge about the world through the power of abstract concepts and mental reasoning, thus giving us an immaterial sense for what is true and what is false. Weighing evidence and coming to a conclusion are rational activities par excellence.

Reasoning leads us from one idea to a related idea; it is a matter of pondering realities beyond that which we experience through our physical senses, thus allowing us to transcend the current situation with the mental power of abstract concepts and mental reasoning. Philosophical giants such as Aristotle and Thomas Aquinas would put it this way: all we know about the world comes through our physical senses but is then processed by the immaterial intellect that extracts from sensory experiences that which is intelligible. Well, it is the rationality of our intellect that makes the world intelligible and understandable; it gives us the power to comprehend the Universe through reasoning. It is the mind's rationality that gives us access to the laws of nature and the structure of this Universe. Laws of nature have to be discovered, not invented; they are not just mental creations but must be anchored in reality.

When scientists or engineers violate these laws, they run into real and actual trouble, and so do we. If we decide to ignore the law of gravity and jump off a cliff, our defiance will not cause gravity to cease working. Likewise, a bridge that has been designed according to the right laws can stand firm, whereas another bridge collapses because its engineers erred in their calculations—perhaps they had the wrong laws in mind. The construction of a bridge would never depend on the right laws and the right thoughts if those laws and thoughts were only creations of the human mind. It would not make sense to say that competent engineers have better mental habits than their inept colleagues. There must be more to it.

Let us see what this entails. It is only thanks to our rationality and intellect that we take the world as an orderly

Chapter 6: Relativists and God

and lawful and comprehensible entity. Interestingly enough, the word "cosmos" in Greek means "order." Rationality assumes order, stability, and predictability in this Universe, for it is to the essence of rationality that there are truths built into the world that reason can apprehend. These assumptions are not scientific output, but rather rational input; they do not come from science but they enable science. Science on its own could never prove that the world is orderly and lawful and comprehensible. We just know it is. Let us see why.

If there were no order in the Universe, it would make no sense to search for laws of nature in physics, chemistry, biology, genetics, and other disciplines. It is only due to the orderly design of the Universe that we can explain and predict—which would be impossible in a chaotic world of disorder and irregularity. In other words, order is proto-scientific and must come first before science can even get started. The tool of falsification, for instance, is necessarily based on this very assumption. Without order, there could not be any falsifying evidence. When we do find falsifying evidence, we do not take this as proof that the Universe is not orderly, but rather as an indication that there is something wrong with the specific order we had conjectured up in our minds. Apparently, falsification is based on order and cannot be falsified by disorder; counter-evidence may falsify a specific theory, but not the principle of falsification itself. In utter amazement, Albert Einstein wrote in one of his letters, "But surely, a priori, one should expect the world to be chaotic, not to be grasped by thought in any way." Einstein often spoke of the "harmony of the Universe"—actually one of the main pillars of science.

Something similar holds for the enigma of this Universe being intelligible, or comprehensible. The notion of intelligibility certainly does not come from science itself.

Scientists assume and know that the world can be understood and taken as intelligible—otherwise there would be no reason to pursue science. So intelligibility is definitely not the outcome of intense and extensive scientific research; it is again a proto-scientific, rational notion that must come first before science can even begin. It does not have to be confirmed over and over again, but it is a precondition for confirmation. We just know that this world is intelligible. This knowledge is so basic to science that it easily eludes scientists. If you were told scientists had discovered that certain physical phenomena are not intelligible, you would, or at least should, tell them to keep searching and come up with a better hypothesis or theory—based on this fundamental philosophical knowledge that says the Universe is "fundamentally" intelligible and comprehensible. Rationality calls for it.

Let's wrap up our discussion for now. Without rationality, we would have no reason to trust our own reasoning. That would be the end of anything we claim to be true—a thought that actually stops all thought. If one cannot trust the rationality of human beings, one is logically prevented from having confidence in one's own rational activities—with science being one of them.

In the meantime, you may have forgotten that the main theme of this chapter is relativism—the idea, or doctrine, that there is no absolute objective truth. Our thesis has been that relativism is the inevitable outcome of what evolutionary biologists and skeptical philosophers have been trying to sell us. But we have tried to show that their efforts are bound to fail. Yet, relativism seems to have survived in our modern culture, and has actually come out even stronger. People who never studied evolutionary biology or skepticism in philosophy have been tainted by relativism.

Chapter 6: Relativists and God

What else can be said against the idea of relativism?

Perhaps the main, potentially destructive problem with relativism is that it may lead to inconsistency, as we briefly mentioned already. The claim of relativism is as follows: "There are no objective truths. All truths are relative." So the question should be: "Is that claim objectively true?" If the answer is yes—yes, it is an objective truth—then the claim leads to contradiction: if the claim is true, it becomes false. We can only avoid contradiction by putting a restriction in the original claim: all truths are relative except the one of relativism. But if we do so, we should ask what entitles someone to make this exception. Apparently, there is at least one objective truth. Why not more then? The problem with a claim like "There is no such a thing as objective truth" is that it claims to be objectively true. We cannot make such a sweeping assertion without also asserting, implicitly, that there is such a thing as objective truth after all.

If so, one could say to a relativist: if there is no truth beyond your belief that something is true, then you cannot hold your own beliefs to be false or mistaken. When you deny that there is something as objective truth, you are in fact insisting in your denial that what you say is objectively true. This problem is not just specific for relativism but applies also to similar statements. If we say that everyone must be tolerant to everyone, except to people who are intolerant themselves, then we are enforcing the intolerance of tolerance. If we say that everyone must be inclusive to everyone, except to those who are not inclusive themselves, then we are enforcing the exclusion of inclusion. In all such cases, we may end up with a demand or rule that is quite dictatorial and authoritarian, allowing no room for anything but itself.

Let's leave these technicalities for what they are worth. But what remains is that relativists basically claim that there are no absolute truths. Taken to its extreme: gravity may be true for you but not for me. As Peter Kreeft put it, "To be a relativist, you must believe that nearly all human beings in history have ordered their lives by an illusion." He also astutely remarks: "There has never been a society of relativists." How can relativists promote relativism by teaching us that relativism is right and absolutism is wrong? Relativism claims everyone is right, absolutism claims some may be wrong. So either there is a real right and a real wrong or there is nothing wrong with being an absolutist, and nothing right with being a relativist. Kreeft then comes to a powerful conclusion, "Relativism is not rational, it is rationalization. It is not the conclusion of a rational argument. It is the rationalization of a prior action."

That's hard to accept for relativists. No wonder, some of them have invoked Einstein's Special Theory of Relativity to defend relativism. They say there is no absolute "now" in the world; "now" is relative to different observers in motion. If you and I are moving with respect to each other, then what is "now" for me is not "now" for you. But it is doubtful whether this interpretation of the theory is right, let alone its extension to the philosophical viewpoint of relativism. In addition to Einstein's understanding, there is Hendrik Lorentz's interpretation, which says there actually is an absolute now in the world, but we just cannot be sure which events in the world are happening now because motion affects our measuring instruments: moving clocks run slow and moving measuring rods contract. Both interpretations are empirically equivalent; there is no experiment one could perform to decide between the two interpretations. So Einstein's theory would not provide a good argument to prove that what is true for me may not be true for you.

Relativism has even tried to infiltrate the last stronghold of objective truth, science. Some philosophers of science—

who are usually not scientists themselves but historians or sociologists who merely reflect on what they happen to know about science—have come up with the idea that science is not ruled by objectivity but by subjectivism, depending on the way scientists look at things. A known exponent of this view is Thomas Kuhn, who claimed that scientific ideas must be put in their sociological and psychological context to let their meaning be revealed—so not in an objective but subjective sense. He made consensus in science a matter of mutual personal agreements codified in a so-called paradigm. Consequently, paradigm choices and paradigm changes are seen as merely depending on the subjective assent of the scientific community. Consequently, changes in paradigm may be so revolutionary that theories from different paradigms can be "incommensurable and irreconcilable," as he called it, lacking a common, objective standard to decide between them.

Where does this take us? Once the road of science is presented as an essentially disconnected succession of paradigms, science has become another victim of relativism, a threat to the objectivity of science and of nature. However, the truth of the matter is that even Kuhn had to admit that "the world remains the same even after it is seen in a totally different perspective following the paradigm shift." In other words, reality is what connects different paradigms. Compare this with different languages: beneath the different words of different languages you find common concepts—and this is what makes translation from one language to another possible. Ironically, the relativism of incommensurability makes each paradigm absolute—its own authority in matters of truth. Stanley Jaki rightly remarks, "Indeed, no great scientist has ever hoped to make a discovery incommensurable with all that had previously been discovered in science." Instead, there is a continuous process in science to search for and to come closer and closer to objective truth, in spite of errors that were made in order to get to the truth.

All scientists tacitly assume in their actions the objectivity of nature and the ability of the mind to grasp it ever more comprehensively. Relativism would be detrimental to this pursuit. There is nothing wrong with looking at scientists and their searching for truth from a psychological, sociological, or historical perspective, but truth itself is not a psychological, sociological, or historical issue. Truth is truth, even if you do not accept it; and untruth is untruth, even if you claim it. Truth is truth—for everyone, anywhere, at any time. If there are many possible interpretations of truth, by definition there is no ultimate interpretation; and if there is no ultimate interpretation, then a person cannot know whether or not his own interpretation is objectively true. In contrast to this view, we need to stress that we do not make truth, like artists; we discover truth, like scientists. Our perception of truth, our understanding of it, and our commitment to it may vary according to the state of art or science or philosophy. But truth itself doesn't change.

But relativists don't give up that easily. Some of them point out that we do have partial access to the truth. Popular in this context is the ancient fable of six blind men who visit the palace of the Rajah and encounter an elephant for the first time. As each touches the animal with his hands, each felt a different part of the elephant, announcing an elephant to be all trunk, all tail, etc. An argument ensued, each blind man thinking his own perception of the elephant was the correct one. The Rajah, awakened by the commotion, called out from the balcony. "The elephant is a big animal," he said. "Each man touched only one part. You must put all the parts together to find out what an elephant is like."

The message is clear. Each one had only found part of the

truth. In an analogous way, people make different truth claims about a certain issue, but no one has the entire picture, just pieces of it. Ultimately, all ideas, beliefs, and theories are supposedly equivalent in being inadequate. Had these people searched more completely, they would have seen their error. However, there is a real problem here with this view and position. To come to this conclusion, we assume there must be someone who must have a full and accurate view of the entire picture—just as the king had of the blind men and the elephant from his balcony. The Rajah was in a position of privileged access to the truth. Because he could see clearly, he was able to correct those who were blind.

If everyone truly is blind, then no one can know who is mistaken. Only someone who knows the whole truth can identify another on the fringes of it. In this story, only the king can do that—no one else. The Christian apologist Greg Koukle words it correctly: "If the story-teller is like one of the six who can't see—if he is one of the blind men groping around—how does he know everyone else is blind and has only a portion of the truth? On the other hand, if he fancies himself in the position of the king, how is it that he alone escapes the illusion that blinds the rest of us?"

Apparently, there are many reasons to reject relativism. Nevertheless relativism keeps doing its devastating work in the minds of many: It keeps sowing doubt and suspicion—no matter whether it is in science, in religion, or even in daily life. The French philosopher Jacques Maritain said it right, "The sole philosophy open to those who doubt the possibility of truth is absolute silence—even mental." No wonder, relativism has been under attack by the Catholic Church. Pope Leo XIII (1810–1903) was the first known Pope to use the word relativism in one of his encyclicals. Later on, Pope John Paul II and Pope Benedict XVI identified relativism as one of the most significant problems for faith and morals today. Benedict XVI spoke of the "Dictatorship of Relativism" in modern secularism. In April 2005, in his homily during Mass prior to the conclave which would elect him as Pope, then Cardinal Joseph Ratzinger said, "relativism, which is letting oneself be tossed and 'swept along by every wind of teaching,' looks like the only attitude acceptable to today's standards. We are moving towards a dictatorship of relativism which does not recognize anything as certain and which has as its highest goal one's own ego and one's own desires." The truth remains that truth cannot be established by majority vote but must find its base somewhere else.

There may indeed be strong reasons to reject relativism as well as the sources it may derive from, but nevertheless, skepticism has left its marks on many of us—not so much as a favorite philosophy, but more like a favorite strategy—an attitude of being skeptic about everything.

Let's make clear first that being skeptic goes much deeper than being critical. In the world of education and in the world of research and technology, people are supposed to speak or write the truth as they see it. If one of them is in error, the responsibility of their critics is to point out where they have made a mistake in reasoning, or where their premises are false, or what they have failed to see or failed to incorporate into their argument. This often requires a critical attitude. But a skeptical attitude goes much further than being critical.

Many people are pretty good at being skeptic about everything. Some even start at an early age, in high school or college. No matter what assertion is being made, they find reasons for doubting it. "How can you prove that?" they ask. And when someone proved A by basing it on B, they'd

Chapter 6: Relativists and God

challenge them to prove B next—and so on ad infinitum. They enjoy playing this game of a skeptic attitude. Nothing is safe for them. Literally everything is suspect in their eyes.

These skeptics deny the validity of nearly all aspects of knowledge, because in their view, we are not supposed to know any truth with certainty. Skeptics find a flaw in every truth claimed. They glorify doubt and suspicion. As Peter Ustinov put it, "Beliefs are what divide people. Doubt unites them." Skeptics have this persistent doubt as to how far they can go in trusting the world around them. No matter where they put their borderline, skepticism ultimately leads to nihilism, claiming that there is no law, no authority, no rationality, no morality, and no purpose to life—and, of course, no God as far as we know. Nihilism denies the very existence of all these fundamental aspects of life, and declares them non-existent, based on the certainty that nothing is certain.

Needless to say that an attitude of doubt makes for a very restrained view on everything in the world—actually so restrained that these skeptics cannot even know whether they have a mind to doubt with. They are so sure that nothing is sure. However, skeptics turn things the wrong way. Granted we often do need to eliminate errors to get to the truth, yet, our ultimate goal is not to avoid errors but to gain truth. We want to know, not to know what we do not know. Our ultimate goal is not to avoid errors, but to gain truth. Eliminating errors is only a means to gaining truth about reality. The fact that we do make errors in our search for truth should not entitle us to lower our standards of truth.

Skeptics, on the other hand, make it their final goal to avoid errors, in denial of the fact that eliminating errors is only a means to gaining truth—so they end up with an empty shell of complete mistrust. How can one be so sure that nothing can be known to be sure? Skepticism is at best a method to avoid errors, but it never leads to truth. It is an activity, not an achievement. It uses a silly slogan like "It is better to travel hopefully than to arrive"—which, as C. S. Lewis pointed out, is nonsense, because if you believe that, you never travel hopefully because there is no hope of arriving. Once we begin questioning the trustworthiness of our brains and senses and intellect and reason, there is no way of establishing their trustworthiness again independently of trusting them.

No matter how many doubts we have, our ultimate goal is always the truth. Truth remains standing. One could even argue that talk about lying does not make sense unless there exists also something like telling the truth. Gilbert Ryle used to say that there can be no counterfeit coins without genuine currency. Even those who swear by the "trial and error" method must admit that errors only exist by the grace of truth. Or take the case that two people have a different answer to a specific mathematical calculation. Does this entitle relativists to state that all answers are worth the same, or that there is no correct answer at all? Even Karl Popper, the champion of falsification and falsifiability, had to admit that the very idea of error is inconceivable without the idea of truth.

The irony is that no one can be certain that nothing is certain. Chesterton diagnosed skepticism very well when he tackled the question whether we can know anything with certainty: "[A] man must either answer that question in the affirmative, or else never answer any question, never ask any question, never even exist intellectually, to answer or to ask." And then he adds, "Most fundamental sceptics appear to survive, because they are not consistently skeptical and not at all fundamental. They will first deny everything and then admit something, if for the sake of argument or often rather

Chapter 6: Relativists and God

of attack without argument." Skeptics are masters of deception; they make us wonder whether we really exist, whether others exist, whether the world exists—and ultimately whether God exists. Skeptics act like criminal lawyers: At trial, they don't have to prove anything in a positive way; all they have to do is raise doubts in the minds of the jurors.

Earlier we mentioned Einstein as saying that the most incomprehensible thing about the Universe is that it is comprehensible, which he actually called a "mystery." Indeed, we seem to have a mystery here. Regardless of the fact that neither human reason nor the Universe can be explained by themselves, the most surprising thing in all of this remains that our minds have the capability to know reality the way it is. There is a deep connect between truth in our minds and the reality in the world around us.

Now the question arises as to what causes this almost perfect harmony of thought and being, of rationality and reality? Put differently, what must nature be like in order for our minds to capture reality the way it is? There seems to be some mysterious conformity between the rationality of our minds and the rationality found in the world around us. Somehow the mind seems to be able to capture reality the way it is. Not only does the physical order we observe in this world appear to be amazingly "consistent," but so does the world of thoughts in our minds. Not only is our rationality consistent, but so is the world itself. It is a consistency that must perplex us. How is it possible that reality can be "grasped" by our thoughts? The mystery we have here is the fact that the rationality present in our minds matches the rationality we find in the world.

We found out already that this dual "consistency" does not come from our genes and was not passed on to us by the animal world. So the question is: where else could it come from? What explains the conformity between the rationality of the mind and the "rationality" of the world? What can explain this match?

The fact that the Universe has an elegant, intelligible, and discoverable underlying mathematical and physical structure calls for an explanation—or otherwise must be left unexplained. Even scientists uphold the conviction—consciously or subconsciously—that there is an intelligible plan behind this Universe, a plan that is accessible to the human intellect through the natural light of reason. Where does this power of reason come from? As John Polkinghorne puts it, "Such a reason would be provided by the Rationality of the Creator." Only the Rationality of the Creator can explain that the world is an objective and orderly entity investigable by the human mind because the mind too is an orderly and objective product of the same rational and consistent Creator. Fr. George Lemaître once spoke about the God of the Big Bang as the "One Who gave us the mind to understand him and to recognize a glimpse of his glory in our Universe which he has so wonderfully adjusted to the mental power with which he has endowed us." Later on, the late astrophysicist Sir James Jeans would put it this way, "[T]he Universe begins to look more like a great thought than a great machine." Apparently, there is an intelligible plan behind this Universe, a plan that is accessible to the human intellect through the natural light of reason.

What is this intellect? It is important to note that rationality is not a matter of intelligence but of intellect. Whereas intelligence can be graded on an IQ scale, intellect cannot. One can be more or less intelligent (or even more or less intellectual), but one cannot have more or less intellect. Since intelligence works only with perception of sense-data, animals may show various forms of intelligence in their behavior, because intelligence is a brain feature and as such an important tool in survival. We find spatial intelligence in pigeons and bats, social intelligence in wolves and monkeys, formal intelligence in apes and dolphins, practical intelligence in rats and ravens, to name just a few. Intelligence is a matter of processing sense-data—something even a robot can do by "cleverly" processing sounds, images, stimuli, signals, and the like

Intellect, on the other hand, is very different from this. Like intelligence, intellect also uses sense-data, but unlike intelligence, it changes perception into cognition. It does so by using mental concepts, which makes sensorial experiences intelligible for the human mind. While reasoning allows us to move from one thing we know to another, the intellect can create concepts through which we are able to understand and know the world around us. So this raises the question what a concept is.

A concept is the result of abstraction from what we have experienced through the senses. For instance, we have seen several round objects and then we abstract from this the concept of "circle." We do not really "see" a circle, for a circle is a highly abstract entity that does not exist as such in the world around us. True, we can visualize a circle without imagining any specific size, but concepts have a universality that images can never have, for the concept circle applies to every individual circle without exception. Besides, a concept has an intricate web of connections with other concepts—in this case, for instance, a "radius," a "diameter," and a "circumference." Even a "simple" concept such as "green" or "greenness" has many connections to other concepts—for instance, green objects turn gray in twilight (the rod effect) and red when receding very quickly (the Doppler effect). As a result, concepts go far beyond what the senses provide: they transform "things" of the world into "objects" of knowledge, thus enabling us to see with our "mental eyes" what no physical eyes could ever see before.

No wonder then that concepts play a central role in how we know the world. Thanks to concepts, we can see similarities that are not immediately evident and not directly tied to what we perceive. Everyone can see things falling, but to perceive gravity one needs the concept of gravity so as to see what no one had been able to see before Isaac Newton. The concept of gravity allows us to "see" the similarity between the motion of the moon and the fall of an apple. Or take concepts such as "carnivore" and herbivore": we do not really see them when we see a dog and a rabbit, but they help us explain why dogs and cats produce clear urine while rabbits and hamsters have cloudy urine. It is through concepts like these that we are able to see similarities that would have eluded us if we didn't have those concepts. We do not really or directly perceive gravity, carnivores, cells, genes, and the like, yet these concepts make the world more understandable and intelligible for us.

It is thanks to concepts that biologists can talk about issues such as evolution and natural selection. Even "relativism" is a concept. Unfortunately for relativism, you cannot have it both ways. If you accept the objectivity and truthfulness of your biological knowledge, including your evolutionary theories, you cannot come to the conclusion that evolutionary theory, in turn, teaches us that all human knowledge is just a product of genes selected during evolution. To claim that the theory of natural selection is the product of rationality, and at the same time, that rationality is supposedly the product of natural selection makes for a "boomerang theory" that undermines its own claims—once we consider it to be true, it becomes false. If I believe that my beliefs are determined by genes, then this very belief must also be determined by genes—which creates a paradox by violating the principle of non-contradiction. Therefore, the theory of natural selection cannot be the product of natural selection itself. When someone like Stephen Jay Gould claims that the mind is merely an illusion produced by the brain, we should seriously question anything Gould says, if his thoughts are just illusions by his own verdict.

Interestingly enough, even Charles Darwin himself vaguely acknowledged this paradox when he said in his Autobiography, "But then with me the horrid doubt always arises whether the convictions of man's mind, which has been developed from the mind of the lower animals, are of any value or at all trustworthy. Would anyone trust in the convictions of a monkey's mind, if there are any convictions in such a mind?" The theory of natural selection makes him wonder whether, as he puts it, "[T]he mind of man, which has, as I fully believe, been developed from a mind as low as that possessed by the lowest animal, [can] be trusted when it draws such grand conclusions." Darwin had good reason to worry about this "horrid doubt."

What Darwin did not seem to realize is that the theory of natural selection can neither create nor explain the rationality of the human mind, but must assume it. If the human mind were really the mere product of natural selection, so would science be, hence nothing we claim to know could then be trusted. The rationality of a person such as Darwin, who discovered the theory of evolutionary theory, or of scientists such as Watson and Crick, who discovered the structure of DNA in genes, must be more than that which they discovered. Otherwise their discoveries would not be discoveries, but very shaky and fragile claims, or not even that. They would be mere illusions concocted by a neural network under the shaky direction of genes shaped by natural selection.

What can we conclude from this? Instead of claiming that

The Eclipse of God: Is Religion on the Way Out?

our rationality comes from "below"—from the animal world, from genes and neurons—it is much more likely it comes from "Above" where God's Rationality reigns. Human rationality is a reflection of God's Rationality. That's where its power comes from. And that's another reason why relativism is flawed. Relativism is an assault not only on our own rationality but also on God's rationality as reflected in creation.

The conformity between the rationality of the mind and the rationality of the world may be a riddle for non-believers, but for religious believers it is actually "a match made in Heaven." This "match made in Heaven" forebodes the end of relativism and skepticism. It ends the eclipse caused by relativism and skepticism. Only God can shine in our darkness. Of course, relativists and skeptics would deny there is such a match. But what arguments have they left to deny such a match?

Chapter 6: Relativists and God

7

Secularists and God

Secularists promote their own kind of ideology—secularism. It is another one of those "isms" with a totalitarian worldview pretention. Secularism and secular humanism put Man on center stage, without leaving any "space" for God. It features Man without a religious dimension. Man has become a solitary individual navigating on his own towards goals of his own. According to Pope John Paul II, people in a secularized society "strive for the good of man, but man who is truncated, reduced to his merely horizontal dimension." They make us believe that we are fully self-made, in full control of our own history and destination. It declares humanity as the measure of all things by pronouncing that all our problems can be entirely solved by using the right human knowledge, technology, reasoning, and judgment.

Since secularists consider all our achievements man-made, they believe also that we can make our own moral values and rules; so our morals are believed to be man-made as well. From then on, everything centers on "me, myself, and I." It should not be surprising then that secularism forebodes trouble for morality.

Chapter 7: Secularists and God

a. How the Eclipse Sets in

Pope John Paul II used to make a distinction between secularism and secularity. It is an important distinction that will help us better understand what is happening in our modern society. Unlike secularism, secularity merely draws a dividing line between religion and state, or between religious institutions and governmental institutions.

Interestingly enough, this dividing line drawn between the Church and the State is a Christian invention—to be more precise, Jesus' "invention." When Pope Benedict XVI discussed the separation of religion and politics—Church and State, if you will—he wrote in his book *Jesus of Nazareth*, "In his teaching and in his whole ministry, Jesus had inaugurated a non-political Messianic kingdom and had begun to detach these two hitherto inseparable realities from one another." In other words, actually in Jesus' words, we should render to Caesar what is Caesar's, but never should render to Caesar what is God's. These two realities are separated, yet not isolated from each other, but rather connected within each one of us. On the one hand, the Church benefits from the State to keep and enforce justice. On the other hand, the State benefits from religious beliefs, which help people respond to each other in a moral and respectful way for the common good. Because of this relationship, Church and State are not each other's opposite, but instead complement each other and support each other.

This principle was further reinforced by the early Church Fathers, as a reaction against the wish of Emperor Constantine and his successors to merge State and Church again in an attempt to control the Church. Let us keep in mind that this line of separation was drawn by the Church, not by the State. After the Reformation, some states tried again to impose new regulations on churches, when the control of religion was handed over once more to the ruler of each individual State. The religious conflicts were mitigated in 1555 as part of the Peace of Augsburg by the principle that the religion of the ruler, either Catholic or Protestant, is that of the people (cuius regio, eius religio). In light of what we discussed earlier, this move was basically un-Christian.

In reaction to situations in which the religion of individuals was made dependent upon the society into which they were born, the United States decided to separate the Church from the State again and gave every person the right to choose whatever religion—or lack thereof—one wishes, without any control of the State. The reason behind this separation of Church and State is the free exercise of religion—a principle that originally aimed not at protecting the State from Religion but at protecting Religion from the State. This way, the USA got the First Amendment and its definition of the first freedom: "Congress shall make no law respecting an establishment of religion, or prohibiting the free exercise thereof." Let us call this secularity, or "freedom of religion."

However, times have changed. Secularism has gone much further in the minds of most secularists. It has gone from "freedom of religion" to "freedom from religion." Whereas secularity merely separates the non-religious realm from the religious realm, secularism is intolerant of religion and imposes its own totally secular standards on everything else, including religion. From now on, religious liberty is understood as "the right to define one's own concept of existence, of meaning, of the Universe, and of the mystery of human life," according to one of its exponents, U.S. Supreme Court Justice Anthony Kennedy. The only commandment in the life of secularists seems to be, "You shall never invoke the name of God, unless you do so in vain."

The term secularism, as it is now mostly understood,

originated in the mid-19th Century in the works of George Holyoake, a British newspaper editor, and his fellow atheists. It is in works such as his that the current usage was adopted in which "secular" is viewed as "free from religion." It has an anti-religious overtone—a vision of the future as devoid of religion, instead of separated from religion. It seeks to eliminate religion, or at the very least to privatize and thus marginalize it. In doing so, secularism reveals itself as totalitarian, for it allows no room in the public space for anything but itself. Secularists want only their views and values to be taught and allowed in public life. They obviously cannot give any reasonable justification for their views. Like all fundamentalists they just assume their views are right, and anyone who disagrees with them must be dealt with.

We see the results of secularism all around us. Many great North American universities were once clearly and openly religious and began under religious auspices and for religious purposes—Harvard, Yale, Princeton, the University of Chicago, Boston University, to name just some of the most prominent. They have become purely secular, or even secularist—indistinguishable from their nonreligious counterparts, except for spacious and now largely unused chapels. Catholic colleges and universities have mostly run the same course. These institutions, which should be educating Catholics to critically examine the categories of the culture they live in, have instead become the main vehicle by which Catholics are indoctrinated into the secularist "values" of their surroundings. What secularists call their "values" are typically pro-abortion, pro-euthanasia, and pro-homosexuality. Again, conformity with the surrounding culture of secularism ranks higher at these institutions than supporting a culture steeped in religious beliefs and moral values.

What this leads to is the disappearance of God—or what

the Jewish philosopher Martin Buber called "the eclipse of God." The secularist society does not allow any mention of God in the public square. It denies there is any religious dimension to a human being. And when God disappears, we lose also what comes with God—not only rationality (see 6.b) but also morality. As a consequence, morality no longer comes from religion, or ultimately from God, but now traces its origin back to our genetic constitution—a product of evolution—or it is reduced to a collection of personal opinions, preferably enforced by a majority vote.

When it comes to morality, secularism is a form of moral relativism: morals are no longer based on objective, universal values, but they are either genetic artifacts, neuronal illusions, politically correct beliefs, or just personal opinions. G. B. Shaw considered them just a matter of "different tastes." We are no longer under any moral obligation—because there simply is no such thing—but we may think we are. The objectivity of morality has become a sense of objectivity, which is in essence a matter of subjectivity. We are not really obligated to act morally, but we may only feel we are. As the philosopher of science Michael Ruse put it, "Morality is just an aid to survival and reproduction, and any deeper meaning is illusory."

Ironically, even relativists and secularists who deny that morality has any absolute authority still hold on to at least one moral absolute that says, "Never disobey your own conscience." So they should then ask themselves the question as to where the absolute authority of a human conscience comes from. They probably find their answer in our genome and in the network of our neurons. Secularists proclaim there is no moral authority other than themselves. Things in the world have the value I myself give them. But if that's true, then the reverse must also be true. If I myself don't "value" something, it has no value. Where do these secularists go wrong? We need to pray again, "God, be our light. Shine in our darkness."

b. How the Sun Reclaims the Day

It is quite possible that secularism started as a reasonable form of secularity: keep Religion and State separate without advancing one at the cost of the other. But that is only how it began. Fr. Robert Barron, now Auxiliary Bishop of Los Angeles, said it right: "The reason that the Bill of Rights—the first 10 amendments to the Constitution—is so important is that it holds off the tendency, inherent in any government, toward totalitarianism, even if that means the totalitarianism of the majority." As a matter of fact, Religion and State can very well complement each other and offer each other what each one is "good" at. Religion has something to offer that the State cannot provide on its own. Religion is needed to fill the voids the State leaves behind, to challenge the State when human dignity is in danger, to heal the wounds the State may cause, to answer questions the State is not familiar with.

But that is not how modern secularism understands the situation. It sees Religion as a threat to the State, the Society, and the Culture. It rejects the impact, not so much of any beliefs—for secularism itself is a belief—but in particular of religious beliefs. We see Western secularization crossing the line here from neutrality to outright hostility toward religion in general and Catholicism in particular. Bishop Barron again: "The secularist state recognizes that its principle enemy is the Church Catholic. Accordingly, it wants Catholicism off the public stage and relegated to a private realm where it cannot interfere with secularism's totalitarian agenda." The assumption behind secularism is that all motives derived from the Christian religion are worthless for the state and for society. Like most other "isms," secularism is a totalitarian doctrine that does not accept any light or guidance from anywhere else. It actually makes for a mild form of fascism. Secularists preach tolerance magnanimously, but only for those who agree with them—"my way or no way."

This makes Iain T. Benson, a Scottish legal philosopher, question the secularists' agenda as follows: "Are we only to allow all kinds of influence as long as they do not come from religion? Why, for example, ought the beliefs of a politician that originate in materialism be acceptable but a critique of materialism animated by religious convictions be unacceptable?" As a matter of fact, everyone has certain "beliefs" and some kind of "faith." So the "secular" cannot possibly be a realm that is free from beliefs or from faith. Yet, that is how many understand the term "secular" nowadays, when they speak of "secular schools," "secular government," etc. These terms are now generally understood to mean "free from any beliefs, in particular from religious beliefs." But it is clear they cannot be free from any beliefs, as the dogma of materialism is at least one of the beliefs still reigning in secularist societies. No wonder a State without Religion becomes easily an authoritarian society. As the legendary Archbishop Fulton Sheen put it, "Once a nation ceases to believe it begins to obey [the Omnipotent State]." Then he quotes William Penn, the founder of Pennsylvania, who warned us: "Men must be governed by God or they will be ruled by tyrants."

How should the Catholic Church respond to this development? The best way is probably what she always used to do in the past—to be leaven in the secular world, light that shines in the darkness, or salt that preserves society. Catholic education in the USA, for example, came about when the Church realized public education did not give her new generation as much as necessary for a human being to become a "complete being," which necessarily includes a religious dimension. The Church's response was not a retreat into seclusion, challenged by public education, but rather an engagement to prepare Catholics better for their service to society based on their Catholic faith. We need something similar today. To preserve their Catholic identity in a secularist world, Catholics should cultivate their identity, not by building walls but by breaking them down, not by constructing road-blocks but by building bridges—in other words, by engaging in society to serve her better through what Catholicism has to offer society. Once you lose your identity and don't know who you are, the wind can turn you in any direction.

The Church has indeed much to offer to society. She does not exist for herself but for the transformation of the world—for the sake of the unborn, the rejected, the disabled, the elderly, the poorest of the poor. It is part of her identity to contribute to society. The Catholic religion wants to make society a better place to live in—for the entire person, not just for a person's material needs. There are many dimensions to a human being—biological, emotional, social, and last but not least religious. Leaving any of these out would be an injustice to any human being. Interestingly enough, secularist parents want to give their children the best they know of in health care and education, but when it comes to religion, they give them nothing, letting them make their own choice when they are grown up. Why not do the same then with education? Well, that is the very inconsistency of secularism.

One of the contributions the Catholic Church has to offer society is her conception of the natural law. The natural law is not something like shari'a law which governs every facet of life, from the great affairs of state and diplomacy to the smallest concerns of the average person, without making a distinction between the affairs of church and those of state. The notion of natural law, on the other hand, is very different from shari'a law. It is based on the reality of human nature—nature as something that is distinct from God, although ultimately dependent on God, so the natural law can at least partially be understood by everyone, even without reference to God. It is the reflection of God's eternal law "written" into our nature. That is why we can know that certain actions are good for us while others are bad, just by the use of reason, even without any input from religious faith.

Thomas Aquinas puts it this way, "the light of reason is placed by nature in every man to guide him in his acts." Just as it is plainly evident that there is order in this world and that like causes produce like effects—there is just no hard proof for it—so it is equally evident that human beings must act in accordance with the natural law. Common sense tells us there is some kind of physical order in nature: stones that fall today will also fall tomorrow; we cannot prove this today, but we can confidently assume it. Similarly, when someone denies the existence of moral laws and moral values, all one can do is invoke the principle of common sense again. Common sense tells us there is some kind of moral order in life: if murder is wrong today it will also be wrong tomorrow. Again, there is nothing we can come up with in support of it—it is just obvious and evident.

Everyone who is not morally blind is able to see this. As a matter of fact, there is not a great deal of difference between a Christian morality, Jewish morality, Hindu morality, Muslim morality, Buddhist morality—although there's a great difference in these religions. Perhaps the best-known universal moral principle is the so-called Golden Rule. In its negative form, it says, "Do not do unto others as you would not have them do unto you." Its positive form is "Do unto others as you would have them do to you." The Golden Rule

Chapter 7: Secularists and God

can be found in Christian, Jewish, Islamic, Buddhist, and Confucian texts, among others. Perhaps the oldest moral code is the Code of Hammurabi from around BC 2250. C. S. Lewis published a list of universal moral principles he called "Illustrations of the Tao or Natural Law." As Peter Kreeft puts it, "We find similar morals, beneath different mores." In other words, what the Catholic Church has to offer is not some outlandish faith, but a faith that comes with reason. Most of all, she has the natural law to offer, which has always focused on the common good of society and is ingrained in human nature, because we are social beings by nature. Whoever refuses to accept this proposition is missing out on something very basic—the common sense of the natural law.

At www.catholicscomehome.org, we find beautifully summarized what we, as the Catholic Church, have done for society: We started hospitals to care for the sick; we establish orphanages, and help the poor; we are the largest charitable organization on the planet, bringing relief and comfort to those in need; we educate more children than any other scholarly or religious institution; we founded the college system; we defend the dignity of all human life, and uphold marriage and family; we are…… the Catholic Church… with over one billion in our family sharing in the sacraments and fullness of Christian faith.

In this context, we should quote Pope John Paul II who famously said, "The Church proposes; she imposes nothing." In other words, there should be no suppression of society by the Church. It's more what she is "for" than what she is "against." She does not put road-blocks but road-markers to show where it is safe to go. Even when she says "no" to certain developments in society, she needs to do so through her Catholic "yes" alternative. Then the Pontiff continues, "An 'adult' faith is not a faith that follows the trends of fashion and the latest novelty." The late Fr. Richard John

Neuhaus made an astute remark in this context: "Few things are more important to the free society than the idea and reality of the limited state.... The role of the limited state is to respect the political sovereignty of the people who acknowledge a sovereignty higher than their own."

When speaking about religious freedom in Philadelphia, Pope Francis stressed how our various religious traditions "remind us of the transcendent dimension of human existence and our irreducible freedom in the face of every claim to absolute power." Then he added, "We need but look at history, especially the history of the last century, to see the atrocities perpetrated by systems which claimed to build one or another 'earthly paradise' by dominating peoples, subjecting them to apparently indisputable principles and denying them any kind of rights."

Then there is another serious consequence when society changed from secularity to secularism. Since a secularist society is supposed to be free from religion, its morality has lost its grounding in God as a consequence. Fyodor Dostoyevsky could not have worded this problem better than he did in his novel The Brothers Karamazov: "It's God that's worrying me. That's the only thing that's worrying me. What if He doesn't exist? What if Rakitin's right—that it's an idea made up by men? Then, if He doesn't exist, man is the king of the earth, of the Universe. Magnificent! Only how is he going to be good without God? That's the question."

The question is, indeed, how man is "going to be good without God." Is that even possible? We will answer this question in two steps. Step one will be that morality does not reside in the genes and did not come to us from the animal world, contrary to what many secularists proclaim. Step two will be that morality can only find its foundation in God, so a morality without God would be floating in midair.

Chapter 7: Secularists and God

Before we do so, we need to find out what morality is, and what it is not. It should be made clear first that morality is not another word for social behavior. These two are very different notions. Whereas social behavior does have evolutionary roots in the animal world, morality does not, as we will see. What is it then that makes morality so different from social behavior?

Morality gives us an "immaterial sense" of what is right and what is wrong in social behavior. The term morality can be confusing, though. The (philosophical) study of morality is usually called ethics, and ethics has added to the confusion by giving us various interpretations of morality. So let us make clear first what morality stands for in this discussion. The morality we are talking about here is our capacity or faculty to distinguish between right and wrong. It is about rights and obligations, about actions others owe us (our rights) and about actions we owe to others (our duties), both being part of the "common good." Through morality we have access to a world of duties and rights—a world beyond our control, although we do have an immaterial sense of what is morally right and what is morally wrong. Morality adds a very different dimension to social behavior. Not everything that is thinkable or possible or reasonable—in rational terms and social terms—is also permissible in moral terms. Thanks to the natural law, social behavior can be evaluated in moral terms of right or wrong.

There are at least four characteristics associated with morality. One is that morality does not come with a specific race, ethnicity, nation, party, or church—it is a common property that belongs to all human beings. Morality is not connected with interest groups or with majority votes, but it is universal in scope—it is the same for everyone everywhere. Moral rules, laws, and values are universally applicable to all of humanity, regardless of race, ethnicity, nationality, culture, or political affiliation.

A second characteristic is that duties and rights have a natural reciprocity: the duty of self-preservation goes with the right of self-preservation; the duty to seek the truth matches the right to seek it; the duty to work for justice comes with the right to pursue it; the duty to protect life is linked to the right of protecting life; the right of receiving religious freedom is also the duty to allow religious freedom; the duty to uphold human dignity is linked to the right to claim it; the right to life comes with the duty to live. In other words, "no duties" means "no rights," and "no rights" means "no duties." No one has the duty to have children, so no one has the right to have children; no one has the duty to marry, so no one has the right to be married; no one has the duty to die, so no one has the right to die.

A third characteristic is that morality is not about what the world is like, but about what the world ought to be like; morality is not a matter of description but prescription. It is not a description of social behavior, but a prescription of what social behavior ought to be like. "Racial equality," for instance, is not a descriptive but prescriptive term; races are not equal in biological characteristics, yet their members do have the same dignity and rights in moral terms. Description and prescription do not coincide. What is the case does not necessarily tell us what ought to be the case.

A fourth characteristic of morality is that it tells us what ought to be done in an absolute sense—no matter what, whether we like it or not, whether we feel it or not, whether others enforce it or not. It tells us what ought to be done—by us, as a duty, and towards us, as a right—otherwise a moral mistake would be made. Whereas science attempts to discover what is the case, ethics as the "science of morality" attempts to discover what ought to be the case for anyone anywhere. As a consequence, morality gives us a moral responsibility. Moral absolutes are like unchanging rocks beneath the changing waves of feelings and practices. They are without exceptions. A morality of mere convention, of man-made and thus man-revisable rules of the social game, is not morality at all, only mores.

The rights and duties of morality have some strong resemblances with the truths and untruths of rationality, which we discussed earlier (6.b). They both are universal (applicable to everyone everywhere), absolute (without exceptions), timeless (even if we do not know the underlying law yet), and objective (a given, independent of us and of any human authority). They are objective, universal, timeless, and absolute standards—no matter whether we are talking rationality, in terms of true and false, or morality, in terms of right and wrong. Just as "truths are true," even when we do not know yet they are true, "rights are right," even though we may not realize yet they are morally right.

What sets morality apart from rationality, though, is that we cannot define moral (prescriptive) notions in non-moral (descriptive) terms. Aquinas' notion of the natural law—written into our human nature and guided by reason—has often been misunderstood. The natural law has nothing to do with the "natural ways" of things. Birds are made to fly, but they don't have a duty or right to fly, because they are not endowed with reason. The natural law is not a law of biology, but a law of morality that does not apply to "irrational beings" such as animals. Animals emit sounds to indicate pleasure or pain, but human beings have reasons in matters of right and wrong. Abraham Lincoln spoke of "an abstract truth applicable to all men at all times." Thomas Aquinas puts it this way, "the light of reason is placed by nature in every man to guide him in his acts."

So whatever is natural in a biological way may not be "natural" in a moral way. Here are some examples. The fact that diseases are "natural" in a biological sense does not entail they are "good" in a moral sense too—that's why we ought to fight them and cure them. The fact that human beings go through a biological process of development does not mean that they also go through a development in human rights. The fact that the "survival of the fittest" may be common in nature does not mean that we should enforce it morally, as is done in eugenics (breeding humans like we breed animals). Morality actually demands that we give the same care to the weakest in society as we give to the strongest. And the fact that some people are richer than others or more intelligent than others does not mean that we ought to value them differently in a moral sense. They may have more clout than others, but they should not have more rights nor fewer duties than others. The fact that human beings differ from each other does not mean they ought to be treated differently in a moral sense. In short, a moral property such as being good or right cannot be reduced to a natural property such as being natural, functional, genetic, more evolved, more developed, better for the majority, or whatever.

This point could be explained further with an example used by the former president Abraham Lincoln, when he was talking about slavery. In his own, rather technical words,

> If A. can prove, however conclusively, that he may, of right, enslave B.—why may not B. snatch the same argument, and prove equally, that he may enslave A?—You say A. is white, and B. is black. It is color, then; the lighter, having the right to enslave the darker? Take care. By this rule, you are to be slave to the first man you meet, with a fairer skin than your own. You mean the whites are intellectually the superiors of the blacks; and, therefore have the right

to enslave them? Take care again. By this rule, you are to be slave to the first man you meet, with an intellect superior to your own.

President Lincoln's point is clear: all the answers some people might come up with to defend their pretended moral claims use relative, descriptive criteria such as a darker skin color or a lower intelligence, whereas moral claims are absolute. Because those criteria are relative, someone with a lighter skin or higher intelligence would then presumably have the "moral right" to enslave someone else. And the same holds for the moral value of human life and human dignity. This value cannot be based on biological standards such as age, viability, vitality, heartbeat, or brain volume, since those are per definition morally irrelevant, and relative besides. There is nothing moral about them; they are descriptive but not prescriptive, relative but not absolute.

In contrast, moral values, rules, and laws are absolute ends-in-themselves—not disposable means-to-other-ends. If moral values were indeed relative, one cannot claim, as almost everyone does, that certain human rights are universally applicable to all members of any culture or ethnic group. Whereas our bodily movements are subject to physical constraints, our social actions are subject to moral ones, based on the natural law, but independent of race, geography, age, ethnicity, nationality, religion, or political affiliation. Let's say it again, moral rights and duties are universal, absolute, timeless, objective, and nonnegotiable standards of human behavior. Therefore, when it comes to morality, we cannot just pick whatever we want. We cannot just vote to decide whether we are anti-slavery and anti-abortion, or not. Abraham Lincoln put it well when he challenged the Nebraska bill of 1820 that would let residents vote to decide if slavery would be legal in their territory:

The Eclipse of God: Is Religion on the Way Out?

"God did not place good and evil before man, telling him to make his choice." In other words, there is no "pro-choice" in morality. Morality obliges us to go, unconditionally, for what is good and right.

Obviously, secularists would object to all of this. They claim that moral values and laws are far from universal and absolute. They would point out that moral laws and values have been subject to change during the course of human history—often determined by a majority vote, so to speak. However, there is a mix-up here. On the one hand, there is a mix-up between moral laws and legal laws. Legal, civic, or positive laws are not identical to moral laws—they should be, but all too often they are not. As a matter of fact, the law of the land is not always a reflection of the moral law. That is the reason why Martin Luther King Jr. called any unjust (legal) law "a code that is out of harmony with the moral law."

On the other hand, there is also a mix-up in this discussion between moral values and moral evaluations. Unfortunately the word "value" is rather ambiguous in our modern culture. Spoken to modern ears, the idea of "objective values" is easily misunderstood as an unintelligible contradiction in terms. Many nowadays tend to associate "values" with the ever changing value of houses and stock, rather than something constant, absolute, and objective. Our secularized age has become crammed with "values"; corporations and universities, for example, are proud to tout their "values." These so-called values allow them to imagine a moral outlook without law, a moral discernment without negative judgments, and moral failure without shame. Besides, politicians often say certain policies go against their "values," but what they actually mean is those policies go against their political wishes. As the Boston College philosopher Peter Kreeft astutely remarks, "God did

Chapter 7: Secularists and God

not give Moses 'The Ten Values.'"

That having been said, the term "moral value" has a very specific meaning. Moral values should not be confused with moral evaluations. Moral evaluations are our personal feelings or discernments regarding moral values. Secularists think that, in making moral evaluations, we create moral values in accordance with these evaluations. So when evaluations change, the moral values and laws are said to change as well. If that were true, our moral values would indeed be subject to various cultural and historical fluctuations; morality would just be a matter of emotions, personal preferences, cultural trends, political powers, and majority votes. As a result, moral correctness should just be a matter of political correctness. Had the slaveholders won the Civil War, so they say, we might see it today as an admirable institution.

In response to this secularists' rejection of the absolute character of morality, it should be emphasized that evaluations are merely a reflection of the way we discern absolute moral values and react to them. Whereas moral evaluations may be volatile and fluctuating, moral values and laws are timeless, universal, objective, and absolute. Think of the following comparison: our current understanding of physical or biological laws constantly needs revision each time we reach a better understanding of those laws in the way they really are. In the meantime, we assume there are absolute and universal laws of nature, although we may not yet have fully captured them in our current understanding and in our existing evaluations. Something similar holds for moral laws. As C. S. Lewis once put it, "The human mind has no more power of inventing a new value than of imagining a new primary color." To use a more specific example, we could ask about Nazi death camps: were they really wrong, or were they just wrong in the eyes of nations other than

Germany after World War II?

We could illustrate this point a little further. A few centuries ago, slavery was not evaluated as morally wrong, but nowadays it is by most people. Did our moral values change? Our evaluations certainly did, but that does not mean moral values did too. Only some people in the past—heroes such as St. Cyprian, St. Gregory of Nyssa, St. John Chrysostom, St. Patrick, St. Anselm, St. Vincent de Paul, to name just a few—were able to discern the objective, intrinsic, and universal value of personal freedom and human rights (versus slavery), whereas many of their contemporaries were blind for this value. Only when we distinguish between values and evaluations can we explain the disconnect that may exist between moral laws and civil laws. Martin Luther King Jr. was right, the law of the land is not always a reflection of the moral law. But not everyone may be aware of that discrepancy, certainly not relativists and secularists.

Whereas civil laws often reflect the current moral evaluations of a nation, moral laws are intrinsically right, even when we do not see yet that they are. Anyone who does not see the evidence of moral laws is morally blind. Although a blind person cannot see the trees outside, the trees are still there; the existence of the trees does not depend on whether the blind person perceives them or not. In a similar way a morally blind person cannot see the moral laws and values out there, yet they are there; their existence does not depend on whether a person with moral blindness can perceive them. Moral blindness can be caused by upbringing, culture, personality, and selfishness, which may temporarily obscure the self-evidence of moral values, principles, and laws.

Just as science needs geniuses such as Newton and Einstein to discover scientific laws, so morality also needs "geniuses" such as Moses, Prophets, and Saints to uncover moral laws. As Jesus would say, "You have heard that it was said … But I say to you …" What he actually says is, whether you "see" it or not, this is the way it ought to be in this world, as this is the way this world was created and designed by the Creator. The fact that some do not "see" certain moral values or laws the way they are, or even violate them knowingly, should not give us any reason to lower our moral standards the way relativists and secularists would like us to do. Just like we should not lower standards in school teaching when some cannot make the mark, we should not adjust moral standards to what everyone can handle or is willing to handle.

Now that we have clarified what morality is, we may be better equipped to revisit our original question as to whether we can be good without God. We will start with step one and argue that morality does not reside in our genes and has not come to us from the animal world as many secularists proclaim when they say that we are "hard-wired" to be moral when making personal judgments regarding good and bad.

To begin with, there is no morality in the animal world that could have been passed on to us through genes and DNA. Animals do not have any moral values or moral rules, so they do not have to control their drives, lusts, and emotions. They just follow whatever "pops up" in their brains—and no one has the right to morally blame them. The relationship between predator and prey, for instance, has nothing to do with morality; if predators really had a conscience guided by morality, their lives would be pretty harsh. Crocodiles may shed tears while devouring their prey, as some say, but we can be certain it is not because of remorse. Dogs may act as if they are "caring," but they just follow their instinct, not some moral code; dogs happen to have such an instinct, whereas cats lack it, since it is not in their genes. Whenever we see social behavior among animals, we can be sure it is not regulated by a moral code.

As a consequence, animals never do awful things out of meanness or cruelty, for the simple reason that they have no morality—and thus no cruelty or meanness. But humans definitely do have the capacity of performing real atrocities. Even kids who bully others should be held accountable and disciplined for their immoral behavior, regardless of their age. On the other hand, if animals do seem to do awful things, it is only because we as human beings consider their actions "awful" according to our standards of morality. Yet, we will never arrange court sessions for grizzly bears that maul hikers, because we know bears are not morally responsible for their actions.

Whereas animals do have social behavior, they have no moral values that rule their social actions—which means no duties, no responsibilities, and consequently no rights. If animals had rights, their fellow animals would need to respect those too. Besides, when fish swim and birds fly, it is hard to say they are exercising their "rights" as they glide about. There are no such things as "animal rights" in the animal world. We, as masters of anthropomorphism, who love to project ourselves into animals, may think animals must have moral rights, because we do—but in fact they do not. We need to acknowledge again that our inability to let animals be animals has something to do with our inability to let human beings be human beings.

But there is also another side to it. Since human beings do have morality, we need to treat animals, God's other creatures, humanely and responsibly—not because animals have that right, but because humans owe it to their Maker and to themselves, being stewards of what their Maker created. For this reason, scientific experiments on live animals (vivisection) have ethical restrictions; in many jurisdictions, use of anesthesia is legally mandated for any surgery likely to cause pain to any vertebrate. Although animals are not human, we certainly are, so we ought to treat them humanely based on morality. As Antoine de Saint-Exupéry wrote in The Little Prince, "You are responsible forever for that which you have tamed."

Apparently, human beings are moral beings, quite unlike their fellow animals. Let it be stated again: our social behavior may have evolutionary roots in the animal world, but morality cannot. Yet, morality is at the core of our being. Knowing already from a very young age on that there is right and wrong, good and evil, that does not necessarily mean we are "hard-wired" to be moral; all it implies is that morality is at the core of being human, is distinctively human, and is part of our human nature. In that particular sense, morality is "inborn"—part of who we are, without being hard-wired in our genes and brains. Those who believe that morality is rooted in their genes must face the possibility that this belief itself then is also rooted in their genes—which makes it another "boomerang" belief. As a dedicated materialist, one needs to go all the way. In the world of materialism, there are no truths and untruths, only matter—and hence, no moral rights and moral duties either.

There is another reason why morality cannot be in the genes. If morality were in the genes, why would we need an articulated moral rule to reinforce what "by nature" we would or would not desire to do anyway? That does not make any sense. If morality is encoded in the genes, a moral code would be completely redundant. Instead the opposite could be argued: morality has the power to overrule what our genes dictate—passions, emotions, and drives. If we let passion govern reason, rather than reason govern passion, there is little hope for morality. The verdict as to what is morally right or wrong is not regulated by genes but by a moral code. If moral behavior were genetic, there would be no need for a moral code as well. We would all act right by mere nature, so it would not even be possible to do something morally wrong.

Reality tells us that far too many people are willing to break a moral rule when they can get away with it. It is hard to believe that they are acting against their genes. Too many parents ignore what some think is an "inborn" responsibility of parenting. Too many spouses violate the sixth commandment, "You shall not commit adultery." Too many folks also violate the fifth commandment, "You shall not kill." When it comes to moral laws, everyone knows about them and yet everyone breaks them repeatedly. Genes do not seem to prevent this. Unlike the laws of nature, moral laws can in fact be ignored (try to do that with the law of gravity!). Mothers who abandon their newborns are very unusual in the animal world, because of genetic constraints, but in human societies they are not so unusual, because maternal responsibility is a moral law that can be ignored.

Obviously, morality can be overshadowed by the tyranny of unruly passions. Those who go against moral laws or ignore them may be steered by passions, but it is hard to believe they go against their genes. Most moral laws do not even have any survival value and therefore cannot be promoted by natural selection. Ironically, the offenders of moral laws—the killers and the promiscuous—reproduce much better than their victims. In general, moral laws do not have any survival value and therefore cannot be promoted by natural selection. Morality and "survival of the fittest" do not go well together. Natural selection is about success at the expense of others; morality is about duties to the benefit of others.

Some might object that sociobiology has demonstrated that seemingly unselfish behavior might very well be biologically advantageous. They refer to examples such as sterile worker bees "unselfishly" helping the queen raise her own progeny. They would explain this behavior as a form of helping one's close relatives, because these carry DNA in their genes very similar to one's own—so-called "selfish genes." Since natural selection is a matter of balancing the benefits against the costs, this would indeed be a way of promoting one's "own" DNA by diminishing one's own offspring (a cost) but increasing the offspring of one's relatives (a benefit). Sociobiologists consider this a biological explanation of "altruism" in the animal world.

This explanation from sociobiology might very well be true, but we should also notice that this is an example of biological altruism—behavior with the effect that one's own offspring is diminished but compensated for by helping relatives. This kind of behavior should not be confused with moral altruism—behavior for the sake of the moral value of helping others, without expecting any advantage in return. Bees have genes to steer their "altruism," but no moral code; we, on the other hand, have a moral code without corresponding genes. What we actually do achieve, which may be a biological target for natural selection, may be very different from what we ought to achieve, which is a moral issue. Whereas natural selection is based on self-preservation at the cost of others, morality is self-sacrifice for the good of others. When firefighters or soldiers on the battle field die in the line of duty, they typically do not give their lives for their relatives' sake. Francis Collins, the former Head of the Human Genome Project and currently Director of the National Institutes of Health, made it very clear that moral altruism goes against natural selection: "Evolution would tell me exactly the opposite: preserve your DNA. Who cares about the guy who's drowning?"

In contrast, one could very well argue that moral laws tell us to do what natural selection does not promote and what our genes do not make us do "by nature." As we saw already, reality tells us that far too many people are willing to break a moral rule when they can get away with it. Morality is about something that is outside the scope of biology, actually beyond the reach of science. Biology is blind to moral values, so it cannot possibly discern anything that is on its "blind spot." Science attempts to discover what is the case; ethics, on the other hand, attempts to discover what ought to be the case. What is the case cannot explain what ought to be the case. Morality can interrogate science, but science cannot question morality—it is beyond its reach.

Therefore, science cannot monitor morality, but it is actually the other way around—morality should monitor science instead. The Tuskegee experiment in which African-American males were research subjects without their consent and to their detriment is universally condemned. Similarly, the research done in Auschwitz by Dr. Josef Mengele on various human patients, who became victims, cannot be justified regardless of the scientific progress that was an alleged goal of the experiments. Cases like these show us what happens when morality does not control rationality. Albert Einstein was right when he spoke of "the moral foundations of science, but you cannot turn around and speak of the scientific foundations of morality."

Nonetheless, secularists keep trying to discard morality by reducing something moral to something non-moral. But how could morality ever come from non-morality? When we define moral notions in non-moral terms, we betray their moral aspect. It is hard to see how non-moral causes such as DNA and evolution could ever produce a moral effect. Besides, as Francis J. Beckwith warns us, we have to face the following problem: "if your belief in the moral law can be attributed entirely to our genes tricking us into believing that there really is a moral law, why not extend that same analysis to all other beliefs that arise from your mind?" So we would end up with many more illusions fobbed on us by our genes—science and math, to name just a few. Do we really want to pay that price? This would amount to losing your mind.

Let me pose the following simple question to clarify the difference between a biological, social, and moral approach: what is wrong with bullying (or any other kind of violent behavior such as rape for that matter)? As a biological feature, it may be very advantageous to have such a gene or allele. As a social strategy, it may be a very effective strategy of banding together against someone else. But as a moral issue, it is plainly wrong. What this simple example shows us is that morality is not the same as and cannot be reduced to biology or sociology without losing something essential. Since moral values add their own, new dimension and perspective to human life, there is not much hope for those numerous attempts of converting moral behavior into a non-moral phenomenon.

Instead, one could make the case that genetic determinism of social behavior is one giant alibi for human responsibility. If the murderer "had" to commit the crime, it is unjust to blame him for anything. Once we declare ourselves no longer responsible for our moral decisions, we think we are off the moral hook. If we wish to be innocent, we must find a way to make the claim that we cannot be held morally responsible (just like animals are not morally responsible for their actions). And some are very creative in finding a way. All you have to do is "geneticize" or "medicalize" bad moral behavior: The victimizer is no longer a person but a disease or pathology caused by genes—a "disease" supposedly beyond our moral control. A popular slogan says, "My hormones made me do this!" Wouldn't defense lawyers love to join the bandwagon of so-called "scientific experts"! St. Paul says, "For I do not do the good I want, but I do the evil I do not want. Now if I do what I do not want, it is no longer I who do it, but sin that dwells in me" (Rom. 7:19-20). He is not blaming something like genes or hormones, but "sin that dwells in me," which leads to the doctrine of Original Sin. That is a moral issue, not a biological one.

So we must come to the conclusion that social behavior may very well have a genetic component, but moral behavior cannot possibly be under genetic control. A gene cannot make something obligated—perhaps more or less effective, more or less successful, or whatever, but never more or less obligated, let alone morally right or wrong. What is right or wrong in a moral sense is not determined by genes—genes cannot make anything right or wrong in a moral sense. Genes may make us act a certain way, but whether such an act is morally right or wrong is a different issue—a moral issue, that is, not a genetic one. Genes can make things either possible or impossible, but never morally right or wrong—the latter of which requires a moral system of laws, values, and evaluations. We are not born with innate scientific truths; they have to be learned. So, too, we have to learn moral truths and norms in order to make correct judgments about how to act.

It is time now for step two: morality comes from God—and therefore, there can be no morality without God. The pivotal question in this debate is how morality can be such a demanding issue—demanding an absolute authority—if it were only a matter of genes, or tradition, or majority votes, or political correctness? Do my genes, or any other natural factors, have the right to demand absolute obedience from me? Of course not! Does society have the right to demand my absolute obedience? Certainly not! Does any person, including myself, have the right to demand my absolute

Chapter 7: Secularists and God

obedience? None of the above!

The only authority that can obligate me is something—or rather Someone—infinitely superior to me; no one else has the right to demand my absolute obedience. And we can easily extend this to the Ten Commandments: they are God's prescription for happiness—two tablets a day. President Ronald Reagan used to say, "I have wondered at times about what the Ten Commandments would have looked like if Moses had run them through the U.S. Congress..." Let no one tell you that these Commandments have become irrelevant in our modern society, given the fact that few of our neighbors possess an ox or an ass for us to covet. It does not take much intellectual effort to modernize "ox" and "ass" into a Jaguar and a luxury yacht.

Interestingly enough, even an atheist such as the French philosopher Jean-Paul Sartre realized that there can be no absolute and objective standards of right and wrong, if there is no eternal Heaven that would make moral values objective and universal. Being an atheist he had to conclude, though, that it is "extremely embarrassing that God does not exist, for there disappears with him all possibility of finding values in an intelligible heaven. There can no longer be any good a priori, since there is no infinite and perfect consciousness to think it." Because Sartre denied the existence of God, he realized very clearly that he also gave up on morality by being an atheist. If there is no God, there cannot be evil either.

The German philosopher Friedrich Nietzsche was another atheist to realize how devastating the decline of religion is to the morality of society, when he wrote, "God is dead; but as the human race is constituted, there will perhaps be caves for millenniums yet, in which people will show his shadow." Nietzsche is saying here that humanism and other "moral" ideologies shelter themselves in caves and venerate shadows of the God they once believed in; they are holding on to something they cannot provide themselves, mere shadows of the past. They are "idols" constructed to preserve the essence of morality without the substance.

Nietzsche clearly understood that "the death of God" meant the destruction of all meaning and value in life. He saw in all clarity how in a world without divine and eternal laws, neither our dignity nor our morality would be able to survive in the long run. No wonder the non-religious philosopher Jürgen Habermas expressed as his conviction that the ideas of freedom and social co-existence are based on the Jewish notion of justice and the Christian ethics of love. As he puts it, "Up to this very day there is no alternative to it." This does not mean, of course, that we must believe in God in order to live a moral life. As Nietzsche put it, we can still venerate "idols from the past."

Because of all of this, we must recognize that morality ultimately comes from "Above." Moral values and laws reside in Heaven. We ought to do what we ought to do—for Heaven's sake! That's where their universality and objectivity reside. The United States Declaration of Independence is in tune with this when it declared that we are endowed by our Creator with certain unalienable Rights—not man-made but God-given rights, that is. When in 1948 the United Nations (UN) affirmed in its Universal Declaration of Human Rights that, "all human beings are born free and equal in dignity and rights," it must have assumed the same without explicitly mentioning it—otherwise all those rights would be sitting on quicksand, subject to the mercy of law makers and majority votes. But the Catholic philosopher Jacques Maritain was right when he said paradoxically, "We agree on these rights, on condition that no one asks us why." The only reason why we do have human rights is because God endows us with rights.

Thomas Aquinas considered these moral laws part of the "natural law," coming from God, and he distinguished them from legal, civil, or positive laws made and upheld by governments. Interestingly enough, without an eternal Heaven where the natural law resides, there would not have been any justification for the Nuremberg trials that took place after World War II—or for any other international court, for that matter. Seen from a purely legal point of view, it would not have been right, or even possible, to bring to trial and punish the Nazi perpetrators who had applied the civil laws that were created and implemented by a regime that had come to power through legal channels—for they were just "law-abiding" citizens following the law of the land. But seen from a natural law perspective, their "lawful" actions were certainly atrocities committed against humanity.

Although the Nuremberg court never referred to natural law directly, in essence it was the deciding factor. It posed a pivotal question: is there some superior law, or are there superior laws, to which even the properly legislated laws of the nations have to be subject? In the mid-12th century, the canon lawyer Gratian had already put it concisely, "Law is what is just"—not the opposite, "Justice is what is law." To put it differently, some things can be legal yet immoral, such as adultery, bribery, and price gauging. And some things are moral but are considered illegal in certain legal systems, such as abolition of slavery, the protection of life in the womb, or free expression of faith.

Many people think it is our moral conscience that tells us about the natural law, about what is right and what is wrong. In a sense that is true, but in another sense it is not. The problem is that our moral conscience can be right at times, but wrong at other times. Therefore, someone's conscience cannot have absolute authority in and of itself. When people say, "Never disobey your own conscience," they forget one can do things "in good conscience," but also "with a bad conscience." So a conscience on its own can be good as well as bad. A person's conscience can in fact be so darkened that the Psalm can say about a sinner, "He so flatters himself in his mind that he knows not his guilt" (36:3).

The truth is that a person's conscience does not speak on its own but it merely reflects the natural law revealed to us by God. Our conscience does not create moral laws but merely receives them. That is the reason why we cannot take our conscience as an entirely private issue that we can form at our own discretion. As Vatican II puts it, "in the depths of his conscience, man detects a law which he does not impose upon himself, but which holds him to obedience." The Catechism calls our conscience "man's most secret core and his sanctuary. There he is alone with God whose voice echoes in his depths" (CCC 1776). So when people follow their conscience, it is important they listen to God's voice, not their own.

It is through the voice of God, in the natural law, that we know about right and wrong, about rights and duties. Without God, we would have no right to claim any rights. If there were no God, we could not defend any of those rights we think we have the right to defend. Instead we would only have (legal) entitlements, or privileges, which the government provides, but no (moral) rights, which only God can provide. John F. Kennedy put it well in his Inaugural Address: "the rights of man come not from the generosity of the state, but from the hand of God." In response to Immanuel Kant, who said we should all start acting in a way that is moral "even if God does not exist," Pope Benedict XVI turned this around and argued that we should do the opposite and live a moral life "as if God existed." Without an eternal Heaven, there could be no absolute or objective standards of right and wrong. If these did not come from God, people could take them away anytime—which they certainly have tried many times.

Contrary to what secularists and relativists believe, moral laws and moral rights must be universal; if they were relative, one could not claim that human rights are universally applicable to all of humanity, regardless of race, ethnicity, nationality, culture, or political affiliation. In the words of Fr. Mark A. Pilon, "Western nations today have lost any valid understanding of natural rights because it has undercut the rational grounds for these rights. Rational grounds ultimately require a lawmaker, far above the limitations of human positive law." Even a secularist society cannot function well, let alone survive, without acknowledging the natural law. Societies and governments that violate the natural law with their legal laws do not last long. The natural law is one of the most precious gifts Religion has to offer the State. The former British Chief-Rabbi Jonathan Sacks worded it wittily, "A world without values quickly becomes a world without value."

8

Atheists and God

All the attacks on religion that we discussed in the previous chapters—materialism, mechanicism, relativism, and secularism— have one thing in common: they paint a picture of the world in which there is no place for God. It is this picture that either led to atheism or originated from atheism. It is a picture darkened by an eclipse of God.

No wonder on May 7, 1965, when Pope Paul VI gave, as usual, his papal address for the opening of the General Congregation of Jesuits in Rome, he gave his "elite troops" a solemn task of grave importance: "making a stout, united stand against atheism." Pope Paul's commission was right on target. Western Civilization had drastically changed and now found itself in a cultural vacuum. For centuries, religion had been part and parcel of Western thinking, but during the 19th and 20th Century belief-in-God was gradually giving away to unbelief-in-God. Unbelief was suddenly "in" and had become a perfectly respectable "belief." Not-to-believe had become as much a right as to believe. A new cult of unbelief had been born.

The legendary Archbishop Fulton J. Sheen gave a good assessment of what atheism is:

> Years ago atheism was an individual phenomenon; today atheism is social, the atheist who once was a curiosity is now a component part of some of the

governments of the world. Once men quarreled because they wanted God worshipped in a certain way; now they quarrel because they do not want God worshipped at all. The wars of religion of the seventeenth century have become the wars against religion of the twentieth century.

Indeed, atheists have become a very vocal group in our society—still a minority, yet on the rise. David Bentley Hart called atheism so much as a "cultural inevitability." The parable of the lost sheep tells us to bring one, the lost one, back into the fold, but nowadays it seems reversed: one is in the fold of the Church, and the ninety-nine others are lost. Somehow we all have been affected, to various degrees, by the virus of atheism. Even when it lies dormant, it can still raise its ugly head. Let's see how.

a. The Eclipse Appears and Disappears

Atheism comes in many disguises. Some forms of it may seem more harmless than others, but they all share the same belief that there is a problem with religious beliefs. This does not mean, however, that atheists have no belief at all. In the words of the philosopher Michael Augros, "Most of them believe in some underlying matter or energy or basic force that simply is, of which nothing else is the cause and which is itself the cause of everything we see." But what most atheists agree upon is that this "force" is certainly not God.

There are many versions of atheism and there are various motives that propel a disbelief in God. Not only do we see them around us, but also within each one of us at certain moments in our lives. Let us analyze their differences and find out where they go wrong. More than ever, we need to pray, "God, be our light. Shine in our darkness."

1a. "I do not know if God exists (or not)."

This version is called agnosticism—a word that the biologists Thomas H. Huxley invented. In his own words, "I neither affirm nor deny the immortality of man. I see no reason for believing it, but, on the other hand, I have no means of disproving it." What Huxley says here about man's immortality, he also applied to God's existence. Agnostics are ambivalent: They neither believe nor disbelieve in the existence of God.

The label of agnosticism may have been a recent invention but the idea behind it is much older. Diogenes Laërtius said already in the 3rd century, "As to the gods, I have no means of knowing either that they exist or do not exist." Agnosticism nowadays applies this idea about "gods" in paganism to the Christian notion of "God"—which is quite a stretch. It asserts that we just do not know whether God does exist or not, and what is worse, we presumably have no way of ever knowing one way or the other (at least not before we die). So this version is not really atheism in the strict sense, for it also says that we have no way of knowing that God does not exist. It just keeps agnostics in limbo; they neither deny God nor affirm God. Sometimes agnostics are also agnostic in the sense that they are not even sure whether they are agnostic or not.

Agnostics swear by logic, and they claim that logic cannot demonstrate the falsity of a belief in God (it is said to be an unbeatable, unverifiable hypothesis), but neither can it demonstrate the truth of a belief in God (it is said to be a daring, undecided hypothesis). This makes the biologist Julian Huxley exclaim, "We should be agnostic about those things for which there is no evidence." Agnostics think that they are not taking any stand pro-or-con at all and therefore that they are safe, secure, and invulnerable to any attacks. It

Chapter 8: Atheists and God

has even been said that we are all born agnostics; atheism and theism is considered something "sold" to us.

Are agnostics atheists? Dan Barker, a former Christian preacher who "converted" to atheism, thinks we are dealing with two different issues: "Agnosticism addresses knowledge; atheism addresses belief. The agnostic says, 'I don't have a knowledge that God exists.' The atheist says, 'I don't have a belief that God exists.' You can say both things at the same time. Some agnostics are atheistic and some are theistic." In general, Barker is right. Agnosticism is not a belief system the way atheism is; rather, it is a theory of knowledge. An atheist denies the existence of God; an agnostic professes ignorance about God's existence. For the latter, God may exist, but reason can neither prove nor disprove it.

As a consequence, agnostics have been divided into two groups: those who deny that reason can know God but they make no judgment concerning God's existence, and those who deny that reason can prove it but nonetheless profess a belief in God's existence. A well-known contemporary instance of the former group is the British philosopher Bertrand Russell; a famous example of the latter group is the German philosopher Immanuel Kant. With some exceptions, modern and contemporary agnostics belong to the latter group.

1b. Do we really not know if God exists?

First of all, let's make clear that there is no need for a hypothesis called "God." God is not a hypothesis that we hold on to tentatively and provisionally until more evidence for or against it emerges. Instead, belief in God is of a different nature. It is more like saying about a spouse, parent, or friend, "I know he or she loves me"—which is certainly not a hypothesis either. A man named Job, in the land of Uz, said something like this about God, "I know that my Redeemer lives." Those who hold on to their faith do not resolve to let nothing count against their belief, but instead they have reason to keep their faith in spite of some seeming counter-evidence. Belief in God expresses someone's faith and commitment, which cannot be tentative without undermining the very faith it means to express.

Second, logic may not be the best tool to prove that God does or does not exist. Chesterton once said, "Atheism is the most daring of all dogmas, for it is the assertion of a universal negative." Chesterton is right; it is much easier to establish that there is a black swan somewhere on the earth than to prove that there isn't one at all. We may perhaps validly conclude that God is unknown (as agnosticism asserts), but it is very hard, if not logically impossible, to conclude that God is in fact absent (as atheism claims). It is just impossible to close a search for God with the conclusion that there is no God. No searches ever conclusively reveal the absence of their object. Absence of evidence is not evidence of absence.

Third, there is in fact empirical evidence for God's existence. The Catholic Church declares that "God, the beginning and end of all, can, by the natural light of human reason, be known with certainty from the works of creation" (Vatican I, Const. De Fide, II, De Rev.). This conviction has strong biblical roots. The Bible testifies that "The heavens are telling the glory of God" (Ps. 19:1) and that God "did not leave himself without witness" as Saint Paul worded it (Acts 14:17), and that "since the creation of the world his invisible nature, namely, his eternal power and deity, has been clearly perceived in the things that have been made" (Rom. 1:20). As we found out in the first five chapters of this book, our Universe shows many clues of God's existence, including the fact that there is order, intelligibility, rationality, and morality. For those who are able to "connect the dots," a new world opens up—the world of religion.

Fourth, we should be careful to demand indisputable evidence for God's existence. Catholic philosophers such as Peter Kreeft from Boston College point out that agnosticism's demand for scientific evidence through something like laboratory testing is in effect asking God, the Supreme Being, to become our servant. Kreeft and other philosophers argue that the question of God should be treated differently from other knowable objects in that this question regards not that which is below us, but that which is above us. Such a stand actually raises the discussion to a "higher level." The question "Does God exist?" is not like "Do neutrinos exist?" God cannot be "trapped" by some kind of ingenious experiment. Religion does use empirical evidence, though, but certainly not experimental evidence that can be verified or falsified by experiments. As a matter of fact, religious believers do allow things to count against God's existence, God's omnipotence, and God's goodness, but they will not allow anything to count decisively against them.

Given these considerations, how should we assess agnosticism then? It may appear to be pretty harmless at first sight. But there is reason to question this impression. First of all, since agnosticism keeps us in limbo, it refuses to give God the honor and worship he deserves as our Maker. Agnostics never gave God their time to study the evidence that points to him. Of course, one can be an agnostic in other things than religion; many people are agnostics when it comes to the existence of flying saucers or extraterrestrial life, because they never took the time to study such issues or to weigh the arguments pro and con. In other words, they are agnostics out of lack of interest. But when it comes to God, lack of interest is a much more serious case. We owe God our interest. But that assumes already that God exists.

Here is a second reason why agnosticism may not be as harmless as it looks. While sitting on the fence—not sure if there is a God—agnostics often act as if they are very sure there is no God. They are theoretically agnostics, but practically atheists. But there is more. Very often agnostics do have a rather negative and highly selective attitude towards religion and religious people in particular—they tend to declare them "stupid." Agnostics think that their own logic is so compelling that everyone who disagrees with their agnostic conclusions must be misinformed or just brainless. So they often call religious people superstitious—believers in supernatural powers that invade and rule our world. Apparently, they treat the Judeo-Christian God the same way Diogenes Laërtius treated the Greek gods.

Accusing Christianity of superstition is often a cheap alibi agnostics use to reject it. It has been said many times that agnostics prefer to remain "sitting on the fence." But how long can one keep sitting there? At the end of life, a coin is being spun that will come down heads (God) or tails (no God). How will you wager? When Blaise Pascal introduced his Wager, he was trying to show that agnosticism is an impossible option. The reason is simple, in the words of Peter Kreeft: "Because we are moving. The ship of life is moving along the waters of time, and there comes a point of no return, when our fuel runs out, when it is too late. The Wager works because of the fact of death." The option of not to wager at all is out of the question; each one of us has no choice but to wager in the face of death, given the possibility that we might be judged by God after death. So by "sitting on the fence," agnostics actually wager against God. It could be said that by refusing to choose, one has already chosen to wager on the idea that picking no religion is safer than accepting a false one.

Chapter 8: Atheists and God

But no matter how we define agnosticism, it should be criticized as a limitation of the mind's capacity to know reality. It actually limits the mind's capacity to know reality to the narrow viewpoint of materialism, scientism, and rationalism. There is no God, agnostics say, because we cannot see him; there are no human souls because we cannot detect them physically; there is no God because we cannot logically or rationally or empirically prove the "God-hypothesis." However, God's existence does not depend on compelling evidence. One of the problems of agnosticism is that it usually demands evidence in a materialistic or scientific sense. The Nobel Laureate and neurophysiologist John C. Eccles called materialism "a religious belief held by dogmatic materialists ... who often confuse their religion with their science."

Pope Benedict XVI accuses agnosticism of limiting itself in claiming the power of reason to know scientific truth only, at the exclusion of religious or philosophical truths. Besides, it is contradictory in its own claims, since agnosticism in itself is not a scientific truth either. Therefore, Pope Benedict considers agnosticism "a choice of comfort, pride, dominion, and utility over truth. It is opposed by self-criticism, humble listening to the whole of existence, the patience and self-correction of the scientific method and readiness to be purified by the truth." In other words, agnosticism tends to stifle the religious sense engraved in the depths of our nature and thus obscures God.

During the 2011 Assisi gathering with some 300 religious representatives, Pope Benedict XVI gave an unexpected twist to agnosticism by acknowledging that agnostics are still engaged in a quest for God. He said that the inability of agnostics to find God is "partly the responsibility of believers with a limited or even falsified image of God. So all their struggling and questioning is in part an appeal to believers to purify their faith, so that God, the true God, becomes accessible." So it is an appeal to all of us to remove the stigma of superstition from the Judeo-Christian faith.

2a. "I find any God-talk non-sense."

Although this no longer appears to be a serious form of atheism nowadays, it used to be rather popular among members of philosophical schools called positivism, logical-positivism, and language-analysis. These schools used to have quite some impact in scientific circles and currently still live underground in many schools, colleges, and universities.

Here we have philosophers who consider any talk about God a violation of the use of common language. Whereas agnosticism regards God-talk unverifiable but nonetheless meaningful, this form of atheism maintains that, if unverifiable, God-talk is ipso facto meaningless. Language is supposed to be either empirical (dealing with facts, like in science) or logical (adhering to rules, like in logic and mathematics), otherwise it is considered a nonsensical abuse of language. Stephen Hawking thinks along these lines as he exclaims, "When people ask me if a god created the Universe, I tell them that the question itself makes no sense."

In this view, religious talk about God would be rejected as neither empirical nor logical. One can legitimately say, for instance, that the root of a plant absorbs nutrients (an empirical statement), or that the root of four is two (a logical statement), but the statement that "the root of a plant is two" amounts to non-sense, as it violates the rules of language by mixing up two different types of using language. And the same supposedly holds for God-talk—it is neither true nor false, but simply meaningless. As a consequence, we should, in the words of the philosopher Ludwig Wittgenstein, be silent about that which we cannot say—or in his own words,

"Whereof one cannot speak, thereof one must be silent." The limits of language are supposed to be the limits of thought.

2b. Why is God-talk not merely non-sense?

Apparently, both atheism and agnosticism accept the statement "a deity exists" as a meaningful proposition that can be argued for or against. But such a discussion obviously makes no sense at all for those who find God-talk nonsense. The fundamental problem of declaring everything that is not empirically verified of logically valid as nonsensical is that it determines ahead of time the outcome these atheists like to see. They define what is legitimate by making sure they exclude what they do not wish to be legitimate. And besides, you wonder whether this claim in itself is either logical or empirical—otherwise is must be meaningless by its own verdict. Some people just have this contemptuous habit of dismissing as meaningless those concepts whose meanings elude them or annoy them, but they do so rather selectively.

One could actually make the case that it is this kind of atheism that shuns debates and refuses to listen to reasonable arguments by limiting ahead of time what makes sense in the debate and what does not. The more you read arguments for atheism, the more you realize it takes a very strong faith to be an atheist—for instance, the faith that God-talk is nonsense. Apparently, not all faiths are religious faiths. Some have called atheism the epitome of blind faith—blind for any evidence and blind for reasonable arguments. We could even call this form of atheism the least reasonable of all faiths—for a faith it is. It is not faith in God, though, but faith in materialism, scientism, and other kinds of ideologies. They do not believe in the real God but they do have faith in their own "gods." Even using reason as a powerful tool in this debate requires some kind of faith—faith that the world perceived through reason is true and that the world itself is reasonable. There is a certain step of faith required in putting all of one's intellectual weight on the pedestal of reason.

Currently, many have come to realize that religious discourse cannot be mere nonsensical babble. Religious believers are usually very well able to explain to others what it is they believe in. The concept of God, for instance, can be made clear to others. As a minimum, it refers to a Primary Cause in the way St. Thomas Aquinas defined God, or to "that than which nothing greater can be conceived" in the words of St. Anselm of Canterbury. Besides, how could religious people ever disagree about what is considered nonsense? Isn't religion constantly dealing with disputes, dogmas, creeds, schisms, and heresies? How could disagreements on such issues ever be possible if religious talk were mere non-sense? There must be some mutual understanding among religious people, otherwise they would have no idea as to what they disagree on.

The atheists we are talking about here make it very easy for themselves: instead of having to deal with the question of what certain religious concepts mean and whether religious statements are true or false, they just discard them as meaningless—as pure nonsense—thus ending the discussion ahead of time. Christopher Dawson, sometimes called "the greatest English-speaking Catholic historian of the twentieth century," was right when he said, "it is impossible to teach men even the simplest theological truths, if they believe that the creeds and the catechism are nothing but words and that religious knowledge is not really knowledge at all." Unfortunately, such a belief that religious beliefs are unacceptable or even meaningless, is still spreading like wildfire in modern society.

Well, the story doesn't end here, as it got an unexpected

twist. The very Wittgenstein we mentioned earlier as defending this form of atheism came to realize the narrow-mindedness of his original views and broadened them considerably later on in life. In addition, he said once he hoped his Catholic friends would pray for him. Well, they did at his death bed; he died shortly afterwards and was given a Catholic burial at St. Giles's Church of Cambridge in England. You never know what you are in for when you declare belief in God nonsensical.

3a. "I know there is no God."

Technically speaking, atheism is commonly understood to be about the absence of belief in God, but most atheists will say it is about the absence of God himself. Atheists in the latter sense are "positively" sure that God does not exist, because they adhere faithfully to the doctrines of positivism, empiricism, and scientism. They reject religion on so-called scientific grounds. You will find this kind of atheism especially in books of scientists such as Richard Dawkins, Daniel Dennett, E. O. Wilson, Peter Higgs, Carl Sagan, Peter Atkins, Francis Crick, Peter Singer, and Sam Harris—all of whom have declared a jihad against religion by abusing science for their own ideological, atheist agenda. The list of names could go on and on, and even seems to be growing.

What do these atheists have in common? They are "devout atheists"—"missionaries" of atheism, so to speak, who want us to believe that believing in God is just impossible because science has shown us there is no God. These atheists tend to believe that modern science is on their side. In their view, science and religion cannot go together. The philosopher Peter Kreeft reminds us of that Western in which one cowboy says to the other: "This town ain't big enough for both of us. One of us has to leave." Well, these atheists like to declare science as the winner, so religion has to leave the town. The declaration "I know there is no God" has become their new creed. Mark Twain put it in a nutshell: "A man is accepted into a church for what he believes and he is turned out for what he knows."

The idea is clear: atheism is based on knowledge; religion is not. When we look through our telescopes or microscopes, we never see God, so we know there is no god—on scientific grounds. Atheists who proclaim they know there is no God like to sit on God's throne that they had declared vacant, and then publicize their own absolute decrees. Their view is probably best summarized by the title of one of Dawkins' popular books—The God Delusion. That's what God is according to this view—no longer non-sense, but a delusion instead. Why? Because science tells us so.

3b. Do we really know there is no God?

These atheists have actually taken on the ideology of scientism, which is a dogmatic, totalitarian "creed" that professes "the real world" is a world of quantifiable entities. They replace the trust religious believers place in God with the total trust they place in science. As we discussed earlier (see 2.b), scientism maintains that science is the only way of achieving valid knowledge, in spite of the fact that scientism itself does not follow its own rule. We found out there are some serious problems with scientism. How could science ever prove on its own that science is the only way of finding truth?

So what we have here is another form of faith-based atheism. It is an immaterial belief that denies everything that can't be dissected, counted, measured, or quantified, including God—and including itself, of course. A sign hung in Albert Einstein's office at Princeton University advised us differently: "Not everything that can be counted counts; not everything that counts can be counted." Science on its own cannot answer questions that are beyond the reach of its empirical and experimental techniques.

Nonetheless, these atheists keep promoting their dogma of scientism, which includes the dogma that there are no dogmas, and no God. As a consequence, they acknowledge only one territory—the territory of science. Whatever it is that science gains must therefore be at the cost of religion. In their view, scientific expansion means religious withdrawal—so religion must be on its way out whenever science advances. But that is exactly where the misconception lies. Science doesn't gain territory at all when it makes new discoveries, but it just learns more and more details about its own fixed and demarcated territory—which is the domain of all that can be dissected, counted, measured, and quantified. The rest is not part of its territory but was given away for other "authorities" to handle.

Therefore, scientists need to keep their scientific hands off of other domains, including the religious domain—which makes for a sound separation between Science and Religion. Science should never forget that it is "blind" for many other than scientific aspects of life. The Austrian physicist and Nobel Laureate Erwin Schrödinger once said about science, "It knows nothing of beautiful and ugly, good or bad, God and eternity. Science sometimes pretends to answer questions in these domains, but the answers are very often so silly that we are not inclined to take them seriously."

Because God is the Primary Cause, God could never be discovered among the secondary causes of this Universe, for God is not one of them. Science is about secondary causes, not the Primary Cause. God is outside its scope, just as everything else that is unseen and cannot be counted or measured is outside its scope. It is scientific arrogance to claim universal validity for local successes in science—in defiance of the fact that the astonishing successes of science have not been gained by answering every kind of question, but precisely by refusing to do so. God cannot be "seen" through telescopes or microscopes. Because God is everywhere, it only looks as if God is "nowhere." That is why there's no reason for megalomania in science. We always need to keep asking for "the rest of the story," for all those things science is "blind" for, including the existence of God.

The troubling part is that an atheist such as Richard Dawkins has never written a word about God; what he talks about is some kind of demiurge—a being among other beings, who differs from all other beings in magnitude, power, and duration, but not a Primary Cause. If Dawkins decides not to believe in God, he should at least have a clear idea of what it is he claims not to believe in. This is a problem with many atheists—they often don't tell you what the god is they are rejecting. They may have a distorted picture of God in mind that is not the God Christianity believes in. The Judeo-Christian tradition actually acknowledges there are many gods, which are called "idols," but there is only one real God. Exodus 20:3 says it clearly, "You shall have no other gods before me." Christians would actually be atheists themselves when it comes to the gods of materialism, scientism, paganism, Hinduism, and New Age. So atheists owe us, and themselves, an explanation of what it is they reject—even if they do so in the name of science.

Apparently, science in itself is not the problem for religion. Reality tells us that there are atheistic scientists as well as religious scientists. Atheistic scientists are not better scientists than religious scientists, nor vice-versa. They both are dedicated scientists who believe in the power of the scientific method. But they differ in one thing. The latter keep an open mind and believe also in the power of religious faith, whereas the former close their mind for anything that cannot be dissected, counted, measured, or quantified. In either case, though, it is not science itself that can decide who is right. Such a decision is a matter of "faith." Therefore, it is not science that "kills God," but rather particular scientists who do so in a very unscientific way.

Unfortunately, those who deny that science and religion can co-exist have gathered huge crowds of "faithful" followers—partly because of their very influential books that have sold millions of copies all over the world. They make us believe that science and religion offer contrary explanations of reality that cannot possibly coexist. They abuse their scientific expertise to make us think they must be experts in everything else too. Again, they are like plumbers trying to fix your electricity at home, or electricians trying to fix your plumbing problems. That is asking a lot of "blind faith" from their followers.

4a. "I consider God an illusion."

This form of atheism demands full-proof certainty. We found out earlier that it is hard, if not impossible, to prove that there is no God, but it is equally hard to prove the opposite—that there is a God. These atheists would agree with Carl Sagan that "Extraordinary claims require extraordinary evidence." So atheists seem to have found a safe strategy for victory. They claim that in order to prove there is a God, we need either empirical proof or logical proof for the existence of God—proof beyond any doubt. And if such is not possible, atheism can declare victory.

Atheists in this category proclaim that there cannot be any empirical proof, because God is not measurable, quantifiable, or touchable, so he is not accessible to our senses. Sam Harris takes this position: "The faith of religion is belief on insufficient evidence." If there is anything "empirical" about religion, these atheists would declare it a product of the mind, a form of wishful thinking, so they say. Hence, religion ends up being an illusion or delusion. When religion tells us that we were made in God's image, these atheists would turn things around and point out that God was actually made in our own image. Carl Sagan is of this opinion: "It is said that men may not be the dreams of the god, but rather that the gods are the dreams of men." Richard Dawkins once said to someone in his audience who asked about the presence of God, "Oh, all sorts of funny things happen in people's heads. But you can't measure them, so they do not mean anything."

Someone else who exemplifies this line of thought was Sigmund Freud. He believed that the adoption of religion is a reversion to childish patterns of thought in response to feelings of helplessness and guilt. We supposedly feel a need for security and forgiveness, and so invent a source of security and forgiveness: god. Religion is thus seen as a childish delusion, whereas atheism is taken as a form of grown-up realism. This makes Carl Sagan exclaim: "You can't convince a believer of anything; for their belief is not based on evidence, it's based on a deep-seated need to believe." Even when these atheists sometimes feel the need to pray for help, they would still believe that the sometimes overwhelming strength of such a need does not in any way show that there is a God to meet that need. The core message is this: there is no irrefutable empirical evidence for God's existence.

In addition to the empirical side of the debate, there is also a logical side. Although the history of Catholic philosophy gives us many examples of what are called "proofs of the existence of God," these "logical proofs" have often come under heavy attack by atheists. Some atheists find a belief in God not only lacking valid logic, but they call them actually illogical. Umberto Eco is one of them: "Isn't affirming God's absolute omnipotence and his absolute freedom with regard to his own choices tantamount to demonstrating that God does not exist?"

4b. Why God is not an illusion?

According to this form of atheism, one can only prove things beyond any doubt in a way that must be either empirical or logical. Let us scrutinize these two claims separately, starting with the empirical side.

Empirical proof "beyond any doubt" is hard to come by. First of all, real "proofs" only exist in mathematics. But even mathematics has to start somewhere with starting points that are called axioms, which are unprovable (that's why there are at least three different kinds of geometry). Only if we accept those axioms can things be proven beyond any doubt. But when we talk about empirical proof, we have left the territory of mathematics. Einstein said it right, "As far as the laws of mathematics refer to reality, they are not certain; and as far as they are certain, they do not refer to reality." In legal court, for instance, it is hard to prove something other than "beyond reasonable doubt."

So science has to face the fact that no scientific statements and concepts are final and proven. They are open to re-evaluation as new data is acquired and novel technologies emerge. Scientific research requires the specialized skills of researchers and the aid of apparatus which is so complicated and so costly, that it is beyond virtually anyone's reach to verify the results. And when there is new and convincing evidence that conflicts with an existing theory, the theory has to be revised. But how? Sometimes the evidence is put aside, sometimes parts of the theory are adjusted, and sometimes other theories that are connected with the theory under investigation are modified. What some call "proven" scientific knowledge is only proven until a new set of empirical data "disproves" what was previously considered "proven." So "empirical proof" is not cast in iron; whatever is true today may not be true tomorrow. Science is always a work in progress.

Because God resides on a level different from scientific issues—not measurable, quantifiable, or touchable—empirical proofs of the experimental type are obviously out of the question in religion. Does this mean, though, that religion is based on a phantom world floating like a castle in mid-air, vanishing into thin air? Certainly not. There might be other strong arguments for God's existence—arguments that are still based on empirical data, but at the same time surpass empirical evidence. This kind of evidence is certainly not of the experimental type, but that does not mean it is not empirical either; we often reason from what is seen, the empirical, to what is unseen, from visible data to invisible facts behind what is seen. This is not a matter of proof but of credibility.

We mentioned already supporting empirical evidence that can be found in the fact that there is design, fine-tuning, intelligibility, rationality, and morality in this Universe. Individually, these may not provide conclusive evidence, but combined they make for a strong case. How could nature be intelligible if it were not created by an intelligent Creator? How could there be order in this world if there were no orderly Creator? How could there be scientific laws in nature if there were no rational Lawgiver? How could there be design in nature, if there were no intelligent Designer? How could there be human minds, if the Universe were mindless?

We have a choice here when answering these rhetorical questions: we either accept that there is no explanation at all

Chapter 8: Atheists and God

for these observations in nature (which is basically irrational)—or we look for a rational explanation of all of this. The only rational explanation seems to be that there is indeed an intelligent, rational, orderly, and lawgiving Creator God who made this Universe the way it is. In this case, belief in a Creator God is more or less like "connecting the dots"—although some may connect the dots differently, and others may connect different dots. But the fact remains that belief in God makes the world so much more understandable. C. S. Lewis beautifully summarized this, "I believe in Christianity as I believe that the sun has risen: not only because I see it, but because by it I see everything else."

Now that the laws of physics themselves receive more and more attention, and now that it has been found they form a single magnificent edifice of great subtlety, harmony, and beauty, Stephen Barr finds reason to declare, "[T]he question of a cosmic designer seems no longer irrelevant, but inescapable." One could certainly take this as "empirical evidence" for the existence of a Creator God. Even Albert Einstein had to acknowledge, "Everyone who is seriously involved in the pursuit of science becomes convinced that a Spirit is manifest in the laws of the Universe—a Spirit vastly superior to that of man." One could also make the case that by denying or neglecting the existence of God, atheism undermines rationality and thus eats away the very foundation of science (see 6.b); it also undermines morality and thus eats away the foundation of societal life (see 7.b).

Besides, even in science, there is so much that we cannot prove in an empirical way but must just assume to be true. How do scientists know that this Universe is comprehensible, that there is some underlying order connecting causes and effects, that there is a "law" stating that every event depends on some law of nature, and so on? If scientists couldn't assume all of this, they would have to give up on all their scientific endeavors. Science cannot be done without a series of assumptions; they are "hidden" like most of an iceberg is hidden under water. The biologist Ernst Mayr speaks of "silent assumptions that are taken so completely for granted that they are never mentioned." Even the principle of falsification depends on the fact—or is it a belief?—that like causes do produce like effects (see 6.b), which is based on the assumption there is some kind of cosmic order operating in the "background." In addition, even in science there is never factual, empirical certainty. Francis Crick, one of the two scientists who discovered DNA, couldn't have said it better: "A theory that fits all the facts is bound to be wrong, as some of the facts will be wrong."

What can we learn from this? As far as science is concerned, there is much more believing in what we know than many want to believe. And, vice-versa, in religion, there may be much more knowing in what we believe than many seem to know. Religion and science share the fact that they cannot exist without certain beliefs. The physicist Paul Davies rightly remarked, "[B]oth religion and science are founded on faith—namely, on belief in the existence of something outside the Universe, like an unexplained God or an unexplained set of physical laws." Faith is certainly not blind but tries to make the best sense of everything there is on the basis of the limited evidence available by "connecting the dots," in spite of the fact that those rejecting religion prefer to disconnect the dots. The Canadian science fiction writer Robert J. Sawyer has one of his characters, Hollus, pose the right question: "'There is no indisputable proof for the big bang,' said Hollus. 'And there is none for evolution. And yet you accept those. Why hold the question of whether there is a creator to a higher standard?'"

Yet, atheists remain suspicious of whatever religion comes up with. If there is anything "empirical" about

Chapter 8: Atheists and God

religion, they would declare it a product of the mind, a form of wishful thinking, so they say, which makes it an illusion or delusion. Atheists have a knack of turning arguments around: God did not create evolution, evolution created god; we were not made in God's image, god was created in our image; God did not create DNA, but DNA created god. Werner Heisenberg tells the story of a discussion among some great physicists. The discussion ended up being dominated by Paul Dirac, who went into a long diatribe declaring religion to be "the opiate of the masses." At the end of the evening someone turned to the brilliant Wolfgang Pauli and said, "You have been very quiet tonight, Pauli. What do you think of what Dirac has been telling us?" Pauli responded. "If I understand Dirac correctly, his meaning is this: there is no God, and Dirac is his Prophet." So there is still reason to question such atheists who refute religion. They are basically saying, "God move over, you are in my seat." Where does their "authority" come from?

Sometimes it is the "authority" of some well-known "experts"—Sigmund Freud, for instance. But it is very doubtful whether someone like Freud really did refute religion as an illusion. First of all, if Freud claims that basic beliefs are the rationalization of our deepest wishes, wouldn't this entail that his own atheistic beliefs could also be the rationalization of his own wishes? Don't we sometimes think what we wish? Don't some people, like ostriches, choose to deny what they fear? Second, C. S. Lewis noticed a serious circularity: "the Freudian proves that all thoughts are merely due to complexes—except the thoughts which constitute this proof itself." Third, even if belief in God were wishful thinking, one could never prove that it is nothing more than wishful thinking. The God one would like to exist may actually exist, even if the fact one wishes it may encourage suspicion. Fourth, if religion is based on a "deep-seated need

The Eclipse of God: Is Religion on the Way Out?

to believe," in Sagan's words, so is materialism.

Let's move on to the logical side of the debate and address the philosophical question as to why our Universe is the way it is, or why it even exists at all. As a matter of fact, our Universe need not be the way it is, and it need not even exist. In other words, the Universe we live in is neither necessary nor absolute, but finite and dependent instead; earlier we said with a more technical term that our Universe is contingent. However, if there is no inherent necessity for the Universe to exist, then the Universe is not self-explaining and therefore must find an explanation outside itself. Obviously, it cannot be grounded in something else that is also finite and not self-explaining (that would lead to infinite regress), so it can only derive from an unconditioned, infinite, and ultimate ground, which is a Creator God (see 1.b). Whoever denies this has only one consistent alternative left: materialism. But how could materialism ever explain the existence of matter, other than by just denying that it requires an explanation? It is hard to see how matter could ever explain itself.

The idea of contingency—that the Universe is not self-explaining and therefore must find an explanation outside itself—is often used as a logical proof of the existence of God. The so-called Five Ways (or "arguments" of God's existence) that Thomas Aquinas mentions are essentially variations of this one way, the way from contingency. If there are contingent beings, there "must" be a necessary Being. "Contingent" means that they do not have to exist; but since they do exist, there must be a necessary Being that causes them to exist. This Being is not a super-being among other beings, but an absolute Being. Well, this Being is what we call God, according to Thomas Aquinas.

It is quite telling that Thomas Aquinas does not conclude his Five Ways with a math-like statement such as "Therefore,

God exists (QED)," but by the less overreaching statement, "And this all men think of as God." Apparently, Aquinas himself did not have the presumption of logically proving God's existence. He is more or less clarifying what we mean when we speak of God, and what this entails. Nonetheless, these "ways" certainly are compelling in a rational sense, working like powerful "pointers" to a Creator God.

Does this mean that we have confirmed the claim of atheists that there is no full-proof logical argument for God's existence? The answer is yes and no. It is not an undisputable proof with logical certainty, but it surely is a very powerful rational argument in favor of God's existence. We should not forget what Thomas Aquinas remarked: "To one who has faith, no explanation is necessary. To one without faith, no explanation is possible." We should also realize that in his days, atheists were not a real force in society or its universities, whereas today, they nearly control education. Besides, no matter whether we deem these "proofs" valid or not, the atheist philosopher Kai Nielsen correctly states, "To show that an argument is invalid or unsound is not to show that the conclusion of the argument is false. It's only to show that the argument does not warrant our asserting the conclusion to be true." In short, to show that the proofs do not work is not enough by itself to deny God's existence. It may still be the case that there is a God.

Besides, we should mention someone who came into this discussion from an entirely different angle. The famous mathematician Kurt Gödel from Princeton University rigorously and mathematically proved in his so-called incompleteness theorem that no coherent system—not even the system of science—can be completely closed; any coherent system is essentially incomplete and needs additional "help" from outside the system. Gödel even went as far as believing that we cannot give a credible account of reality itself without invoking God. Gödel was said to be very cautious to mention this belief in scientific circles, because he considered it potential dynamite. But what he did tell us is that our capacity to know truth transcends mere formal logic. In other words, there are truths that we cannot "prove." The truth of God's existence may certainly be one of them.

5a. "I never see or experience God."

And then there are those atheists who no longer feel any need to protest or even deny God's existence, because they are completely absorbed by what they can see, feel, hear, and touch in their surroundings. As far as God is concerned: out of "sight," out of mind. At best, he lives in an imaginary world that we have concocted in our own fantasies. In a world of what can be seen, there is no space for the unseen. These atheists are basically "empiricists" or "positivists" who believe only what they can see, hear, or touch. Since God is not someone they can capture this way, God has become a "non-entity" in their lives. They are blind for what cannot be seen and deaf for what cannot be heard.

Their point is that they only accept what our human senses can capture: that which is visible, audible, or tangible. We never bump into anything devoid of shape, size, and location. We cannot even imagine anything without shape, size, or location—and that's why anything "religious" or "spiritual" is out of the question, or at least not of our interest. Consequently, everything related to God has been evacuated to an unseen, illusionary, and therefore "unbelievable" world that is foreign to these atheists and that they have no need of. God has become fully eclipsed.

Chapter 8: Atheists and God

5b. Do we really never see or experience God?

Is there really no space for what we cannot see? Not only has science been masterful in discovering things we never thought existed, but science has also come up with entities that cannot be "seen" or "touched." We all experience gravity in life but we cannot see it (that is, until Newton came along).

There may be so much more to life than what "meets the eye." Not being able to see or touch some specific entities does not necessarily negate that they exist. The invisible or the unseen may very well be as real and factual as what is visible and seen. As St. Paul teaches us, "look not to the things that are seen but to the things that are unseen, for the things that are seen are temporal, but the things that are unseen are eternal" (2 Cor. 4:18). The invisible or the unseen seem even necessary for us to better see and understand the visible and seen. To use Ryle's example again: Although Oxford University cannot be "seen," it is nevertheless a very real entity, vital to understanding the unseen unity behind all the seen university buildings combined.

Once applied to religion, this opens up a wide and rich domain of "invisible things" that are so vital to Christianity. It is called the spiritual realm—the super-natural world behind the natural world, if you will. God is the Creator of "what is seen and unseen," of "what is visible and invisible," in the words of the Nicene Creed. We need to look beyond the natural to see the supernatural, beyond the present to see the eternal, beyond the visible to see the invisible, beyond the material to see the spiritual. This does require faith, but certainly not "blind" faith. St. Paul made it clear that we can see the invisible God through the visible: "his invisible nature ... has been clearly perceived in the things that have been made" (Rom. 1:20).

The Eclipse of God: Is Religion on the Way Out?

Some call this awareness merely a matter of faith, in a condescending way, but it is this very basic faith in the existence of God that we need in both science and religion. As we said several times before, science is actually a faith-based enterprise, for even in science, it takes faith to study and understand this Universe. In religion, on the other hand, we also need some basic faith, before we can believe in what religious faith tells us in more detail based on God's revelation. It is a kind of basic faith that we can accept and rationally understand independently of any specific religious faith. It is called "general revelation" telling us that God is all-good, all-knowing, all-present, and all-mighty. On this basis, the so-called "special revelation" from the Bible and Judeo-Christian Tradition can be built up. Through special revelation we know, for instance, that God came into the world through Jesus Christ and that God is Triune (Father, Son, and Holy Spirit). In other words, we have in the Bible one source of information about reality, and in nature another source of information about reality. Deism may get us halfway but theism takes us the rest of the way.

It is ironic that the "unseen world" of the Judeo-Christian Faith gave us not only the first hospitals and the first universities, but also the first scientific developments. Believing in an "unseen" Creator God entails that nature is not a divine but a created entity—which opens the door for scientific exploration (otherwise we would not be allowed to "touch" the divine). In this view, the invisible God is ultimately the source where the visible Universe, with its order and intelligibility, stems from. To find out what this order looks like is to "interrogate" the Universe by investigation, exploration, and experiment. Through scientific experiments we can "read" God's mind, so to speak. The visible world finds its ultimate explanation in an invisible God. Atheists who cannot look beyond what is visible end up with a complete riddle as to how the human mind is able to grasp the order of the Universe. David Bentley Hart is right: "The very notion of nature as a closed system entirely sufficient to itself is plainly one that cannot be verified, deductively or empirically, from within the system of nature." So the notion of nature as a closed system must be a form of "blind belief"—no less "blind" than the religious beliefs these atheists like to call "blind."

Let us get some support for this view from three scientists—experts in the field of "touchable" entities. The first one is the German physicist Robert Pohl, the inventor of the solid-state amplifier. After each demonstration and explanation of some physical experiment in his class room, he used to conclude his experiments with the words "And that gives us all the more cause for wonder." He had a profound message for his students: there is more than what the eye can capture and the ear can register.

The second one is the nuclear physicist and Nobel Laureate Werner Heisenberg who once said: "The first drink from the cup of natural science makes atheistic… But at the bottom of the cup, God is waiting." Interestingly enough, Pope Pius XII had said already in 1951 that "true science discovers God in an ever-increasing degree—as though God were waiting behind every door opened by science." Indeed, in the words of G.K. Chesterton, science is racing toward the mysteries of faith with the speed of an express train. In other words, the unseen can be found in and behind what is seen.

And last but not least there is Max Planck, who revolutionized physics with his quantum theory. It was his observation that "the greatest naturalists of all times, men like Kepler, Newton, Leibniz, were inspired by profound religiosity." And then he goes on "For the believer, God is the beginning, for the scientist He is the end of all reflections." Interestingly enough, Aquinas said something similar much earlier: "All our knowledge has its origin in sensation. But God is most remote from sensation. So he is not known to us first, but last." Elsewhere Planck says, "All matter originates and exists only by virtue of a force which brings the particles of the atom to vibration. I must assume behind this force the existence of a conscious and intelligent mind. This mind is the matrix of all matter."

It is needless to say that atheists have never gotten yet to the bottom of the cup, to the end of all reflections, to the invisible world behind the visible world. But they may someday. Because God is omnipresent, he seems to be "nowhere," yet he is only seemingly absent. They say about fish the last thing a fish would discover is water; well, atheists are in a similar predicament as far as God is concerned. David Bentley Hart put it well, "If one could sort through all the physical objects and events constituting the Universe, one might come across any number of gods (you never know), but one will never find God." God is certainly not a secondary cause but the Primary Cause. God is not just one item, no matter how superior, in a class of items, but the very Source from which their being is derived.

6a. "I do not dare to believe in God."

Some atheists do not want to be on the bandwagon of any kind of faith, and certainly not of faith in God. Faith is a scary, forbidden word in their vocabulary—the opposite of knowledge. Faith comes with too much uncertainty. As the physicist Carl Sagan puts it, "I don't want to believe. I want to know."

Many of these atheists tend to equate any kind of faith—especially faith in God—with "blind faith," not worth our trust. Benjamin Franklin had already stated, "The way to see by faith is to shut the eye of reason." The biologist E. O.

Wilson is another one who likes to put religion against what we know through science: "Blind faith, no matter how passionately expressed, will not suffice. Science for its part will test relentlessly every assumption about the human condition."

These atheists persistently put faith—especially religious faith—in opposition to truth, knowledge, facts, and science. It began with Friedrich Nietzsche: "Faith means not wanting to know what is true." Then Thomas Huxley added: "[S]kepticism is the highest of duties; blind faith the one unpardonable sin." Or take Richard Feynman, "Religion is a culture of faith; science is a culture of doubt." Then there was George Bernard Shaw: "It is not disbelief that is dangerous to our society; it is belief." And rather recently Richard Dawkins had to say: "Faith is belief in spite of, even perhaps because of, the lack of evidence." And then he goes on, "There's no point of having faith if you have evidence."

The overall message is clear: there is an unsurpassable divide between scientific evidence and religious faith. It is very obvious that these atheists persistently put religious faith in opposition to truth, knowledge, facts, and science. Religious faith is always blind faith, in their view. No wonder religious faith is at the losing end—leaving mere darkness behind.

6b. Why should we dare to believe in God?

Evidently, there is no belief in God without some form of faith or trust, for religion always requires a final step of faith, a final surrender. But isn't that true of many other things in life? We found out earlier that scientists must believe in order and design, in rationality and comprehensibility—without such a belief they cannot function the way they should. There is no other way than to trust your own reasoning. Whether they like it or not, whether they realize it or not, scientists actually harbor quite some "blind" faith that they do not question. So, in a logical or empirical sense, atheists have no more and no less power of "absolute proof" than religious believers. The call for proof asks for more than it can deliver.

Sometimes we need understanding before we can believe and trust; at other times we need faith and trust so we can understand. It is as hard, if not harder, to prove what you believe than to prove what you doubt. According to Alvin Plantinga, belief in God is what philosophers call a basic belief: "It is no more in need of proof than the belief that the past exists, or that other people have minds, or that one plus one equals two." So faith is not to be contrasted with knowledge; rather, faith is itself a mode of knowledge, and knowledge always requires some faith.

In other words, just take the risk of believing that the Universe is orderly and comprehensible, otherwise you lose out on scientific progress. Just risk believing that the past exists and that other people have minds, otherwise your life will be hampered. In the same vein, just take the risk of believing that God exists, and this faith will change your life dramatically forever. It is actually startling how some atheists devote their entire career to make others believe that there is no space for beliefs. Yet, they are absolutely sure in believing that nothing in religious belief is sure. They doubt any kind of religious belief, except their own beliefs.

The Catechism speaks of two different kinds of doubt—voluntary and involuntary doubt (CCC 2088). Involuntary doubt is something we all experience. It is the kind of doubt the apostle Thomas had when others told him they had seen the Lord. He had his doubts in the face of what seems to be too good to be true. It is the kind of doubt we all experience time and again when surrounded by unanswerable questions—aroused by the great mysteries of life. This is the kind of doubt that may lead to anxiety. In contrast, the form of atheism we are discussing here is a voluntary kind of doubt, rooted in a deliberate refusal to let God enter into our lives. We should point out, though, that blind belief is worth as much or as little as blind unbelief.

When you start to doubt whether you really exist, whether your mind knows anything, or whether matter exists, your doubts are entirely unwarranted. There isn't much, perhaps even nothing, to corroborate your doubts. But when you doubt whether Martians really landed on our planet, or whether life is the result of evolution, your doubts may not be unwarranted but require further critical investigation. Atheists would say their doubts about God belong to the second category and require a critical analysis. However, it could be argued that their doubts make for a voluntary kind of doubt, rooted in a deliberate refusal to let God enter into their lives. Religious believers, on the other hand, might consider such doubts about God unwarranted—as much so as the doubt regarding your own existence or the love of your dear ones.

In all such cases, most of our beliefs—and therefore, most of our doubts—depend on other witnesses and the testimony of others. Much, or perhaps most, of what we know or claim to know comes to us from "hearsay." What we know about science came to us through teachers and textbooks. Doubting such information would amount to declaring them as part of a conspiracy of lies. In science, we can only advance by standing on the shoulders of predecessors. Those who are not trustworthy should be banned from the scientific community. As Stephen Barr puts it, "For a person to accept as knowledge only what he had discovered and proved for himself from direct personal experience would put his knowledge at the level of the Stone Age."

The Eclipse of God: Is Religion on the Way Out?

Something similar holds also for what we know about religion and God; such knowledge also came to us through witnesses—parents, teachers, pastors, and friends, but ultimately through the testimony of apostles, prophets, Church Fathers, and Saints. They told us the basics, showed us the way, and lived a religious life. So in religion too, we stand on the shoulders of predecessors. Doubting their information is an attack on their credibility and authority. But again, those who turn out not to be trustworthy should be banned from the religious community. True, unlike scientific statements, religious statements cannot be tested by experiment, but they can be tested by checking the trustworthiness of their witnesses. And, of course, "the proof is in the pudding." Whether it is in science or religion, thanks to the testimony of others, we can belong to a community of scientists, learners, or even believers.

We have stressed already several times that atheism is as much a belief as the religious beliefs that it is trying to wipe out from the face of the earth. Nevertheless, atheism is a very powerful force in our secular culture that has gathered a growing number of "converts" into its ranks—more so by persuading them than by convincing them, or just by making it look more fashionable. Atheism is portrayed as "the right thing to do," by making it look as if its opposite, religious faith, is against reason and counter to reality. Christopher Dawson was very aware of this: "The great obstacle to the conversion of the modern world is the belief ... that there is no such thing as religious knowledge."

Where atheists go wrong is when they put religious faith in opposition to truth, knowledge, facts, and science. Religious faith is not just a matter of a personal belief or a subjective opinion—instead it is about facts. Why should we believe something? Because others believe it? Not so! Because it feels good? Not so! The only reason is: because it

Chapter 8: Atheists and God

is true. The existence of God is not blind faith but a factual matter. It is a factual issue of yes or no: God either exists or he doesn't—that's not a matter of opinion. You can have your own opinions, but you can't have your own facts. Whereas science cannot be as "factual" as many scientists may have hoped for, religion is more "factual" than many of its enemies like to admit. Frank Cronin of Aquinas College expresses this as follows: "If it turns out God doesn't exist, it isn't that our faith was wrong—our facts were wrong. Our beliefs, no matter how sincere or pure, must correspond to reality.... Our faith is wrong because we got the facts wrong."

Cronin also says,

> Without an appeal to an intangible reality such as God, reason and its demands for evidence and rational proof are reduced to mere sensations. Leaving God out of the cosmos reduces reason to an effect caused by neural activity,... no more real than a mirage, an illusion or a hallucination. If reason is indeed real, it must be truly real, actually and factually real. Now, it does not have to be physically real to be truly real. Reason is a mental, intangible reality, the product and substance of a mind. But it still must be real.

For those who still do not dare to believe in God, the philosopher and physicist Blaise Pascal created the Wager that we mentioned earlier. Once it is shown that there are only two options, theism and atheism—not three, theism, atheism, and agnosticism—then the rest of the argument is simple. Peter Kreeft describes Pascal's Wager as follows: "If God does not exist, it does not matter how you wager, for there is nothing to win after death and nothing to lose after death. But if God does exist, your only chance of winning eternal happiness is to believe, and your only chance of losing it is to refuse to believe." In other words, atheism is a terrible bet, for it gives you no chance of winning. As Pascal put it, "If you gain, you gain all. If you lose, you lose nothing."

The Wager certainly has a haunting power. Needless to say that a Wager decision is less based on faith and trust than on fear. No wonder it has been criticized by some. The Harvard law professor Alan M. Dershowitz, for instance, considers it "a questionable bet to place, since any God worth believing in would prefer an honest agnostic to a calculating hypocrite." But it is hard to deny there is something to this Wager, especially when death comes into the picture. Even atheists pray in desperate circumstances, which is sometimes expressed as: "There are no atheists in foxholes."

It is worth noting that many former atheists ultimately did change their minds when they got confronted with death. Even Woody Allen once joked he wasn't afraid of death but didn't want to be around when it happens. Indeed, life is short, so it may not be wise to waste your time "wagering" in the "windowless cell" of atheism, not even agnosticism. The philosopher William Lane Craig describes the consequences of atheism in very clear terms: "If there is no God, then man and the Universe are doomed. Like prisoners condemned to death, we await our unavoidable execution."

7a. "I declare God to be beyond my reach."

Some atheists have another reason for calling religious faith a form of "blind faith." Their argument is that God, if there is one, is "per definition" entirely beyond our reach. They believe that terms like "God's transcendence" and "God's infinity" necessarily make the infinite, transcendent God completely inaccessible to the finite human mind.

Chapter 8: Atheists and God

Marquis de Sade said long ago: "Anything beyond the limits and grasp of the human mind is either illusion or futility." Peter Atkins claims something similar: "Religion, in contrast to science, deploys the repugnant view that the world is too big for our understanding."

In other words, these atheists may not really deny God's existence, but they consider it so far beyond their reach that they rather remain entirely silent about God. Otherwise they would have only two options left. The first one is that our talk about God would be considered so open-ended that it becomes completely inadequate and empty. In that sense, religious faith would indeed come very close to "blind" faith. The other option is that we can only speak about God in purely negative terms—"God is not this… and God is not that…" The problem with this latter approach is that one cannot merely say that God is not this and not that, without saying something positive. A negative definition of God proceeds by elimination—it can begin, it can go on indefinitely, but it can never do its job. The best we could ever say this way is, "Oh God, if there is a God, save my soul, if I have one."

This latter solution comes close to Hinduism. Since religious truth is said to transcend all verbal definition, the core of Hinduism does not depend on the existence or non-existence of God, or not even on whether there is one God or many gods. If you cannot say anything right about God, then you cannot say anything wrong either, so the reasoning goes. As a result, anything allegedly goes in religion. If one religion is true, then all of them must be true. Some hail this as "one faith but many beliefs." This view leads almost inevitably to some kind of relativism in religious matters. It makes God the "Great Unknown" who cannot possibly be known by any human being, let alone any religion. So all we claim to know about God must be in essence inadequate. As a consequence, all religions would end up being equivalent in being inadequate.

What some atheists conclude from this is the following. If God were transcendent in the sense of unknowable, we should stop talking about God right then and there, as there is no way to speak about the unknown, not to mention the unknowable. How could we possibly speak about the unspeakable? Clearly, these atheists may not really deny the existence of God, but even if they do believe in God, they do not know anything else about God—perhaps not even whether God exists. For this reason, they refuse judgment on God's existence, because they feel that the subject is unknowable—beyond the reach of human knowledge—and therefore no judgment can be made.

7b. God is not beyond our reach.

The kind of atheists we just mentioned often take the fact that there are so many different religions as an argument against religion in general. G. K. Chesterton was eager to debunk this argument:

> It is perpetually said that because there are a hundred religions claiming to be true, it is therefore impossible that one of them should really be true.... It would be as reasonable to say that because some people thought the earth was flat, and others (rather less incorrectly) imagined it was round, and because anybody is free to say that it is triangular or hexagonal, or a rhomboid, therefore it has no shape at all; or its shape can never be discovered."

The mere fact that many religions refer to the same God does not entail that all religious conceptions of God are

Chapter 8: Atheists and God

equivalent in being inadequate. It is indeed a frequently heard argument that all religions worship the same God—no matter whether they call God by the name of Yahweh, Allah, Brahman, or you name it. This seems to be especially true of the so-called monotheistic religions such as Judaism, Christianity, and Islam. The argument used here is based on the distinction between reference and description. Yahweh and Allah, for instance, have the same reference—referring to the same God in Heaven— although their descriptions are rather different. There are similar cases. Aristotle's sun refers to the same sun as Galileo's sun, but their descriptions are very different. The same can be said about the Morning Star, the Evening Star, and Venus: They come with different descriptions but refer to the same thing in the sky. Based on this distinction, the argument goes as follows: If, according to monotheism, there can only in principle be one God, then Christians, Jews, and Muslims must be worshipping the same God.

This is often called the idea of "common ground." It is based on the notion that if we abstract enough from particular beliefs about God, we will eventually arrive at some "god" on whom we can all agree. In this view, there must be more that unites religions than what separates them. However, this common "god" refers to some abstraction about which nothing much can be said. This raises the question: Is the "common ground" approach a viable option? It is hard to see how it could be. Declaring all religions as equal is as dubious as the statement that all dogs are equal. Equal in what sense? It is very obvious that there are many differences between dogs, although they all eat dog food. Religions are definitely not equal in the sense of all being true, as there are obvious contradictions between them. If the descriptions of God in different religions are in contradiction with each other, then they cannot all be true at

The Eclipse of God: Is Religion on the Way Out?

the same time. So we have to decide which description is true. In other words, there must be more to it than having the same reference.

Yet, it remains true that God's transcendence is what unites the orthodox forms of Judaism, Christianity, Islam, Buddhism, and to a certain extent even Hinduism. But that is probably where the similarities end. Religions are definitely not equal in the sense of all being true, as there are obvious contradictions between them. A clear example is the fact that the Qur'an denies the Trinity, the Divinity of Jesus, and even his Crucifixion, which are essential to most of Christianity. When religions contradict each other, at least one of them must be false, for contradictory statements cannot be both true at the same time. The title of a recent book raises a pertinent question, "Is the Father of Jesus the God of Mohammed?" Or are they essentially different? Both Muslims and Christians would agree they are different. If Christians believe—as they do—that Jesus Christ is God's all-inclusive revelation, then there can be no correction or addition to it. Benedict XVI was right when he expressed a deep respect for Muslims, but that is not the same as having a deep respect for Islam.

Atheists who accept God's transcendence consider this discussion useless because they believe that a transcendent God is unknown and unknowable—beyond our knowledge and beyond our reach. Whatever we say about God is necessarily off the mark. But is this really true? Is God indeed totally unknowable? There is some confusion here between "unknown" and "unknowable." We may not know everything about God, but that does not mean God is unknowable. It is a confusion that this form of atheism shares with Hinduism, a religion that does not care whether there is one God or many, not even whether God exists or not—for all our God-talk is in essence off the mark, since

Chapter 8: Atheists and God

God is not only unknown but also unknowable. However, the irony here is that any kind of religion that wants to abstain from any true statements about God must at least accept one true statement, namely that God is such that human beings cannot make true statements about God. But then the question arises: where could this one particular statement about God come from, given the assumed fact that we cannot say anything about God? Who told us that God is unknowable?

The answer probably is that some philosophers in line with Immanuel Kant told us so. Kant—a man who never left his own hometown, by the way—drew Heaven and Earth completely apart from each other by driving a wedge between God and the world. Kant claimed to have shown, once and forever, that God's existence can never be proven nor refuted (but he also assumed that you cannot know that anyone exists beside yourself). In human experience, so Kant states, there can be no space for God; if there were, God wouldn't be God anymore. So if God is really God, God cannot possibly fit into our human experience. In Kant's view, Heaven on the "other side" is totally separated from Earth "on this side." Not only is God considered "other" than the world but even "totally other." Not only did Kant make god unknown but also unknowable. Hence, we could never cross that infinite gap. All that remains is silence—a glorified version of atheism.

However, the statement that God is "other" than the world does not entail that God is "other" in the sense of being beyond anyone's reach and completely separated from us. We may not know everything about God, but that does not mean God is unknowable. Apart from God's transcendence, Judaism and Christianity invoke another religious concept, called God's immanence, which states that God is "in" the world, in spite of God's "otherness," and thus reveals himself to us. The Catechism (2129) ties this together: "It is the absolutely transcendent God who revealed himself to Israel." We know God through his Creation (in general revelation) and through his acts in history (in special revelation). A created world, by definition, is not divine, yet it can reveal us something about the Divine. The way Jews and Christians know about God is through the world, not without the world. They know about the unseen God through what is seen in his Creation. God is "part" of everything in this world, although he is not a "physical part" of it.

The concept of immanence counterbalances the other pole, transcendence. God is the Infinite Majesty, and yet he is intimately involved with everything and everyone. In his book Jesus of Nazareth, Pope Benedict XVI speaks of "God, who is as much in this world as he is beyond it—who infinitely transcends our world, but is also totally interior to it." Immanence adds a new dimension to transcendence. Since we were created in God's image, we also share "in the light of the divine mind," in the words of Vatican II. That is how we can know something about the Unknown. The Catechism (1028) puts it this way: "Because of his transcendence, God cannot be seen as he is, unless he himself opens up his mystery to man's immediate contemplation and gives him the capacity for it."

We need to be aware, though, that the way we know something about God cannot be the same as the way God "knows" things. On the other hand, human knowledge and divine knowledge cannot be wholly unrelated either, because the Creation is somehow a reflection and manifestation of its Creator, God. Thomas Aquinas would say that God's goodness, justice, wisdom, and mercy can only be true by what he calls "analogy," which combines likeness and unlikeness—or immanence and transcendence, if you will. God's wisdom, for instance, resembles what we understand

Chapter 8: Atheists and God

by wisdom, but at the same time it transcends human wisdom. In that sense, God is unknown—but not unknowable. Therefore, our concepts do not literally or fully capture the infinite being of the infinitely transcendent God. We do not capture things with our concepts like in a power grip. It is rather a participation in intelligibility that the Creator gave us. Blaise Pascal expressed this tension well when he said, "It is incomprehensible that God should exist, and it is incomprehensible that he should not exist."

So this doesn't entail at all that our religious concepts and conceptions are empty and useless. Even when we say, "God is beyond our conceptions," we say something meaningful and factual about God. Truth is truth, even if you don't accept it; and untruth is untruth, even if you claim it. In other words, some religious conceptions may be true, while others may be wrong. Because God's transcendence is also a fact, a true reality, we cannot just say about God whatever we choose. That's why Catholics have a Creed. The way we understand God and know God penetrates everything else we do in life. If we say we love God, we need to know who God is. You cannot love what you do not know, for you want to know the person you love. Knowledge, truth, and love are strongly interconnected. Each time we encounter someone, even God, we want to know whom and what we encounter. Pascal had remarked already, "Human beings must be known to be loved; but Divine beings must be loved to be known."

In fact, the concept of truth is at the core of all world religions, especially of a religion such as Christianity. When the apostle Paul tuned in to the philosophical mind of his Greek audience in Athens, he did refer to the idea of an unknown God: "I found also an altar with this inscription, 'To an unknown god.' What therefore you worship as unknown, this I proclaim to you." (Acts 17:23). But Paul certainly didn't imply that this unknown God is also unknowable, for he was quick to add, "Now what you worship as something unknown I am going to proclaim to you."

8a. "I no longer need God as a hypothesis."

This stance is particularly popular among scientists. They do their research as if there were no God. As the legendary biologist J.B.S. Haldane put it, "My practice as a scientist is atheistic. That is to say, when I set up an experiment I assume that no god, angel, or devil is going to interfere with its course." He is right: in a way scientists are atheists by profession.

More in general, one could say that in science there is no place for God as some kind of working hypothesis. The French astronomer Pierre-Simon Laplace is often quoted in this context. When given a copy of his latest book, Napoleon Bonaparte received it with the remark, "They tell me you have written this large book on the system of the Universe, and have never even mentioned its Creator." Laplace answered bluntly, "I had no need of that hypothesis." At one time, the laws of nature had been seen as pointing to a lawgiver; now they are seen as constituting in themselves, and by themselves, a satisfactory explanation of reality (see 1.b).

The fact that there is no place for God in science as a hypothesis, is reason for some atheists to claim there is no place for God anywhere in life at all. They battle with those religious believers who want God to keep a "foot in the door" by invoking divine interventions for any "gaps" in our scientific explanations. The problem with invoking God as a scientific hypothesis for scientific gaps is that science will eventually close more and more of these gaps. This gave the

Chapter 8: Atheists and God

atheist Richard Dawkins good reason to say, "[G]aps shrink as science advances, and God is threatened with eventually having nothing to do and nowhere to hide." From here it is only a small step for him to say, "[R]eligions still make claims about the world that on analysis turn out to be scientific claims." Somehow atheists like Dawkins think science is on its way to replace religion with science. We no longer "need" God, they say, since science has explained how things really are.

8b. Why do I still need God?

When some scientists reject God entirely, we need to ask them which god they are rejecting. Whether they realize it or not, they may not have the real God in mind, but rather some corrupted version of God. What could this corrupted version be? Where does it come from?

First of all, let's make clear that there is no need for a hypothesis called "God." We could never call God a hypothesis that we stumbled upon or used in our scientific endeavors. Besides, God is never considered a provisional hypothesis in the sense of an explanation we adopt until a better one might happen along. God is not a "working hypothesis," but he is a Primary Cause, who should not be degraded to the secondary causes science is dealing with (see 1.b). Because hypotheses are always open to disproof and thus should only be tentatively held, God is not a hypothesis that we hold on to tentatively and provisionally until more evidence for or against it emerges.

Nevertheless, some religious believers have given these atheists the wrong image of God with their belief in a god that the theologian Dietrich Bonhoeffer called a "god of the gaps." In Bonhoeffer's own words, "[H]ow wrong it is to use God as a stop-gap for the incompleteness of our knowledge.

If in fact the frontiers of knowledge are being pushed further and further back (and that is bound to be the case), then God is being pushed back with them, and is therefore continually in retreat." How right he is when he added, "We are to find God in what we know, not in what we don't know."

Because a "god of the gaps" is a misconception that actually obscures the real God, it makes no longer sense to maintain, like Dawkins does, that religions only make claims about the world that on analysis turn out to be scientific claims. Neither does it make sense to honor science at the cost of religion. Religion and science deal with separate questions. The so-called "faith-science conflict" is an imaginary creation that originates on both sides of the divide: either with religious believers who have a superstitious kind of faith, or with atheists trying to pick a fight with a superstitious form of religion. If this were a real power-battle, atheists would most likely end up on the winning side. But there is no winner, because there should not be any conflict.

The God that these atheists are actually rejecting is very often merely a "god of the gaps," not the real God. It is important to emphasize, though, that there is a huge difference between the two. We need to admit that God is not, cannot, and should not be a hypothesis in science, nor can he be one of the secondary causes that science deals with. But God can indeed be seen as an assumption of science—as the best, and perhaps only, way of explaining the order, lawfulness, and intelligibility of this Universe. Scientists have the right to reject a "god of the gaps," but when they reject the Creator of this Universe, they reject the real God—the Primary Cause of this Universe, if you will—and thus indirectly they reject the very foundation of their own scientific work.

Even if we consider the laws of nature as constituting in

themselves, and by themselves, a satisfactory explanation of reality, as many scientists do, they still need to face the question as to where these laws of nature ultimately come from. That is an entirely different question that cannot be answered by science itself. But again, the answer does not lie in a god-of-the-gaps, but in the real God, the Maker of Heaven and Earth.

9a. "I can live without God."

Once God has been removed from our life—which is atheism—we have not much more left than mere humanism. It is "humanism without God," often called secular humanism. It is one of those "ism" ideologies, similar to its "cousins" capitalism and communism. What these three doctrines have in common is a foundation of materialism; we find a social form of materialism in humanism, a collective form of materialism in communism, and an individualistic form of materialism in capitalism (not to be confused with a free-market economy). All three share a vision of the human person that is incomplete: it has no longer a religious dimension. None of them has any "need" for God.

This kind of humanism declares human beings as fully sufficient in themselves, fully self-made, and in complete control of their own history (see 7.a). Humanism declares humanity as the measure of all things. When humanists say they serve people, not ideas, they have to realize this in itself is an idea too, actually an ideo-logy. Secular humanism is a philosophy of life which views man as the "supreme being" on Earth, so there is no need for or no space left for a Supreme Being in Heaven. It pretends that all our problems—personal, social, technological, and what have you—can be entirely solved by using the right human knowledge, technology, reasoning, and judgment. We are supposed to be in full control of ourselves and should further free ourselves through economic, technological, and social liberation. From then on, not Heaven but the sky is the limit.

True, there are some humanists who may be dedicated to humanity because of their belief in God, who created us after his own image. But in secular humanism, we are dealing with humanists who have no longer any need of God. The British Humanist Association explicitly states, "Positive atheists—humanists—simply believe that within the confines of a mortal life and the Universe we live in, we have all the resources we need to live meaningful and ethical lives." These humanists believe it is a mistake to think that we need anything more, or that anything more actually exists. Apparently, belief in God is a waste of time in their eyes. So they go as far as claiming, "The religious element, in fact, distorts moral motivation."

The French philosopher Denis Diderot said already during the Enlightenment, "Whether God exists or does not exist, he has come to rank among the most sublime and useless truths." More recently, atheists have taken a similar position. Isaac Asimov, for instance, expressed as his opinion: "I don't have the evidence to prove that God doesn't exist, but I so strongly suspect he doesn't that I don't want to waste my time." Bill Gates put it more directly: "Religion is not very efficient. There's a lot more I could be doing on a Sunday morning."

9b. Why we can't live without God.

Indeed, for many people, belief in God has been replaced by humanism. Humanism has no need of God. It usually bathes in practical materialism, "which restricts its needs and aspirations to space and time," says the Catechism (2124). The Man of humanism is setting out on his own to know and master his cosmos—all of it. Secular humanism "falsely considers man to be 'an end to himself, and the sole maker, with supreme control, of his own history'" (CCC 2124). It considers man as the "measure of all things," in spite of the religious belief that Man can only know himself in reference to God. As Pope John Paul II put it, "Without the Creator, the creature disappears." When we throw God out, we throw Man out as well—and therefore humanism as well.

The question remains, of course, from where humanists derive their motivation of doing good for humanity. Earlier we found out that morality needs an anchor in Heaven (see 7.b), so it is hard to see how it could be anchored in humanism itself. Why should whites care about blacks, or the rich about the poor, or the strong about the weak, if it were not for the religious fact that we are all children of the same God, made in his image and likeness? This fact makes us very unique beings. As Fr. James Schall, S.J. puts it, "we are the most interesting figures in the cosmos. We are the beings in the Universe that can reject what we are."

Of course, one can be moral without being Christian. We can be moral without knowing why we are moral beings. When humanists "do" the same good things as Christians, perhaps one could say that they actually still live off of Judeo-Christian capital—without them being aware of it—venerating shadows of the past, in the words of Nietzsche (see 7.b). Sometimes they base their acts on the Golden Rule, presumably free of religion: do to others what you want to be done to yourself (Tobit 4:15; Matthew 7:12; Luke 6:31). Yet, a worldview without God looks like a jigsaw puzzle with some large and vital pieces missing—take away religion and it just doesn't look complete. So belief in God does not distort moral motivation, as many humanists think, but actually bolsters it.

The Eclipse of God: Is Religion on the Way Out?

Contrary to secular humanism, in Christianity it is Christ who is the measure of all things—not the old Adam but the new Adam. That is why it is tempting to ask humanists what to do when disaster strikes us, when things do not go the way we had planned, when we become victims of injustice in our man-made systems—in short, when self-made people reach their own limits? Don't we all know that life doesn't owe us a living? Suffering actually shows us that we are not in control of our lives but need divine assistance. In addition, we should ask these humanists: isn't it striking that Christianity actually has the Cross at center stage in its religion; it claims there is some mysterious salvation for us in carrying our crosses in life—for the benefit of ourselves and the benefit of others. No wonder the Cross is a touchstone for Christians, but at the same time a stumbling block for non-Christians, including many humanists.

And besides, since the existence of our world is contingent, not a necessity, our world would be nothing, literally, if there were no God. Without God, there is a permanent void in our lives—a void that may easily go unnoticed because it is a void. In the words of Pope Benedict XVI, "Again and again man falls behind the faith and wants to be just himself again; he becomes a heathen in the most profound sense of the word." These "heathens" of the humanist type just have no need to believe in God because they think they are completely self-sufficient. They do not need God, they do not even want God, because such a God would undermine humanism—the power of Man, the power of "Me, myself, and I."

The Catechism (2126) considers this "a false conception of human autonomy, exaggerated to the point of refusing any dependence on God." Autonomy does not mean that we can become whatever we please, without being accountable to anyone. Autonomy means instead that we become more and more aware of our deepest self. We understand ourselves best in the light of God. When people try to build their own tower of Babel into Heaven, they become divided from each other and lose their common heritage, their common language, and their common sense; it calls for Pentecost to unite them again. In one of her novels, Flannery O'Connor gave a good description of what this kind of atheism leads to: "Where you come from is gone, where you thought you were going to never was there, and where you are is no good unless you can get away from it. Where is there a place for you to be? No place."

There is this gravestone of an atheist, perhaps a secular humanist, in the town of Thurmont, MD that could not express things better: "Here lies an Atheist. All dressed up and no place to go." That's where humanism without God ends. As a matter of fact, humanists miss much more than just some great holidays; they also miss out on a destination in life, on a power that far surpasses what humans can attain on their own.

10a. "I cannot believe there is a just God."

Some atheists have a completely different "style" of defending atheism. They have encountered so many problems in life that they cannot believe anymore there is a loving God who takes care of his people. The main obstacle for these atheists is often the problem of evil. The existence of evil certainly poses a huge problem for a belief in an all-powerful God. Long ago, the Greek philosopher Epicurus worded the problem as follows: "Is God willing to prevent evil, but not able? Then he is not omnipotent. Is he able, but not willing? Then he is malevolent. Is he both able and willing? Then whence cometh evil? Is he neither able nor willing? Then why call him God?"

More recently, the English writer Virginia Woolf worded the same problem: "How could any Lord have made this world? ... there is no reason, order, justice: but suffering, death, the poor." We find a similar concern in the works of the atheist Jean-Paul Sartre. He had a keen awareness of evil and human perversity. He says, "We have learned to take Evil seriously.... Evil is not an appearance.... Knowing its causes does not dispel it. Evil cannot be redeemed." Yet he also says that since there is no God and since we therefore create our own values and laws, there really is no evil.

Many atheists struggle with a related problem: How does an all-powerful God deal with human freedom? If God is almighty, human beings must be powerless. Christopher Hitchens once spoke of belief "in a sort of benevolent dictatorship." The French atheist and philosopher Jean-Paul Sartre worded the dilemma of God versus human freedom as follows: an almighty God doesn't leave room for free human beings, whereas free human beings do not leave room for an almighty God. This puts God and Man in a power battle. Sartre opted in favor of human freedom over divine omnipotence and thus became an atheist. In his eyes, and in those of many atheists, God had lost the power battle.

What these atheist have in common is their problem of how to understand the religious belief that God is all-powerful, all-knowing, all-just, all-present, and all-loving. A contemporary British atheist has remarked that if he were asked why God does not exist, he would simply say, "Bone cancer in children." At least these atheists seem to know which God they are rejecting.

10b. Why we can believe in a just God.

Interestingly enough, it was the then-atheist C. S. Lewis who once tried to prove that God did not exist, because the

Chapter 8: Atheists and God

Universe seemed so cruel and unjust to him. But then he realized, "in the very act of trying to prove that God did not exist—in other words, that the whole of reality was senseless—I found I was forced to assume that one part of reality—namely my idea of justice—was full of sense.... If the whole Universe has no meaning, we should never have found out that it has no meaning: just as, if there were no light in the Universe and therefore no creatures with eyes, we should never know it was dark. Dark would be without meaning." Thus atheism turned out to be too simplistic for the turned-around atheist C. S. Lewis. He realized that by asserting "evil exists," he used an ethical standard in order to define good and evil—and such an absolute standard implies the existence of God (see 7.b). We only know of eclipses when we know what they cast their shadow on.

At those moments when life does not seem to make sense, especially when death, sickness, loss, and suffering strike us—at those moments, we experience our own powerlessness and ultimate limitation to the fullest. We become either bitter or better. These are the moments when we could easily turn angry or disappointed in life, even to the point of being "depressed" or "paralyzed." That is when some people end up losing all their faith and hope in an all-powerful, all-knowing, all-just, all-present, and all-loving God. They just cannot deal with this latest loss, this latest disaster, this latest disease in their lives. They may always have considered God as an intervening God—that is, intervening on their request. However, a religion that promises immediate answers to prayer and instant awards for good behavior is merely a commercialized version of religion. God is not a cosmic vending machine. Through prayer, we may get what we need—not what we think we need but what we do need. God answers our needs, not our wants. So where does this leave us when it comes to evil?

First of all, there is physical evil—evil not caused by human beings, but evil that seems to come with nature, such as natural death, famine, diseases, earthquakes, tsunamis, and other catastrophes. How can this kind of evil be reconciled with an all-powerful and all-loving God? There have been many answers to the question of physical evil.

One of them is that our world is bound to follow its God-given laws of nature. Therefore, we should distinguish between what God wills and what he allows. Thomas Aquinas says that God "neither wills evils to be nor wills evils not to be; he wills to allow them to happen." God does not will earthquakes, but he allows them when they are a consequence of the laws of nature—in the same way as God does not will wars but allows them when humans use their freedom to start them. In other words, there is God's positive or providential will and then there is God's permissive will; therefore, not everything that happens in this Universe is directly willed by God's providence—that would amount to a denial of autonomy of secondary causes and human activities. To say that God "allows" or "permits" evil does not mean that he sanctions it in the sense that he approves of it, or even wants it. God's creation is not perfect yet, but is on its way to perfection—and we, human beings, have been made participants in his creation; we are God's "co-workers" in bringing his creation to perfection. God wills perfection but allows imperfection on the journey to perfection. As the Catechism (302) puts it,

> Creation has its own goodness and proper perfection, but it did not spring forth complete from the hands of the Creator. The Universe was created 'in a state of journeying' (in statu viae) toward an ultimate perfection yet to be attained, to which God has destined it. We call 'divine providence' the

Chapter 8: Atheists and God

dispositions by which God guides his creation toward this perfection.

Calling God all-powerful or almighty does not mean God can do whatever he wants. Does God have the power to create a square circle, for example, or can he make a stone so heavy that he himself cannot lift it, or can he undo what happened in the past, or can he undo the effects of secondary causes? When Thomas Aquinas dealt with these questions, he was very definite in his answer: God being all-powerful does not mean that God is able to do what is logically contradictory. When something is against reason, God cannot do it. Doesn't this put God at the mercy of our own reason, though? Not at all. God cannot act against his own nature, which includes Reason. St. Augustine would add to this that God cannot do what he does not will.

What made Aquinas so sure on this issue? The answer is that God is reason and freedom, so he cannot act against his own nature by doing what is contradictory. God is absolutely free, but his freedom is not arbitrary, so he cannot go against what is true and right. How do we know this? Well, our own power of reason is rooted in creation and thus participates in God's power of reason. If our reason tells us that something like a square circle is impossible, then we see this with our very intellects which were created by God and are participating in God's reason. Aquinas concludes from this, "Hence it is better to say that such things cannot be done, than that God cannot do them." So atheists who reject an Almighty God reject him because they take God's omnipotence the wrong way. They take it as the capability to do anything whatsoever. So if God cannot do certain things, then he cannot be omnipotent, they say.

Another answer to the problem of physical evil turns the world completely upside-down. When speaking of physical evil, we find ourselves already in a mental, spiritual, even moral context. When speaking of "evil," we are asserting somehow that evil "should" not exist—and that's why we call it "evil." We are in fact evaluating physical suffering as wrong or bad—something no animal would be able to do. A prey does not consider the predator "evil"—perhaps painful, literally, but not evil. When giving birth, animals may experience physical pain, but not suffering in the sense of something "bad." So the "thorns and thistles" may have always been there, but since the Fall in Paradise, they were felt not only as painful but also as distressing, as something "evil." After the Fall the world did not change, but we did. Hence, even the cause of physical evil is ultimately sin. Without sin, physical evils would not rankle or embitter us.

There certainly is something to this answer. Only humans take diseases and catastrophes as something that should not be, as something that seems to be acting against them personally. Only humans can get depressed. Animals may "dislike" these things, but they do not question them in terms of "Why me?" They feel pain, but not evil or suffering. They do not have a "me," and since animals do not know about good and bad, they cannot ask why bad things happen to good animals. Only humans know of God, so they ask the question "Is something wrong between God and me?" or "Why do bad things happen to good people?" Without God, we could not even speak in terms of evil. Thanks to God, we know what the world "should" be like if we look at it from a "God's-eyes-view." We know of "evil" because we have an idea of "good" and of what things should be like if everything were "good"—the way God intends them to be, before the Fall. This also explains why humans, unlike animals, can suffer threefold—in anticipating suffering, in experiencing suffering, and in reliving suffering.

So why do "bad" things happen to people? God's creation

is "in a state of journeying toward an ultimate perfection yet to be attained," according to the Catechism (302). God's creation is not perfect yet, but it is on its way—and we, human beings, have been made participants in his creation; we are his "co-workers" in bringing his creation to perfection. God wills perfection—his providential will—but allows imperfection—his permissive will—on the journey to perfection. So physical evil is part of the imperfection we are still surrounded by. God guides his creation toward this ultimate perfection with divine and loving Providence. As co-workers we can bank on God's Providence, so the Universe can ultimately reach its destiny. To those who say suffering is a "proof" against God, one might respond it is actually a "proof" for God, since suffering shows us that we are not in control of our lives but need divine assistance.

This takes us from physical evil to moral evil—evil not caused by nature, but evil that humans cause themselves. How can there be moral evil and suffering? The answer is quite simple: moral evil is a consequence of human freedom. God has given human beings the freedom to act for or against him, so God acts through persuasion, not by coercion. Sartre would protest, of course, and say that an almighty God doesn't leave room for free human beings, so free human beings would leave no room for an almighty God. However, Sartre was wrong on that issue and created a false dilemma. There is no reason why we would have to question God's omnipotence, or even his existence, if there is human freedom. There is no reason to assume that God and Man are in a power battle.

The fact that we do have freedom actually points to a Creator after whose image we were made: how could we be free if there were no God who has freely created us after his image? St. Hippolytus once clarified "the significance of the proverb, 'Know Yourself,' that is, discover God within yourself, for he has formed you after his own image." God does not rob us of any decisions we make ourselves. He is in fact the one who gives us decision-making power; he allows us to become causes of our own. God is the Primary Cause who is the cause of all other causes, including the causes we can become ourselves. In a God-less society we may have more liberties but we end up with less freedom. God invites us to share in his own happiness, which is infinitely better than any "happiness" of our own design. So it is certainly not a "benevolent dictatorship."

Let us use the following analogy to explain how an almighty God can give us freedom. A sovereign king can pass a law that makes him no longer sovereign—which is somehow what God did out of love for the world. God does not need us, but he wants us. He set limits to his own omnipotence by setting no bounds to human freedom. When it comes to our salvation, we are certainly at God's mercy, but he has also chosen to be at our mercy. God could perhaps have chosen to eliminate the possibility of evil and evil-doing, but then God would have also taken away the possibility of good and doing-good. We would have become puppets on the world scene. Instead, God lets the actors on the world stage be free actors, who may not act the way the Author of the play would like them to act. God wills perfection but allows imperfection. We may not know what the future holds, but we do know that God holds the future. That's why we can believe in a just God, in spite of seeming counter-evidence.

11a. "I just never think of God."

Here we come upon a completely different form of atheism. It is the kind that no longer feels any need to protest or deny God's existence, because atheists of this type no longer perceive anything spiritual or religious in their lives; they suffer from some kind of "spiritual amnesia"; they have completely lost their religious dimension. They are not so much atheists as heathens who have never heard of God and have never even thought about God. These people live in a very noisy and busy world, entirely transformed into a secularized world and filled with radio and TV, loudspeakers and earphones, which overpower and squash everything else.

Here we have atheism in its simplest form: I just never think of God. This form of atheism is not of the theoretical kind that makes one believe there is no God, but rather of the practical type that makes one act as if there is no God. It is a form of secularism that leads to a lifestyle marred with complete unawareness of God (see 7.a). It doesn't deny God, it doesn't fight God, it just ignores God. It doesn't notice the eclipse of God, because it never saw the world before the eclipse set in. It leads to a life without a "fourth dimension"—without a religious or spiritual dimension. The only thing left in life is the "rock-solid" reality of food, money, sex, and material possessions—all of which will collapse when we die. We are dealing here with heathens and pagans; they are not really non-believers, because they never thought of the idea there is a God to believe in. Even the word God is completely missing in their vocabulary. They just live a life without God, and have no idea of what they are missing.

11b. Why do I want to think of God?

This is a "brand" of atheism that has actually forgotten about being surrounded by a culture once steeped in Christianity, because currently that culture has become highly secularized in habits and practices (see 7.a). The Catechism (2088) calls it "spiritual blindness." When agnostics protest "I do not know if God exists" or when other

The Eclipse of God: Is Religion on the Way Out?

atheists declare "I do not believe that God exists," they may not realize it but both their protest and their assertion imply at least the concept of God; they imply that there is now a void that was once filled by faith in God. It has left a "God-shaped hole" inside each one of us that only God can fill—and nothing else. As St. Augustine put it in his *Confessions*, "What place is there in me to which my God can come, what place that can receive the God who made heaven and earth? Does this mean, O Lord my God, that there is in me something fit to contain you?"

Unfortunately, this "God-shaped hole" has rather quietly become empty and vacant in the lives of many. It creates like a permanent eclipse. How could anyone forget what the world was like before the eclipse? Our freedom, our democracy, our health care system, our scientific achievements, our educational system, our charitable institutions, and many other blessings wouldn't be what they are, or they might not even exist, if they didn't have Christian roots nourished by God. So you wonder how some people can live in complete ignorance of such an obvious fact.

Let's keep in mind that, for centuries, it was unthinkable in the Western world to even deny God's existence. Although atheists are still a tiny, yet very vocal minority in the Western World (± 4% in the USA), our society is changing fast. More and more people are no longer aware of this growing void, as they have no memory of the way life used to be; they live obliviously in complete religious ignorance. They are quietly leading a life of religious amnesia—aimless and clueless. Pope Benedict XVI recently mentioned how the air we breathe in our societies is often polluted by a non-Christian, even a non-human mentality, concerned only with worldly things and lacking a spiritual dimension. It is a life of heathens. The bottom has been taken out of their lives; they have lost their "sixth sense" and their "fourth dimension."

Chapter 8: Atheists and God

And they don't even know it. They are spiritually illiterate. They never give God or religion any thought. They have forgotten about their roots—God and religion. Pope Benedict XVI used to say that "without memory there is no future." Only when we know where we came from do we know what we are heading for.

It is not that many of these heathens explicitly dismiss any basic kind of faith in God. They do not dismiss it, for one cannot dismiss what one has never received. They just never heard of it or never thought of it. It never crossed their minds. They have no way of seeing the world through the eyes of religious faith because they were never given that opportunity. When schools create graduates that are illiterate, we protest, but somehow we accept that schools, including the "school of family life," creates "graduates" who are spiritually illiterate. As the Communications expert Robert P. Lockwood puts it, "Children without faith not only become adults without faith, but adults who will pass that faithlessness on to their children." What parents instead should hand on to their children is the rich tradition of their Catholic Faith. Tradition means literally: something we "pass or hand on." Unfortunately, our culture doesn't appreciate what has been handed on to us, because it is often considered second-hand.

Pope Benedict XVI used to speak of a "massive amnesia in our contemporary world." Indeed, we have lost our cultural memory, even to the point of disregarding the Christian roots of Western Civilization. We need what Elie Wiesel, a survivor of the Nazi concentration camps, called a "memory transfusion" to bring the wisdom of the past back into our consciousness. David Bentley Hart is right, "The reason the very concept of God has become at once so impoverished ... is not because of all the interesting things we have learned over the past few centuries, but because of all the vital things we have forgotten." Sometimes someone like Pope Francis can help people to recover traces of lost memories. As he said in his speech on religious liberty in Philadelphia, "Remembrance saves a people's soul from whatever or whoever would attempt to dominate it or use it for their interests."

Here we have atheism in its simplest form: I just never think of God. Pope Benedict XVI calls it "secularism," which leads to a lifestyle marred with complete unawareness of God. He also calls it "paganism," turning us into complete heathens. A thoroughly secularized world is a world without windows or skylights—a prison cell, that is. Atheism and secularism start slowly and then erode all Christian elements in society, layer by layer, and next set off a mudslide that has the destructive capabilities of an avalanche, wiping out everything on its way. So we all end up in the mud. Where God is absent, nothing can be good.

When such a thing happens, when the eclipse of God has set in, when we lose sight of God and lead a life "as if there is no God," we may also lose the foundation of morality, because we no longer know why certain things are not permissible. Without morality, we would be mere animals again. Without moral values, we could even lose our judicial laws, which have been protecting us so far to the extent they were in tune with the natural law. All of this will ultimately lead to the nihilism of no-law, no-authority, no-rationality, no-morality, and no-purpose to life. When Aleksandr Solzhenitsyn, in his 1983 Templeton Prize lecture, tried to locate the root of the evils of the 20th century—two world wars, three totalitarian regimes with death camps, and a Cold War—he discerned a profound truth: "Men have forgotten God." What does this lead to? The writer Fyodor Dostoyevsky had already given us the answer when he said that without God, all things are permissible.

This is probably the scariest kind of atheism so far, because it doesn't raise its voice in protest or denial; it just lives and grows like a mushroom in complete silence and ignorance until its season is over. It quietly lives in a world of materialism, scientism, relativism, and secularism, where people are possessed by their material possessions—and they seem to be happy there, because they no longer know of any other goods. They are quietly leading a life of religious amnesia—aimless and clueless. As the saying goes, those who do not remember tend to repeat past errors. What this leads to is well described by Chesterton: "For when we cease to worship God, we do not worship nothing, we worship anything." When "God is dead," we must worship idols instead, for we are by nature worshippers. Indeed, those who are unaware of God usually end up serving other "gods" such as materialism and scientism. As Psalm 106:19-20 puts it, "they made a calf, bowed low before ... the image of a grass-eating bull."

12a. "I hate any belief in God."

There is at least one more kind of atheism left, which is by its very nature a belligerent form that wants to spread far and wide by propagating itself through books, TV, and other media. It is on its way to becoming a real "cult"—a cult of people who vehemently refuse to believe in God and want you to believe that believing in God is "evil" and needs to be attacked or even eradicated. These people consider spreading their message of God-hatred to be their "holy war," their "sacred mission," a Jihad against God. It does not question God, it does not deny God, but it hates God. George Orwell referred to this kind of atheists when he said about someone, "He was an embittered atheist (the sort of atheist who does not so much disbelieve in God as personally dislike

Him)."

There is something very peculiar about this form of atheism: it tries to constantly remind us of God while maintaining God does not exist. How could one hate something that is not there? Why would one persistently prove to people the non-existence of a being that is not supposed to exist anyway? Cardinal Stefan Wyszyński, the late Primate of Poland, who dealt most of his life with the aggressive atheism of Soviet Communism, has an astounding answer to these questions: in order to hate God, you must first have faith that there is a God, for only when you firmly believe in God will you be able to hate him. That was his explanation for the fact that the Communist media in his country used to persistently mention God in their God-less propaganda against God.

12b. What is wrong with hating God?

Why is this form of atheism so aggressive? Why on earth would one want to fight religion, which doesn't hurt anyone in any way? As a matter of fact, we have nothing to fear from Christianity; it doesn't endanger the common good but makes the deepest contribution to it; it actually gave a push to respect human rights and establish democracy, and it played a main role in education and health care from its very beginning. If I were an atheist, I would say let religion just die quietly! But fortunately, religion keeps burying its undertakers. The long-time atheist Oscar Wilde, who eventually died a Catholic in 1900 on November 30, once said that, of all religions, Catholicism is the only one worth dying in.

Some might counter that Christianity has its missionaries—so atheism should be allowed to have its own "missionaries" as well, even its own "chaplains" in the armed

Chapter 8: Atheists and God

forces. The problem with this stand is that Christianity has "Good News" to spread, with the goal of helping people in their daily lives and saving them from eternal damnation, whereas atheism has only "bad news" to bring—their message being that, at the end of life, "there is no place to go." It is actually not a message of God-denial but of God-hatred. Why would anyone want such a message to spread or to help it spread?

What is going on here? The philosopher William Lane Craig gives us a plausible answer: "No one in the final analysis fails to become a Christian because of a lack of arguments; he fails to become a Christian because he loves darkness rather than light and wants nothing to do with God." The key line here is that such a person "wants nothing to do with God"; he wants no part of the Light, but cherishes the eclipse instead. There is actually aversion, disgust, and hatred involved. So the pivotal question is this: what is behind the deep-seated hatred that these atheists nurse against religion and against God?

Let's face it, there is only one force that hates God's Creation more than anything else—and that force is Satan. Satan is not an atheist in the regular sense. Satan knows that God exists but wants no part of him. It is Satan's ultimate goal to demolish all Christian elements in society and to damage the human image that was made in God's image. Satan prowls about the world for the ruin of souls. He is not an atheist himself, yet he loves to spread atheism.

Could Satan be the real instigator of this aggressive form of atheism? It is hard to say "no" to this question. As a matter of fact, destructive atheism could very well be part of a much larger picture—a cosmic warfare, so to speak, between Good and Evil, between God and Satan. It is God's aim for each one of us to attain Heaven after death, whereas Satan's aim is to ensure that as many people as possible miss that eternal goal. Do not take God and Satan as two eternal principles locked in permanent conflict (as it is in Dualism and Manichaeism, CCC 285), for Satan and other demons are fallen Angels who were originally created good by God (CCC 391), but they decided in their freedom to go against their Creator. Obviously, Satan is a reality; and evil is something real to watch out for.

It is only the religious "eye" that sees all of history as a cosmic and constant warfare between God and Satan, waged everywhere and daily—"24/7." It "sees" how life is more of a battleground than a playground. It "sees" how the power of evil and the light of Satan enabled men such as Hitler, Stalin, Mao, bin Laden, and ISIS to spellbind and enslave the minds and spirits of millions, creating hell ahead of time, right here on earth. This explains how such people could have sold their souls by following "orders" that stem from sources far beyond their own resources. Only religious people are able to see this dimension in history that historians usually miss. They are able to see what is unseen behind all that is seen.

And now we witness again how the power of evil, the "light" of Satan, is enabling atheists to spellbind and enslave the minds and spirits of millions, creating havoc on earth with religious erosion and mudslides. These atheists have been happy to sell their souls to their new "master." No wonder the reality of evil goes far beyond material and physical powers; it goes even far beyond what human beings can do on their own. Aleksandr Solzhenitsyn is very adamant about the way atheistic communism operated in the former Soviet Union: "Militant atheism is not merely incidental or marginal to Communist policy; it is not a side effect, but the central pivot." Whether it is Stalin or Mao or Hitler or bin Laden or ISIS, the key question is: could they have ever done what they did relying on their own human power alone? The answer seems to be a definite "no."

Is there any indication that this explanation is correct? For people who do not have a "religious eye," it may be hard to accept the existence of satanic forces, but we do have confirmation from an unexpected source—exorcism. Exorcists always need to distinguish demonic possessions from mental or psychiatric disorders, and they use at least three symptoms to identify people as possessed. First, those people have the ability to see hidden sacred objects, which they always want to be removed. Second, they have an extraordinary physical strength, going far beyond normal human strength. And third, they show an aversion to the sacred—e.g. they begin to curse, remove holy pictures from their houses, refuse going to church, etc.

This is not to say that all atheists are "possessed," but they appear to be at least "under the influence" of evil forces—and this seems to be even more evident in the case of aggressive atheism fueled by God-hatred. If there is a cosmic warfare waging between God and Satan—and in the Catholic view, there is—militant atheists are definitely on the wrong side in this battle. They show a clear aversion to anything sacred and try to remove it with all the strength they have. Unfortunately, they get tremendous help from the satanic realm of evil, which gives them the power to do even more than they could ever do on their own.

This explains how such people can follow "orders" stemming from sources far beyond their own resources. They churn out endless propaganda against God through books, mass media, and the internet—and are rather successful in doing so. The fuel behind all their convictions is some satanic force engaged in a battle against God's creation—which is the role of Satan, the "father" of all lies, the great divider who knows how to remain hidden behind the scene. Satan is happy to lend such people some "spiritual" help from "beyond." That is why these atheists seem to feel empowered from "on high" to declare to the whole world that there is no God, and that they are "his prophets." But you wonder whose prophets they really are.

b. We end up with "I believe in one God."

Here is the turning point we should close our discussion with: "I believe in one God, the Father Almighty, Creator of Heaven and Earth." The difference between atheists and religious believers is not that the believers know what to point to for their religious beliefs, whereas atheists do not. The difference is that the believer sees what is pointed to as evidence of God's existence and the atheist does not. The evidence is there in the world to be seen by anyone who has eyes to see it—both believers and non-believers. Everyone sees it, but not everyone sees it as evidence.

As to whether non-believers can actually learn to see it as evidence requires something like a "Gestalt Switch." Think of the famous duck-rabbit picture; one has to make a mental switch to see the rabbit after seeing the duck in the same picture; they are both there to be seen, but only after going through a "Gestalt Switch." Such a switch requires a mental switch, for the image on the retina does not change. Can the evidence the religious believer sees ever convince the atheist? It cannot until the evidence is seen for what it is—evidence instead of counter-evidence. That requires a "switch." True, it is empirical evidence to be seen by anyone who has eyes to see it. But it is not empirical in that it can be seen by all people who have eyes in their heads. To quote C. S. Lewis again, "I believe in Christianity as I believe that the sun has risen: not only because I see it, but because by it I see everything else."

Belief in God's existence, his omnipotence, and his goodness is only possible after some kind of "switch" that

Chapter 8: Atheists and God

makes for a turning point in someone's life. No one knows this turning point better than those "life-size" atheists who have gone through it all and, at last, were able to make the switch and came to see the Divine Light. They could finally see the Sun behind the eclipse. There are many of them who finally discovered—often after a hard and long battle—how they were deceived and had sold their souls. You can find their life stories everywhere—on the internet, in books, in articles.

The list of former atheists and agnostics is quite impressive: Ronda Chervin, Francis Collins (former leader of the Human Genome Project, and currently director of the National Institutes of Health), Dorothy Day, Cardinal Avery Dulles SJ, Peter Hitchens (a brother of the atheist who recently died), C. S. Lewis, Gabriel Marcel, Malcolm Muggeridge, Joseph Pearce, Charles Péguy, Aleksandr Solzhenitsyn, St. Edith Stein, Allen Tate, Evelyn Waugh, Simone Weil, Dr. Bernard Nathanson (the abortionist who became a Catholic pro-life advocate)—and this list could go on for quite a while.

Let me mention one of them more in particular, the French philosopher and renowned atheist Jean-Paul Sartre whom we mentioned several times in this book as an astute atheist. Toward the end of his life, by then blind, in poor health, but still in full possession of his faculties, the man whom most people know as an uncompromising atheist had a profound conversion. In the early spring of 1980, he shared much of his time with an ex-Maoist, Benny Lévy (writing under the pseudonym Pierre Victor), and the two had a dialogue in the ultra-leftist Le Nouvel Observateur. It is sufficient to quote a single sentence from what Sartre said during this dialogue: "I do not feel that I am the product of chance, a speck of dust in the Universe, but someone who was expected, prepared, prefigured. In short, a being that

The Eclipse of God: Is Religion on the Way Out?

only a Creator could put here; and this idea of a creating hand refers to God." Doesn't this sound like a profession of faith—actually much to the consternation of his life-long girlfriend Simone De Beauvoir, who spoke of the "senile act of a turncoat"? It is hard to deny that, at last, the blind and old man had been cured from his "mental myopia." He was finally able to make the "switch."

Why did it take him so long? What we often see in the lives of atheists is a certain disconnect between what they know and what they prefer to know. Thomas Aquinas was very aware of this disconnect: "Whereas unbelief is in the intellect, the cause of unbelief is in the will." No matter how strong the empirical and rational evidence is in favor of God's existence, some atheists choose not to accept God's existence as a fact because they don't like the way the world looks to them with God in the picture. They act like smokers who know smoking is unhealthy, but nevertheless keep smoking. It is the will, says Pascal, which "dissuades the mind from considering those aspects it doesn't like to see." Instead of worshipping the real God, atheists prefer to worship their own gods, such as materialism, scientism, evolutionism, and the like.

In other words, often atheism is not a rational conclusion but rather a matter of choice and preference. Even the best arguments won't work for those who are not willing to even listen to them. Atheists often do not will what they know, but they know what they will. They must will to see what they don't like to see. The British philosopher Anthony Flew seemed to be this way. For more than fifty years he scrutinized arguments for and against God before finally abandoning atheism in favor of theism. One could say in general that if someone is not interested in whether God exists, or vehemently rejects God, it is almost impossible for such person to be won over by any kind of empirical evidence

Chapter 8: Atheists and God

or rational arguments. Take the atheist biologist Richard Lewontin and self-proclaimed Marxist who once defended materialism when he wrote, "[W]e cannot allow a Divine Foot in the door." The keyword is "allow": If we would allow that, then... Apparently, we are dealing here with a choice made before evidence is brought in. Atheists often invest a great deal of time and energy in fleeing the very God they deny or reject. But isn't flight itself the recognition that there is something from which to flee?

Nevertheless, even those who choose not to believe in God may decide later on to choose differently. Let's hope and pray that you had a similar conversion yourself, if needed, when you made your way through this book, and that you feel better equipped now to face the attacks of scientists, relativists, secularists, and atheists who keep coming your way. Atheism is a poison that requires an antidote. St. Augustine gave us the right antidote: "To fall in love with God is the greatest of romances, to seek him the greatest adventure, to find him the greatest human achievement." Just join Sartre who had finally seen a glimpse of the Light that Pope Benedict XVI has been speaking off so unrelentingly. Better late than never. Fortunately, in Christianity, it is never too late in life.

Conclusion

John Paul II used Buber's image of the "Eclipse of God" to speak of an "eclipse of the sense of God and of man" as "the heart of the tragedy being experienced by modern man." Pope Benedict XVI also used this image to describe what he saw as the single most serious and urgent problem of our time. He saw the "eclipse of God" as not just a loss of traditional religious faith, but a more profound loss of man's whole sense of transcendence, his consciousness of the Absolute.

Pope Benedict was speaking of a growing blindness and deafness to the Eternal, a loss of insight into what lies beyond the finite horizon. He remarked that "with the dimming of the light which comes from God, humanity is losing its bearings, with increasingly evident destructive effects." This made the Pontiff conclude, "[T]he overriding priority is to make God present in this world and to show men and women the way to God."

The "eclipse of God" points toward the loss of an infinite horizon, and its replacement with a purely finite scope—which means that our freedom has no longer a higher goal or reference point, that moral values have become merely personal preferences, that technical ability becomes the criterion of truth, and that science has been given the last word. Because of this "eclipse of God," we are living now in the real "Dark Ages." This causes not just a moral disorientation, but also a metaphysical and existential crisis. It is an existential threat that affects the core of our very existence.

And what does this crisis lead to? It means that life itself has become absurd. It means that the life we have is without ultimate significance, value, or purpose. When that happens, God has become eclipsed, and we need to remove what obscures him. We painted this picture of the eclipse in every chapter of this book, but we also found out that life does not have to be eclipsed. We discussed many reasons why this wave of materialism, mechanicism, relativism, secularism, and atheism does not have to be that way and can be reversed. Thank God, eclipses are only temporary, so the Sun can reclaim the day again. It is not the sun that is in darkness during an eclipse, but the earth is.

G. K. Chesterton once told the story of an English yachtsman who slightly miscalculated his course and discovered England under the impression that it was an island in the South Seas. The explorer, he said, "landed (armed to the teeth and speaking by signs) to plant the British flag on that barbaric temple which turned out to be the pavilion at Brighton." Having braced himself to discover New South Wales, he realized, "with a gush of happy tears, that it was really old South Wales."

We could easily apply this story to what we experience in modern society as discussed in this book. By the compass of science, relativism, secularism, and atheism, we may easily get off-track and sail away from God's territory. But hopefully, perhaps with the help of this book, you may find yourself back in God's land. What you thought was a new God-less land turns out to be the same land where God was found before—the God of old. And thus you begin to recognize first one and then another of the old familiar landmarks. The good news is that searching for truth will always eventually lead you back to God, as we pray, "God, be our light. Shine in our darkness."

Psalm 139 could not express this experience better:

> Where can I go from your Spirit? Where can I flee from your presence? If I go up to the heavens, you are there; if I make my bed in the depths, you are there. If I rise on the wings of the dawn, if I settle on the far side of the sea, even there your hand will guide me, your right hand will hold me fast.

Conclusion

Index

A

Adler, Mortimer J. 103
agnosticism 189
Allen, Woody 221
altruism 78, 178
animal 47
anthropic coincidences .. 55
anthropomorphism 175
Aquinas, Thomas 9, 12, 13, 15, 22, 47, 62, 63, 104, 110, 114, 118, 125, 134, 137, 163, 168, 183, 197, 209, 210, 215, 227, 239, 240, 255
Aristotle 15, 19, 123, 125, 137, 224
Asimov, Isaac 233
atheism 84, 187
Atkins, Peter 15, 30, 56, 198, 222
Augros, Michael .9, 10, 33, 55, 71, 111, 188
Augustine 240, 245, 256

B

Barker, Dan 190
Barr, Stephen 17, 22, 35, 61, 62, 72, 101, 108, 206, 218
Barron, Robert 160
Beckwith, Francis J. 179
Benedict XVI .74, 144, 145, 156, 185, 194, 225, 227, 235, 245-247, 256, 257
Bennett, Daniel 72
Benson, Iain T. 161
Berkeley, George 109
Bernard, Claude 27
bifurcation 126
Big Bang theory 6, 7, 19
body and soul ..114-116, 118
Bonhoeffer, Dietrich 231
Book of Genesis 5, 21
Brain plasticity 104
Brenner, Sidney 78
Buber, Martin.... 1, 159, 257
Buchner, Eduard 26

Index

C

capitalism 232
Carroll, William E. ... 17, 20, 21, 64
Casimir, Hendrik 45
causality 9, 64, 71, 126-128, 130, 133-136
chance ...... See randomness
Chesterton, G. K. 42, 72, 82, 109, 130, 147, 191, 214, 223, 248, 258
Church and State .. 156, 157
Collins, Francis 64, 85, 178, 254
common ground........... 224
communism . 232, 249, 251
conscience 159, 174, 184, 185
contingency 209
Copernicus, Nicolas 58, 124, 131
cosmology......... 3, 7, 13, 19, 20-22, 125
Craig, William Lane 221, 250
creation ...3, 63, 69, 70, 72, 191
origin vs. beginning ..18, 19
out of nothing... 7, 14, 17-19
spontaneous 8, 14, 53
Crick, Francis ...29, 34, 48, 98, 108, 152, 198, 207
Cronin, Frank............... 220

D

Darwin, Charles ..5, 47-51, 58, 60, 65, 66, 68, 73, 108, 132, 133, 152
Darwinism 48, 49, 60
Davies, Paul 30, 207
Dawkins, Richard ...52, 56, 57, 66, 68, 70, 81, 98, 108, 198, 199, 201, 203, 216, 230, 231
Dawson, Christopher .197, 219
death 94, 193, 221, 251
deism.................36, 37, 213
delusion. 93, 199, 203, 208
Dennett, Daniel............ 198
Dershowitz, Alan M. 221
Descartes, René 27, 99, 115, 125
Design
  cosmic.... 51, 67-72, 206
  in biology............ 51, 60
determinism...........89, 180
Diderot, Denis.............. 233
Dostoyevsky, Fyodor ..165, 248
doubt.....202, 204, 217-219
dualism 113, 114, 251
Dulle, Jason 86
Dulles, Avery................ 254
Duve, Christian de 69

262

E

Eccles, Sir John ... 102, 114, 194
Eco, Umberto 204
Einstein, Albert 15, 20, 41, 87, 108, 125, 134, 135, 138, 141, 148, 173, 179, 200, 204, 206
empirical vs. experimental 93, 141, 192, 200, 205
Epicurus 236
eugenics 49, 169
evil 56, 170, 176, 180, 182, 236, 248, 251, 252
   and Satan 250
   moral 242
   physical ... 239, 241, 242

F

falsification ... 123, 138, 147, 207,
fermentation 26
Feser, Edward 41
Feyerabend, Paul 41
Feynman, Richard 216
fine-tuning 55, 70, 205
First Cause (See Primary Cause)
Five Ways 209, 210
Flew, Anthony 60, 255
Fodor, Jerry 102
Francis, Pope 165, 247
Frankl, Viktor 102
Franklin, Benjamin 216
free will 89, 90, 98
freedom from religion .. 157, 165
   human 237, 243
   of religion 157
Freud, Sigmund .. 203, 208
Futuyama, Douglas 56

G

Gilbert, Walter 78
god gene 2, 79, 81-86, 88, 90
god of the gaps 231
Gödel, Kurt 210, 211
Gould, Stephen Jay 152
Grand Unified Theory 44
Gratian 184
gravity 7, 8, 14, 21, 54, 68, 91, 108, 133, 137, 151, 177, 212

H

Habermas, Jürgen 183
Hacker, Peter 117
Hahn, Scott 21
Haldane, J. B. S. 107, 229
Haldane, John 135
Hamer, Dean 79
Harris, Sam 198, 203
Hart, David Bentley 16, 60, 188, 214, 247
Hawking, Stephen .. 7, 8, 14, 45, 55, 195

Index

Heisenberg, Werner 208, 214
Herodotus 122
Heschmeyer, Joe............ 36
Higgs boson................... 18
Higgs, Peter................. 198
Hill, James 134
Hippolytus...................242
Hitchens, Christopher . 237
Hitchens, Peter 254
Holyoake, George.......... 158
homunculus fallacy . 99, 117
Hoyle, Fred................. 6, 71
Hubble, Edwin 6
Human Genome Project ... 64, 77, 78, 85, 178, 254
humanism ... 155, 182, 232, 234-236
Hume, David 125-128, 130, 133-135
Huxley, Thomas H. 49, 189, 216

I

immanence............226, 227
intellect.. 110, 114, 123, 131, 137, 147, 149, 150, 240, 255
intelligence.....................121
intelligibility......... 138, 192, 205, 213, 228, 231
Islam.............103, 224, 225

J

Jaki, Stanley....39, 135, 142
Jeans, Sir James 149

John Paul II ..155, 164, 234, 257

K

Kant, Immanuel ..125, 185, 190, 226
Kass, Leon...................... 67
Kennedy, John F.......... 185
King, Martin Luther.....171, 173
Kreeft, Peter 10, 18, 141, 164, 171, 192, 193, 198, 220
Kuhn, Thomas 142

L

Laplace, Pierre-Simon . 229
laws of nature 37, 51, 70, 73, 91, 92, 137, 138, 172, 177, 229, 231, 232, 239
Leibniz, Gottfried 70, 105, 214
Lemaître, George 6, 22, 149
Leo XIII........................ 144
Lewis, C. S. 45, 50, 59, 61, 107, 147, 164, 172, 206, 208, 237, 238, 253, 254

Lewontin, Richard 256
Lincoln, Abraham .168-170
Lockwood, Robert P.... 246
Lorentz, Hendrik.......... 141
Louis, Ard 46

M

Marcel, Gabriel.............254
Maritain, Jacques. 144, 183
Maslow, Abraham 42
materialism 57, 62, 91, 92, 105, 106, 161, 176, 187, 194, 196, 201, 209, 232, 233, 248, 255, 256, 258
matter and form 115
Mayr, Ernst...................207
mechanicism 1, 26-29, 31, 32, 34-38, 60, 100, 187, 258
Mendel, Gregor 47, 77, 133
Merleau-Ponty, Maurice ... 125
Mettrie, Julien de La 27
mind.... 1, 35, 91, 94, 97-99, 101, 107-119, 128-130, 133, 143, 148-153, 172, 194, 203, 214, 215, 217, 221
Minsky, Marvin 98, 117
models 31, 45
monism....................... 114
moral values 155, 158, 163, 170-175, 179, 180, 182, 183, 247, 257

morality 1, 2, 87, 146, 155, 159, 163, 165-170, 172-183, 192, 205, 206, 234, 247
Muggeridge, Malcolm..254

N

Nathanson, Bernard 254
natural law ... 162-164, 166, 168, 170, 183-186, 247
natural selection 47-53, 65-70, 73, 81, 107, 128-133, 136, 151, 152, 177, 178
Near-Death Experiences (NDEs) 103
neo-Darwinism 48
Neuhaus, Richard John 164
Newman, John Henry....64
Newton, Isaac.... 58, 70, 71, 108, 132, 151, 173, 212, 214
Nielsen, Kai 210
Nietzsche, Friedrich....182, 183, 216, 234
nihilism 146, 247

O

O'Connor, Flannery 236
order 19, 61, 72, 73, 87, 128, 136-138, 148, 163, 192, 205-207, 213, 214, 216, 217, 231

vs. randomness.... 2, 53, 54-58, 61-63, 73
Orwell, George 248
Out-of-Body Experiences (OBEs) 103

P

Paley, William 54, 65
paradigm 142
Pascal, Blaise .73, 95, 191, 218, 219, 226, 253
Paul VI 187
Pearce, Joseph 254
Péguy, Charles.............. 254
Penfield, Wilder 101, 102
Perry, Ralph Barton 42
physical constants... 54, 55, 70, 73
Pilon, Mark.................... 186
Pinker, Steven 114
Pius XII 214
Planck, Max...108, 135, 215
Plantinga, Alvin ...106, 131, 217
Pohl, Robert 214
Polkinghorne, John C. 17, 18, 74, 105, 115, 149
Popper, Sir Karl 114, 147
Primary Cause ...9-15, 18-19, 33, 51, 57, 58, 63, 64, 71, 197, 200, 201, 215, 230, 231, 243
Protagoras 122
Providence...... 1, 37, 62-64, 239, 242

Purpose
  in biology 51
  in life 59
  in science 51
  vs. chaos 56
  vs. randomness 56

Q

quantum tunneling 8, 16, 17

R

randomness 2, 53-58, 61-63, 73
  and mutations 53
  and Providence 62
  as primary cause......... 57
  vs. purpose 57
rationality 87, 128, 131, 136-139, 146, 148, 149, 151-153, 168, 179, 205, 206, 216, 247
reason.................... 147-149
relativism .. 1, 121, 122, 125, 128, 130, 139-145, 151, 153, 159, 187, 222, 248, 258
religion 81
revelation 213, 225, 227
rights vs. entitlements. 185
Rorty, Richard M. 122
Royal Society of London 44
Ruse, Michael 65, 159
Russell, Bertrand 190

Ryle, Gilbert 41, 99, 118, 147, 212

S

Sacks, Jonathan 186
Sade, Marquis de......... 222
Sagan, Carl ...3, 8, 29, 198, 202, 203, 209, 215
Saint-Exupéry, Antoine de 175
Sanders, James 'J.C.' 115
Sartre, Jean-Paul 182, 237, 242, 254, 256
Satan......................250-252
Sawyer, Robert J. 207
Schall, James............... 234
Schrödinger, Erwin 200
science and religion 22, 74, 114, 198, 200, 202, 213
scientism...... 31, 38-45, 88, 194, 196-201, 248, 255
secularism 1, 31, 145, 155-160, 162, 165, 187, 244, 247, 248, 258
secularity 156-157, 160, 165
Shaw, George Bernard ...50, 65, 98, 119, 159, 216
Sheen, Fulton J. 161, 187
Simpson, George Gaylard . 56
Singer, Peter.................198

skepticism 78, 125, 128, 130, 135, 139, 145-147, 153
Smolin, Lee 8
sociobiology 177, 178
Solzhenitsyn, Aleksandr ... 247, 251, 254
Spencer, Herbert......49, 68
spirituality....79-84, 86, 88
St. Anselm (c. 1033-1109) 173, 197
St. John Chrysostom (c. 347-407) 173
Stein, Edith 254
Swinburne, Richard......114

T

Tate, Allen 254
teleology 51, 52, 64-66, 68, 69
theism........36-38, 84, 190, 213, 219, 220, 255
time............. 6, 9-13, 17-21, 28-30, 63, 72
transcendence 86, 221, 225-228, 257
Twain, Mark 199
twin studies 79, 83

U

Ustinov, Peter 146

Index

V

vacuum 8, 16-18, 187
values vs. evaluations ..171-173, 181
Vilenkin, Alexander ... 8, 16
Voltaire 84

W

Wager of Pascal ...193, 220, 221
Wagner, Andreas 69
Wallace, Alfred 68
Watson, James.29, 88, 108 152
Waugh, Evelyn 254
Weil, Simone 254
Weinberg, Steven 71
Whitehead, Alfred North.. 126
Wilde, Oscar 249
Wilson, E. O. ...29, 88, 198, 216
Wittgenstein, Ludwid 112, 195, 198
Woolf, Virginia 237
Worner, Tod 36
Wyszyński, Stefan 249

About the Author

Gerard M. Verschuuren is a human geneticist who also earned a doctorate in the philosophy of science. He studied and worked at universities in Europe and the United States. Currently semi-retired, he spends most of his time as a writer, speaker, and consultant on the interface of science and religion, faith and reason.

Some of his most recent books are:

- *Darwin's Philosophical Legacy—The Good and the Not-So-Good* (Lanham, MD: Lexington Books, 2012).
- *God and Evolution?—Science Meets Faith* (Boston, MA: Pauline Books, 2012).
- *What Makes You Tick?—A New Paradigm for Neuroscience* (Antioch, CA: Solas Press, 2012).
- *The Destiny of the Universe—In Pursuit of the Great Unknown* (St. Paul, MN: Paragon House, 2014).
- *It's All in the Genes!—Really?* (Charlestown, SC: CreateSpace, 2014).
- *Five Anti-Catholic Myths—Slavery, Crusades, Inquisition, Galileo, and Holocaust* (Kettering, OH: Angelico Press, 2015).
- *Life's Journey—A Guide from Conception to Growing Up, Growing Old, and Natural Death* (Kettering, OH: Angelico Press, 2016).

About the Author

- *Aquinas and Modern Science—A New Synthesis of Faith and Reason* (Kettering, OH: Angelico Press, 2016).
- *Matters of Life & Death—A Catholic Guide to the Moral Dilemmas of Our Time* (Kettering, OH: Angelico Press, 2017).
- *Faith & Reason: The Cradle of Truth* (St. Louis, MO: En Route Books and Media, 2017).
- *The First Christians: Keeping the Faith in Times of Trouble* (St. Louis, MO: En Route Books and Media, 2018).
- *Forty Anti-Catholic Lies: A Mythbusting Apologist Sets the Record Straight* (Manchester, NH: Sophia Institute Press, 2018).
- *Broken Hearts in a Broken World* (St. Louis, MO: En Route Books and Media, 2018).
- *The Myth of an Anti-Science Church—Galileo, Darwin, Teilhard, Hawking, Dawkins* (Angelico Press, October, 2018).
- *At the Dawn of Humanity: The First Humans* (Kettering, OH: Angelico Press, April 2019).

For more info:

http://en.wikipedia.org/wiki/Gerard_Verschuuren.
He can be contacted at www.where-do-we-come-from.com.

www.ingramcontent.com/pod-product-compliance
Lightning Source LLC
Chambersburg PA
CBHW032151080426
42735CB00008B/659